In the Shadow of Freedom

Three Lives in Hitler's Germany and Gandhi's India

In the Shadow of Freedom

Three Lives in Hitler's Germany and Gandhi's India

LAXMI TENDULKAR DHAUL

zubaan

ZUBAAN
An imprint of Kali for Women
128B Shahpur Jat
1st Floor
New Delhi 110 049
Email: contact@zubaanbooks.com
www.zubaanbooks.com

First published by Zubaan 2013

ISBN 978 93 81017 66 1

Zubaan is an independent feminist publishing house based in New Delhi, India, with a strong academic and general list. It was set up as an imprint of the well known feminist house Kali for Women and carries forward Kali's tradition of publishing world quality books to high editorial and production standards. 'Zubaan' means tongue, voice, language, speech in Hindustani. Zubaan is a non-profit publisher, working in the areas of the humanities and social sciences, as well as in fiction, general non-fiction, and books for young adults that celebrate difference, diversity and equality, especially for and about the children of India and South Asia under its imprint Young Zubaan.

Typeset in Bembo 11/14 by Jojy Philip, New Delhi 110 015
Printed at Raj Press, R-3 Inderpuri, New Delhi 110 012

In loving memory of my parents
Indumati and Ayi Ganpat Tendulkar

Contents

Foreword

Not until the publication of Patrick McGilligan's monumental biography of Fritz Lang in 1997 had the name of Ayi Tendulkar rung a bell among experts of German cinema during the Weimar Republic (1918–1933), or even in the community of scholars who have done extensive research on Indians living in Germany between the two world wars. The latter included students, radical activists engaged in the cause of Indian independence, artists, filmmakers and a handful of businessmen. Some of them are well-known: the communists M.N. Roy and Virendranath Chattopadhya, the socialist leader Ram Manohar Lohia, former President Zakir Hussain, filmmakers Himansu Rai and V. Shantaram. Ayi Tendulkar does not figure in the list.

This is odd, to say the least, for Tendulkar had forged strong links with institutions and personalities that shaped Germany's tumultuous politics and culture in the decade preceding the triumph of Nazism. On the strength of his proximity to leaders of the freedom struggle in his early youth – Mahatma Gandhi, Jawaharlal Nehru and Vallabhbhai Patel – he wrote extensively on Indian affairs for influential left-wing publications in Berlin. He also enjoyed a reputation in the city's intellectual circles for his scholarly achievements and, not least, attracted much attention for his love affair with, and subsequent marriage to Thea von Harbou, wife and collaborator of Fritz Lang, arguably the most talented film director during the Weimar era.

Now, fifteen years after the publication of McGilligan's biography, Tendulkar's daughter, Laxmi Dhaul has provided an exhaustive, sensitive and often moving account of the life of this brilliant and complex man. She tracks the trajectory of his life through its many, colourful vicissitudes before, during and after his sojourn in Europe by drawing on recollections of family members and her research in archives of the period available in Germany and India.

My own introduction to her is a story in itself. The reference to Tendulkar in the McGilligan biography – which I read only two years ago – ignited my curiosity, not least because, as I was rapidly to discover, our two families had known each other. My father instantly recalled Tendulkar down to the last detail of his sartorial elegance, his swashbuckling manner, his huge, Mercedes car and, above all, the way he courted and married a lovely and feisty girl named Indumati Gunaji. My paternal grandfather knew the Gunajis well in Belgaum and was full of admiration for Indumati and her sister because they had a mind of their own – a rarity in women in that city's deeply conservative society. In no time at all I managed to contact Laxmi, who took me into confidence about her project to let the world know a thing or two about her exceptionally gifted parents.

My own interest in the cultural and political scene in Berlin during the Weimar years took an altogether different turn after Laxmi spoke to me in some detail about her father's relationship with Thea von Harbou. Their vastly different backgrounds of race and class, not to speak of the big difference in their ages (he was 17 years younger than her), lent the relationship, forged as it was in the wake of Adolf Hitler's rise to power, a magnetic quality. And so it is that thanks to Laxmi I began to explore the life of von Harbou to discover some clues about her fascination for the ruggedly handsome, debonair, dark-skinned Indian.

The Patrick McGilligan biography of Fritz Lang provided the clues in ample measure. So did a website dedicated to her. Indeed, in recent years there has been a renewed interest in her life and achievements among scholars specialising in film studies. Its main merit lies in the fact that much of the harsh criticism aimed at her by writers of an earlier generation – particularly Siegfried Kracauer and Lotte Eisner – for promoting an exclusivist idea of Germany through her novels and film-scripts and for her allegedly ambivalent attitude towards the Nazi regime has been placed in a less contentious context. All the same, the Thea von Harbou that emerges from recent literature still retains something of the aura of mystery that surrounded her in her lifetime.

Born on 27 December 1888, Thea had a privileged childhood despite the limited financial means of her Prussian family that belonged to the minor nobility. She studied in a convent and with private tutors who taught her several languages, introduced her to the world of arts and letters, and nurtured her precocious talents as a writer and a connoisseur of music. She earned the sobriquet of a child prodigy when a magazine published a short story of hers when she was barely thirteen. At that same age, she privately published a volume of poetry too.

However, determined to earn her own living, she chose, when she was just eighteen, to become an actress, much against the wishes of her father. That is when she met and subsequently married an actor named Rudolf Klein-Rogge. The couple, after nearly a decade of performing on stage, moved to Berlin where Thea devoted her time and energy exclusively to writing. She drew her inspiration from classic German myths and legends. Her novels, as M C Gilligan remarks, 'became patriotic and morale-boosting, urging women to sacrifice and duty while promoting the eternal glory of the fatherland.'

Thea's long and distinguished career as a scriptwriter began when the director Joe May decided to adapt one of her novels for the screen. It was May who introduced her to Fritz Lang in early

1919. The two hit it off instantly, not least on account of their shared interest in India. Tragedy marked their love affair. Lang's wife, Lisa Rosenthal, a Russian Jew, shot herself with her husband's pistol after she found him and von Harbou in a clinch. To this day, it is not clear whether this was a case of suicide or murder.

Lang and von Harbou got married in Berlin in August 1922. A year earlier they had worked together on a screen-play for a film entitled 'The Indian Tomb.' It reflected their common passion for Indian culture, or rather for an extremely exotic idea of Indian culture. Over the next decade, she scripted all the films he directed. Many were hailed then, and continue to be hailed today, as the most outstanding examples of German Expressionism. They include 'Dr. Mabuse, the Gambler' in two parts, 'The Nibelungen' also in two parts, 'Metropolis', 'The Spy', 'Woman in the Moon' and 'M'.

Their marriage foundered as Lang continued to chase younger women though he claimed that the reason was his wife's growing fascination for the Nazis. Matters came to a head when, in a scene reminiscent of the episode concerning Lisa Rosenthal, Lang, who had arrived earlier than expected at his apartment, found Thea in bed with her Indian lover – Ayi Tendulkar. The two had met courtesy a common friend – Conrad von Molo, who had travelled extensively in India and written about Mahatma Gandhi's non-violent movement for papers in Berlin. Laxmi Dhaul gives a fine account of the Indo-German marriage, of Thea's career as a filmmaker during the Third Reich, of her internment in a British camp after the war and of how she was finally cleared of the charge of collaboration with the Nazi regime.

What stands out in this account, however, is the fact that though she was an intensely nationalist German, Thea von Harbou had no love lost for the anti-Semitic barbarity of the Nazi regime. She was progressive too in that she took the lead to campaign against a law that made abortion illegal. Equally significant was her generosity towards Indians who had taken up cudgels against

British colonial rule in India. She helped them with money, food and shelter and, above all, with encouragement in their struggle for India's freedom. Indeed, when Tendulkar's young Indian wife, Indumati, and her infant child spent six months with her in Berlin, she looked after them as only a mother would.

But here is the reason why the mystery about this exceptional woman persists. Until her dying day, there were three framed photographs in her apartment which she dusted daily: one was of Ayi Tendulkar, another of Mahatma Gandhi and the third of Adolf Hitler.

Dileep Padgaonkar
Pune 2012

Thank you

It was my mother's dream that there be a book that told her story. She gave me her letters, the essays she wrote and the newspaper clippings she had kept carefully tucked away in her cupboard. And she told me many stories, allowing me to enter the world of her memories This is her story and I am happy to share it with you. I've tried to piece it together from whatever material I was able to find, and from accounts of people who knew both my mother and father. I wish, though, that I had started writing this book earlier, for by the time I got round to it many of the people I would have liked to have spoken to, had passed away. My father was the centre of our lives and I dedicate this book to his memory and to that of my mother.

I have been helped and encouraged by several people in writing this story. My husband Harry was tremendously supportive in helping me collect data, enabling me to travel and meet people, and indeed to write this book. He has been part of the saga of retelling the history of my parents. I am happy to present my children Veda, Mikhail, Karan and Juhi, and my niece Rohini Tendulkar with a document that belongs to their heritage. Also, I would like to acknowledge my aunt, Anuradha Kittur, and cousin Shanta Tendulkar for sharing their photographs and memories with me.

I also dedicate this book to those who are no longer with

us but have helped me along the way, namely my dear cousins, Narayan and Baburao Tendolkar and Vinayak Tendulkar, Shital, my daughter-in-law who was untimely taken away from us.

I would like to acknowledge my gratitiude to Dr Guenther Lothar for his kindness and help in giving me information, translating my father's articles from *Berliner Tageblatt* and travelling with me to Thea von Harbou's grave. I got to know so much more about Thea von Harbou's support for the Indians who were stranded in Berlin, through him. The website on Thea von Harbou created by Dr Gunther and his colleagues, Dr Keiner and Dr Kagelmann, was truly a wonderful way of contacting them.

I thank Urvashi Butalia for her guidance and for editing my book and publishing it under her banner Zubaan. I would like to thank Rosalyn D'Mello, Mita Kapur and Rasma Haidri for assisting me with my initial drafts. Friends who I have to thank include Sandeep Jolly, Soomesh Sharma, Gitanjali Khanna, Rajiv Tandon, R K Purohit, Deepak Rao, Shekhar Krishnan and several others.

Laxmi Tendulkar Dhaul

1

The Beginning

My bed is strewn with letters and photographs that have, for long, been stacked away. There's an old folder with letters my father wrote to me when I was at school – short ones, some typed, some handwritten, replies to questions I put to him, letters saying how much he missed me. I found them in an old plastic bag. I was 20 when I lost him. I look at all these pieces of paper, and I am reminded of the difficult days my father went through when he had to let go of the company he had built from scratch. He never said a word about that to any of us.

Among the scattered papers on my bed are scraps with bits of verse written in Marathi by my mother. A creative woman, she always felt life had been something of a mixed bag for her. She was proud to have been associated with many of India's national leaders during the freedom movement and independence. But she also had this nagging sense of failure – she felt she had never managed to accomplish anything because of the circumstances of her life. Among the papers are letters from Gandhi to both my parents about the conditions he laid down for their marriage in 1945. There are colour postcards from my elder brother and from several of my parents' German friends: fragments from my parents' lives, kept very carefully by my mother in a cigar box.

There are photos of Thea von Harbou, the German film maker who was married to my father. Theirs was an unusual love story.

Thea von Harbou was a pioneer in the world of cinema – best known for the classic black and white silent movies that she scripted and co-directed in Germany with her then husband, Fritz Lang. She married my father in 1933 after Fritz Lang, himself a noted film director, left Berlin for Hollywood. They stayed together for several years and then, in 1939, my father left Berlin for India. I grew up hearing Thea's name – I was told she was something of a celebrity in Berlin, both as a film maker and a writer. But she was also quite controversial for having joined the Nazi party, although she claimed she had done so only to defend her Indian friends in Berlin. In my family though, she was just a much loved and generous friend.

There's a letter from a woman called Alexandra Passini to me. Her daughter Veronique and son-in-law Gregory Peck came to India in 1979 when the Hollywood blockbuster *Sea Wolves* was being filmed in Goa. Veronique somehow managed to track me down and explained how her mother had been married to my father in 1922 when they were both students in Paris (his first wife, he married three times after that, so a total of four marriages!). Alexandra also sent me a letter with a photograph of both of them when they were young.

I have been working on this book for the last four years, collecting information, reading through what I have – my mother's handwritten recollections, my father's letters, the documents I managed to collect, those that other people gave me. I've been talking to people who knew them, and trying to find a way of documenting their extraordinary lives. It hasn't been easy: when parents are alive, children seldom ask them questions about their lives. After they're gone, it's too late. And then, if you do decide to write, how do you find the 'right' voice, and indeed how do you know what the right voice is?

It took me a long time to understand that. At first, when I

Tendulkar and Laxmi 1960

started writing, I tried to recreate my parents' voices as I knew them, writing the account in the imagined voice, first, of my mother and then, of my father. But somehow this didn't feel right. I then wrote the entire manuscript as a fiction narrative but though it made for a great story, even to my own eyes, it felt wrong. Something was missing. I wasn't sure what. Then my publisher, Urvashi Butalia read it, and she said to me, 'the thing really missing in the manuscript is you. We don't know enough about you, why you felt impelled to write this book, what it means to you...' She suggested I go back to everything I had, all the papers, documents, stories, and search my memory for anecdotes, that I look at what my parents' friends told me about them, and that for the bits I did not know much about, I explain that they were either conjecture or hearsay. That way, we'd have a much more honest manuscript.

This then is the story of my parents Indumati Gunaji and Ayi Tendulkar, and of my father's relationship with Thea von Harbon.

It's the story of how they met, how world events shaped their lives, and who they were influenced by. But it's also much more, it's the story of two countries, and two histories that are, in strange ways, linked through the lives of these two individuals and all those who became part of their lives. It's the story of pre-war Germany, of the lives of creative people in Hitler's time, of the pressure to assimilate and the compromises that it brought; it's the story of Gandhi's India, of his campaigns for non-cooperation, and of how people responded to them, giving up their lives, often their loves, for the cause. But above all, it's a story of love – an unusual love, between a man and two women, and a deep friendship, between the two women, born out of their love for the one man.

Early Years

1973 was the year that Pablo Picasso died. Elvis and Abba were big stars in the field of popular music. There were no cell phones, no video players and no laptops. Indira Gandhi was the Prime Minister of India, and the US President Nixon had been impeached for Watergate. I was 17 and had just returned to Mumbai after spending several years studying in an Irish convent in Kodaikanal in South India. I had finished school and begun to apply for admission to college. I had two choices: the government-run Elphinstone College or St Xavier's, which was run by Jesuit priests.

My father was in Bombay at the time and was quite excited about my going to college. He had just celebrated his 70th birthday, and was recovering from two major heart attacks. Having lived a rich, colourful life, he was finally settling into retirement. His major preoccupation at the time, it seemed to me, was to be in touch with and involved in what was happening in my teenage world. He loved having visitors over, enjoyed spending time with my young friends, reading books and discussing politics, but most of all he wanted to be part of my world, and for me to be part of his. He would insist on my accompanying him when he went to see his doctor or dentist or even his chartered accountant. At the time I never imagined those would be his last few years with us, and I would constantly make a fuss when he made what I thought were unreasonable requests for my time and company. In hindsight,

I realize that his motive in making me do 'real life' things was so that I could fend for myself when he was no longer alive.

I had applied for a bachelor's degree in science, and to be eligible for this I needed to have excellent grades. Each college normally displayed about three lists over a three-day period which featured the names of accepted candidates. I was crestfallen when I couldn't find my name on the first list at St Xavier's. I did get into Elphinstone College, but my father wasn't too keen on me going there.

"I will come with you to meet the Principal of St Xavier's," he declared to me the morning I was setting off to find out whether I had made it to their second list. I was horrified at his suggestion – I didn't want to be seen with a parent in college, and anyway I anticipated that the outcome of the meeting would be disastrous. But I didn't have the courage to tell him not to come. So I waited in trepidation as he got ready and I watched him comb his sparse salt and pepper hair. He wore his characteristic white Khadi suit with white shoes and sprayed himself liberally with his favourite cologne – 4711.

We entered the tall and somewhat intimidating gates of the college and walked into a campus filled with teenagers like me who were all there to find out if they'd been accepted or not. I was uncomfortable. I didn't want to be seen with my father. A few acquaintances waved at me and I waved back and found my father also waving back at them which amused me. My dear father wanted to be involved in every aspect of my life! We had to wait for at least half an hour to meet with the principal, Father Lancelot Pereira, a Jesuit priest originally from Goa. When he finally managed to get free, he asked what he could do for us. My father introduced himself and started to talk to him about his life, how he had grown up in Goa, how he had been sent to Germany. He then recounted an incident about his college life when he was a student in Gottingen University. Apparently, he attended classes taught by a very distinguished professor. One day, the professor called him aside. He was upset because he had noticed Tendulkar falling asleep in his classes. My father described how he had hung his head in shame. He had then gone on to explain to the professor that he worked in a factory all night in order to earn enough money to cover his expenses and tuition fees, which was why he'd fall asleep in class, out of sheer exhaustion.

"Tendulkar, that is a very touching story," the professor had said to my father. "What I will do is give you a book to read, it's a textbook I've written. I want you to read it and come to me after two weeks and I will examine you. If you pass my test I will make sure you are recommended for a scholarship and fee waiver from the University so that I do not have to face the disturbing sight of one of my more intelligent students asleep in class."

"Father Pereira," my father said, coming back to the present. "I know my daughter is a brilliant girl."

I kept my eyes glued to the floor, I was horribly aware that something frightening would happen in the next few minutes

"Why don't you give her a book to read? Then you can test her on it. If she passes, then maybe you can consider granting her admission."

At the time I had just returned from boarding school and had begun to discover how exciting the world was outside of a convent. I was part of a large group of friends and all of us were catching up on all the fun we thought we'd missed. I didn't want to spend the few days I had left before college started, locked up at home studying.

But my father had different ideas – and different plans. He dreamt of my becoming a researcher in Biochemistry. It turned out that Father Pereira was a scientist and a professor at the Microbiology lab. He had even started his own research lab called Caius. I had heard my friends talk about the Caius lab as it was one of the few Microbiology labs in Bombay, and even had a large computer made by Wang Laboratories! That was the era before personal computers, and my college friends spoke about the Caius

lab with great awe and respect. The two men hit it off instantly. I
don't think Father Pereira had encountered such an unusual and
enthusiastic parent before. He took us to Caius lab immediately,
and presented me with a copy of *Molecular Biology of the Gene* by
James Watson, a scientist who had won the Nobel a few years ago
along with his colleague Francis Crick for their discovery of the
structure of DNA. They had found that the genetic protein chain
had a double helical structure which helped them explain how
the gene structure was able to duplicate itself during cell division.
My father was thrilled to meet Father Pereira. I dared not look
up at him smiling! This was his current favourite topic and he
constantly spoke about Molecular Biology and Biochemistry being
the sciences that were going to change the nature of scientific
research in Biology. He was excited and felt that I was on the
right path.

I watched in horror as Father Pereira handed the hardbound
book to me. I saw a gleam in his eyes that was similar to what I'd
seen in my father's eyes. And I wondered what I had let myself
in for.

"Yes Laxmi. Please read this book and come back after two
weeks," Father Pereira said.

I was really upset. Over the next two weeks I leafed through
the pages of the book and stared at the complex circular figures
of inorganic molecules and other energy chains such as the
Krebs cycle. I knew this was a textbook for those pursuing a
masters degree in Biochemistry, but what was I to do with all the
information. Poor me! Did no one understand that I had been
out of school for barely six months?

The outcome of the meeting was that I did, eventually, get
admission into St Xavier's College. Father Pereira examined me
after a fortnight and realized that I had not understood anything,
and correctly suspected that I had not read the book thoroughly
either. He gave me a two-week grace period and told me that
he would only examine me on the first three chapters. I was

embarrassed and I really struggled with the book. I didn't let my father down on the second attempt. He was so thrilled with the news that I had finally been admitted to St Xavier's that on his next trip to Mumbai from Belgaum, he spent a lot of time flipping through my textbooks and asking me about all my professors.

"Why did you tell Father Pereira about that incident with your professor in Germany?" I asked him soon after.

"Well, he was one of the most important influences in my life," he replied.

We were on the lawns of the Brabourne Stadium at the Cricket Club of India, Mumbai which was right across from our building. I could tell my father was in a talkative mood and that he was willing to talk to me about his life and his experiences.

"From the time I was in school I was drawn to the Satyagraha movement," he said. "I went to Gandhi's ashram in Sabarmati, in Ahmedabad. As it turned out, I stood first in the exams held by the Tilak Vidyapith in Ahmedabad, where there must have been at least 850 candidates."

I listened, fascinated. He was laying down tough standards for me, I thought.

"I was too young to sit for the board exam in my hometown in Goa. It was 1920. I was just fifteen, and the minimum age was sixteen. My teachers advised me to go to Ahmedabad instead. I still remember the journey. My parents had died when we were still young boys and we had no money, so I did the entire journey on foot and it took me about a fortnight! I walked part of the distance, sometimes I got a lift from farmers in their bullock carts, sometimes from truck drivers who let me stand at the back with the goods they were transporting.

"Once the exams were over, I went to the Sabarmati Ashram and came into close contact with Gandhi and Vallabhai Patel. Both remain important influences in my life. I worked for Vallabhai Patel as his secretary, and handled his correspondence. In the evenings, I gave tuitions in Sanskrit to a few people.

"In fact, I remember an incident where I was chosen to recite a passage in Sanskrit at an important function in Gandhi's Ashram. Sanskrit, like Latin, is not a spoken language. I felt very privileged, but I was also very nervous, and in the middle of my speech, I noticed Gandhi nodding in appreciation. I got distracted and stopped reciting. I was tongue-tied. There was pin drop silence in the auditorium. It took me a few moments to pick up the thread of my words and resume."

"Shortly after, I was selected for a Topiwalla scholarship to an English University. Every year, a few of the brightest Indian students are offered this scholarship to qualify for the Indian Civil Service."

"How fascinating Papa! But how did you land up in Germany?" I asked.

"I accepted the scholarship and left for London. But I found it difficult to get admission to the subjects I wanted to study in the University of my choice. Someone suggested I travel to Paris, and that is where I went. I spent four years in Paris, at the École Normale Superieure. I was able to pick up French very easily and in fact fell in love with a very beautiful Italian girl called Sasha (Alexandra) Passini who was also studying in Paris. We were married for a short time. Her daughter Véronique is married to a famous Hollywood actor called Gregory Peck. You must have seen his films. Véronique and Gregory both came to visit me in 1952 or 53 before they were married!" I had heard this story several times from my mother in much more detail but I never tired of listening to it. In my view, Gregory Peck was definitely the best looking film star I had ever seen!

My father went on with his narrative. "After I had finished my studies in Paris, Sasha and I parted company, and my elder brother Purshottam who was studying in Germany, convinced me to do my post graduation in Germany as he felt that not only was the standard of education excellent, but it was also much cheaper than anywhere else in Europe."

"But what about German, was it a difficult language for you to learn?" I asked.

"Yes, it took me some time initially, but since I already spoke about six different Indian languages, I think I picked it up fairly quickly. I went in 1922, a long time ago," he said. He told me that the incident that he had narrated to Father Pereira was about his time as a student in Gottingen University, where he studied during the day and worked in a factory at night.

"Initially, a professor called Schubring helped me out. He later became my father-in-law, his daughter and I were both students in the same class, and we were married for a while."

"Were married? So then this was your second wife?" I inquired, perhaps boldly, but I was now getting more and more curious. I had heard my mother mention that she was his fourth wife but I hadn't really paid much attention to what she had said. I just took it for granted. Now for the first time I was able to trace the chronology of his life. Suddenly I wanted to know everything about my father.

"Yes, Laxmi," he continued, "but it was really my relationship with her father that had the most impact on me. Professor Schubring gave me a lot of support at University. I completed my PhD in Applied Mathematics in 1930. It took me seven years during which time I was a Humboldt scholar at Berlin University for two years. I visited India in 1930 as a special correspondent for a leading German daily, *Berliner Tageblatt*, and I reported on the political scene in India during that year. After returning to Germany, I joined the technical college in Berlin in 1932 to study Mechanical Engineering. I got my degree four years later in June 1936 and was ranked first at Berlin Technical College."

At this point he took off his glasses and wiped them with a handkerchief. I noticed that his movements had become a lot slower since his recovery from two heart attacks.

"I took the engineering course hoping to make a contribution to the development of my country. I was greatly impressed by the reconstruction efforts which I saw in the first years of Hitler's regime in Germany and I remain greatly inspired even today by what I saw then of the German people, their discipline and their work ethic. On 16 July 1936 I received a letter from the chancellor of the Berlin Technical University, Gehimart Friedrich Romberg, who had heard of my success in the exams and wrote to me. I still remember what he said: 'I am happy to count you amongst my best students with whom I have come in contact during the last 35 years as a professor. And as a student who is very close to me. To students of your type, I feel closely bound for the whole of my life. I wish you good luck on your way through life with your young years, your strong will and your strong capacity for creative work. You have a duty to help your Fatherland. I want you to become like Max Eyth, the maker of industrial Germany. You should become the Max Eyth of India. If I live to see this, I shall be happy and proud that I had the privilege of being your teacher.'"

I realized what an accomplishment this must have been – completing a PhD while simultaneously working in Berlin. For a young man from rural India, with absolutely no family backing it was quite extraordinary.

I remember hanging out at the St Xavier's canteen with some of my friends who were cinephiles. We would go to the Alliance Française in Mumbai where classic films from the forties and fifties were screened. One day I casually asked them whether they had heard of Fritz Lang. They had, they said.

"Oh," I continued, "Do you know that my father was married to Thea von Harbou, Fritz Lang's ex-wife?"

They looked at me and I could not help noticing a slight smile on their faces as they looked at each other. Clearly they thought I was making up the story. During my school years I'd been careful never to mention anything about my parents to my schoolmates as I didn't want my friends to know that my

St Xaviers college, Mumbai

parents were different from theirs. I didn't want to tell them about my parents' German connections, or the Gandhians and the politicians who were very close to them. Now, in college, I don't know what made me blurt it out, but I instantly regretted having done so.

It was only about a year later that one of my cinema friends came up to me and said, "Laxmi, you remember you told us about your father and Thea von Harbou? Well, we believe you, we read that Thea von Harbou was married to an Indian named Ayi Tendulkar." This was in 1973. There were no computers then, and we never imagined that in a few years there would be such a thing as the internet and Google which could help you check things in the blink of an eye.

People often asked me why my father was called Ayi. In Marathi Ayi means 'mother' and that seems to be a strange prefix for a man to have. I asked my father why he always wrote his name as Ayi Ganpat Tendulkar. "I took the name Ayi as a pen name when I was writing articles in German newspapers. It means bird of wisdom in Latin." I have tried several times to find out more about this but have never been able to. Most people who knew my father would call him Doctor or Doctor Sahib, and only his brothers called him Ganpat.

My Parents
Tendulkar and Indumati

Belgundi is a small village about 15 kilometres from the city of Belgaum in Karnataka. It is the village that my grandfather lived in. He was a caretaker and managed several farms owned by landlords in Belgaum. Both my father and his older brother were born in Belgundi, and they studied under my grandfather who was a strict disciplinarian. My father loved being in Belgundi. I remember he told me once that as children they would run up the hill and sit under the jamun tree during the break their father would give them.

Years later, my father purchased the whole hill bit by bit, and built a beautiful glass house at the very top. The jamun tree, now a hundred years old, still stands there. It is one of the few things that remains from that time, a marker of the place and a witness to many histories and stories.

On one of our family trips to Belgundi, My father was in a slightly pensive mood, and he actually described and wrote down in the form of a table the chronology of events in his life. I preserved that piece of paper, and have used it as my most valuable guide in writing this book. I always knew I would one day write a book – this book. Years after my father wrote it, I found that piece of paper again – carefully tucked away in a 'special place' –

the kind you can never remember when you need to. I reread it and memories of that day flooded back. My eyes were wet and I realized that I had not understood the significance of losing my father when I was 20. Had he been alive for a little longer, how different my life would have been! I had lost my biggest support and source of love.

I remember that when I came home from boarding school during the holidays, I always met my parents individually because they lived apart. But each time the moment arrived for me to go back to school, I would ask my mother, "Ma do you think Papa will be alive when I return?" She would reassure me, "He is a strong and healthy man, nothing will happen to him." I was always conscious that everyone else's parents were in their late thirties and forties and mine were in their sixties and seventies. I remember every night I would pray to God to give them both a long life. When I lost my father to a massive heart attack in 1975, I was 20 and he was 71. I was grateful that I had at least got to know him.

My trips to Belgundi as a child were always adventurous. There was no electricity and in the evening, just before dinner, the generator would be turned on. If the generator didn't work, we'd use a hurricane lamp that was known by the locals as 'petromax'. It was difficult to sit too close to a petromax because of the large number of insects it attracted. There was no television in India till the early '70s and, if there were no visitors, we would sit around either playing rummy or listening to my father narrate stories from his life. A few pegs of whisky always helped him to relax and become talkative. He held us spellbound with stories from his life.

Those evenings were magical: the house he built on top of the hill was big with large French glass windows commanding a magnificent view. Houses with large glass windows were rare in the sixties in Belgaum and people would come from all over to see this one. The kitchen was about 40 feet away from the house, and in between was a lush green bamboo plantation. Papa insisted on warm plates at dinner, especially on cold damp monsoon nights. Our cook Babu had become quite adept at pouring hot water on the plates and wiping them just at the entrance of the dining room. We had beautiful French china and yet the meal was a simple fish curry and rice with beans, cooked the way Papa remembered them from when he was a child. The contrast between the simple Indian food and the sophisticated crockery and cutlery struck me as strange. I was a child and loved eating rice with my fingers which was strictly not allowed in front of my father! I would reluctantly eat with a fork, but the stories more than made up for this – I'd be listening to them rather than eating! On such evenings, the stories featured a strange mixture of the east and west, and I have pieced them together bit by bit to create the narrative that is to unfold.

Papa had told me how the plague was a curse in Belgaum as it would recur frequently, killing hundreds of townsfolk each time. During such epidemics, the more affluent would move to the safety of their country estates in nearby villages. His father had been assigned the duty of managing several such estates. He had found it easier to stay in the village rather than to travel the 15 km distance to town every day. His young wife, too, had no objections to staying in the village. She was mostly busy looking after their four children.

My father was the second of four sons. His father was proud of him. He showed tremendous potential as a leader, though he was often rebuked for bullying his older brother Purshottam who was two years his senior. The four boys were taught at home by their father, and though they played with village children their age, they were made to follow a strict academic regime. They were taught to read and write and their father also introduced them to rudimentary mathematics and made them recite Sanskrit shlokas and other Hindu texts.

My father would describe his mother's smile, her habit of

covering her head with the end of her sari while breastfeeding his younger siblings. He remembered her funeral pyre being lit by his father near the river when he was just eight. The four young boys had tears in their eyes not only because of the loss of their mother but also from the smoke and the confusion. Soon after, his father took his four sons to Goa to live with their maternal grandmother. The boys were enrolled in a Jesuit missionary school where the medium of instruction was English. Shortly afterwards, when their father died, the boys were helped by other members of the Brahmin community that they belonged to. My father ended up going to Ahmedabad, and was then sent to England and eventually Germany to study.

My parents came from simple backgrounds, but like thousands of others, their lives were affected by political developments at the time. The years around World War II saw the rise of leaders such as Hitler who tried to control the world through aggression and warfare. And then there were people like Gandhi, who used his particular weapon of non-violence and passive disobedience, satyagraha, to fight British colonialism in India.

Both my parents told me many stories about this time. In her last few years, my mother kept herself busy with writing. Later, I found books and notepads filled with essays and anecdotes in Marathi, written in her artistic hand. Many of those – along with stories I heard from relatives – became the material I mined for this book. In 1984, my mother built a school in Belgundi and dedicated it to the memory of my father. She named it 'Tendulkar High School'. She wanted to distribute a book about him during the inauguration. She'd put together some 200 pages that she had carefully written and she handed these over to me just a couple of weeks before the inauguration, but there wasn't time to put them together in book form, so we made a book of photos that we distributed at the event. When I began to put this book together, I was so grateful that my mother had taken the trouble to write about my father. Her 'memoir' in Marathi was invaluable in helping

Indumati Gunaji

me gather material. I have translated and reproduced parts of it below to give the reader an idea of what their lives were like.

Indumati's Manuscript

My daughter Laxmi is after me to tell her my recollections and describe what I remember about my encounters with Gandhiji, my impressions of him and how our lives were affected by the incidents leading to the independence of India and the freedom struggle. It all seems a very long time ago and a lot of water has flown under the bridge. Today's world is so different from the world we knew. But when I look back and remember the incidents associated with Independence, I realize that I was indeed very privileged to come across such wonderful leaders and personalities. I have tried here to give an accurate description of these incidents and my personal experience and to describe how I got involved in the freedom movement.

In a strange way Bapu wanted to test me. He wanted to test my love for the country and he wanted to test my love for Dr Tendulkar. Because of this, he agreed to marry us on condition that we would wait five years, and we were finally married in 1945. Believe me, those five years were indeed an eternity then. I think the events leading to my marriage with my husband were intended to test whether our first aim was to serve the nation. Once he had officiated at our marriage, Bapu made us promise that we would not have children till India became free. Our wedding was unique and very different from other marriages held in the ashram. The garlands we exchanged were made of Khaddar yarn spun by Bapuji himself. The vows we took were to first serve the nation! Bapuji insisted that a Harijan priest marry us and we were given instructions to read the 12th chapter of the Gita the morning before. The world has changed so much now …

My mother grew up in a small town called Belgaum in a sheltered Saraswat Brahmin family. Belgaum is exactly midway between Mumbai and Bangalore. Even today, it is considered a pensioner's paradise. Belgaum is very close to both the Karnataka and Maharashtra borders, and just a few kilometres from the Goa border. At that time, Goa was run by the Portuguese and because of its proximity to Belgaum the British developed Belgaum extensively. It had a Divisional Commissioner and various army battalions stationed there.

My mother was born in 1912 and had five brothers and one sister. They grew up in a lovely atmosphere. It was unusual for girls to study then, but their father, N V Gunaji was a writer and a scholar, and was progressive in his thinking. He encouraged his daughters to study. In fact the two Gunaji sisters were the first girls in Belgaum to learn swimming and even rode bicycles. This always created a problem because often they had people following them until one day my aunt became tough with their followers and brandished a kitchen knife that she always carried with her! It was unusual to find this kind of behaviour in Belgaum, but the girls participated in all the sports alongside their brothers and were never treated as 'women' as was the custom at the time. My aunt Anuradha Kittur still tells me how their father encouraged all of them and gave them the confidence and freedom to think independently. She once said:

"Your mother's preoccupation with the freedom struggle had an impact on the rest of us, and two of our brothers were sacked from the British Army because your mother participated in the Congress activities against the British. She was older than I and she was very beautiful. She was my father's pet, he was always partial to her. I assisted my mother in all the household tasks while my sister was exempt from housework. She had poise and grace and was very artistic. She attracted a lot of attention and had many suitors. She always refused everyone and soon started to wear Khaddar and got seriously involved in the freedom struggle."

My mother writes:

I was young, idealistic and patriotic and I had pledged my life for swaraj – self rule. The first time that I heard about the political situation – the struggle for independence – was when I was eight years old (1920). Mahatma Gandhi came to Belgaum and I remember that the freedom fighters were trying to collect funds for the Tilak fund. I have strong recollections of people donating whatever they had – money and jewellery. I can still picture the women taking off their golden bangles and mangalsutras and putting them in the collections. It was the first time that I had heard Mahatma Gandhi speak, and though I could not understand what he spoke about, I was very impressed by him at that time.

Later, in December 1924, when I was 12 years old, the 39th Indian National Congress was organized in Belgaum and Mahatma Gandhi presided over the session. I had registered as a volunteer and had the important duty of serving water to all the delegates and participants. I remember seeing Vallabhai Patel, Kaka Saheb Kalelkar and many other eminent Congress workers. I was very impressed with Shaukat Ali and Mohammed Ali and watched them when they went on their 'prabhat pheris' (morning rounds with music and song) with their green flags. They were tall, fair and very imposing! Other leaders were Motilal Nehru, Chittaranjan Das, N.C. Kelkar, a young and shy Jawaharlal Nehru, Acharya Kripalani, Rajendra Prasad, Sardar Patel, Sarojini Naidu, Madan Mohan Malaviya, C. Rajagopalachari, T. Prakasham, Pattabhi Sitharamayya and Swami Shraddhananda.

The whole of Belgaum crowded to get a glimpse of so many important leaders. Even Annie Besant attended the meeting although she came very late. The session was dynamic and it motivated and enthused all present and made them committed workers and nationalists. The water tank sunk especially for the supply of water to the venue was called Pampa Sarovara which is still there today and is known as the 'Congress well'. The entrance was decorated in the style of the famous Virupaksha temple in Hampi and lit with so many lights. Gangubai Hangal, the famous classical singer who was quite young then, had been invited to sing patriotic kannada songs. There was also a Khadi and Village Industries exhibition.

I was too young to realize the significance of the Congress session – that it was the grand scale on which it was organized that marked the turning point in the freedom struggle. Gandhiji had expounded his philosophy of non-violence and his approach of strengthening the party at the grassroots. It was only after the Congress in Belgaum that the spinning wheel became the sacred symbol and instrument to bring about political, economic and social consciousness among people and non-violence became the most powerful weapon to fight repression and violence. I was too young then to realize all this but I do know that witnessing

Mahatma Gandhi addressing the volunteers: in the background are Shaukat Ali, Mohammed Ali, Jawaharlal Nehru, Abul Kalam and Maulana Azad, Belgaum, 23 December 1924. © GandhiServe

Mahatma Gandhi giving his presidential speech at the open session of the Belgaum Congress, 23 December 1924. © GandhiServe

this wonderful charged event changed my life forever and I, at the tender age of 12, knew that I too would be involved in the national freedom struggle somehow.

I could not resist the call of freedom. How should I describe the lure to join the freedom movement?! I felt the atmosphere was electric and the movement was building up to boycott the British. I would get up before daybreak and join the prabhat pheris and I'd participate in all the other activities. I would be moved when I read about Gandhiji's activities.

Although I was my father's favourite child, he took the decision to ask me to leave the family house! The reason why he threw me out was because he did not approve of my involvement with my husband-to-be, Dr A G Tendulkar. I could never understand why so many people objected to my marrying Tendulkar. He was very distinguished looking with jet black hair and what you noticed first when you met him were his intense and piercing eyes. Obviously I had stars in my eyes and I was very much in love with him. I thought he was the most brilliant person I'd ever met and definitely, the most charming. I was impressed by the fact that he had lived abroad for seventeen years at a time when very few people even travelled abroad. It did not matter to me that he had been married to two European women before and that his current wife was a famous German film maker named Thea von Harbou. I just believed him when he told me that he wanted to help me in serving the nation, that his reasons for returning to India would be fulfilled by marrying me. I trusted him when he said that he wanted to settle down in India and have children. I empathized with him when he told me that he had come back not only because of World War II but because his heart belonged to India, and after having lived in London, Paris and Berlin he longed to eat rice and Goan fish curry and hear the delicate sounds of glass bangles while he was served his food! I believed him when he told me of his vision of building the nation together. I wanted to nurture this hugely talented man who said he was so much in love with me. I never understood why my father and then Bapuji and other wonderful leaders in the ashram were against our marriage.

How was I to know that I was the only one to believe these words of promise and motivation? It was obvious to everyone that we were so ill-matched. Tendulkar was experienced and very European. I was a simple though stubborn and strong-headed young woman from a conventional middle class family. But would I have heeded their advice? No, not at all! I was young, beautiful and maybe just a little arrogant as are most young girls who are confident and outgoing. I was always ready and eager to try something new.

It was a difference of two cultures. We had been brought up in a very conservative and traditional atmosphere where we were made to do yoga and read the Bhagavad Gita and other texts each day. Through Tendulkar, I caught a glimpse of what I thought Europe must be like. It was a naive belief but that was all that I knew then. My father's attempts to dissuade me from my friendship with Tendulkar pushed me further into it. Although I had seen Tendulkar's 'western' side he had a warm and generous side and most importantly he wanted to dedicate his life to the progress of our nation.

In retrospect, I look back at my life and I realize that if I had a chance to live my whole life again I would possibly do it just the same way as I did the first time round. Tendulkar fulfilled his promises to me, yes, he dedicated his life to building the Bagalkot Cement Company, he educated young people, he helped people and was always larger than life. We have two wonderful children.

They were hard times that we grew up in as my father had given up his job at the Municipal Corporation. He was a prolific writer – author of several religious books and translator of the Bhagavad Gita, he had also documented the lives of renowned Indian saints such as Shirdi Sai Baba and Ramana Maharishi. The living that he made through his writing was meagre and as we were seven siblings we supported each other through our education.

My second exposure to the freedom movement was through Gangadhar Deshpande, the 'Lion of Karnataka'. He was my

A young Tendulkar

father's friend. I was working at a khaddar district exhibition fair organized by the Khadi Gramudyog in Belgaum when Gangadhar Rao Deshpande and the famous Congress politician Moraraji Desai were walking around visiting the stalls. I was standing behind the counter of one of the stalls when these great luminaries came up to my stall. They asked me who I was and were pleased to know whose daughter I was as they knew my father. Morarji Desai was a very charming man and graciously presented me with my first Khaddar sari that same day, making me promise that henceforth I would wear only khaddar.

Ganagadhar Rao Deshpande was a wonderful guide and mentor to me thereafter. I told him that I would also like to join in the service of the nation. He suggested that I go to Wardha which is near Nagpur and not very far from Sevagram and join the Mahila Ashram there as Rector. The Mahila Ashram was sponsored by Jamnalal Bajaj, and the women who stayed there were the wives and daughters of freedom fighters who were imprisoned or on the move. There were also some young girls there – in all there were some 50–60 women. They all followed a regime similar to the one followed at Bapu's ashram in Sevagram. We would go often to the Sevgram ashram for public prayer meetings and other gatherings. We followed the same routine everyday: we'd wake up at 4 a.m., have breakfast by 7 a.m. after community prayers or work. After breakfast we had to go for a morning walk, and then do whatever work was assigned to us, namely helping in the kitchen, cleaning latrines or washing utensils, chopping vegetables, grinding, etc. Bapu would spin khadi every evening at 4.30, and at 5 p.m. there would be an evening meal followed by the prayers.

When I was first taken there, Gangadhar Rao Deshpande presented me to his distinguished friend Shri Jamnalal Bajaj. Jamnalal Bajaj had a large amount of land in Wardha and was very keen that Bapu start an ashram there. It was here that the Mahila Ashram was set up, and it was like a training ground for women who might have to spend time in jail. For several years, the Mahila Ashram was under another famous Gandhian, Acharya Vinoba Bhave. When I went there, I was made Rector for a few months.

I was also to teach several subjects including English and was to brush up on my Hindi. I found life there so hard! For breakfast they gave us sooji (semolina gruel) and some chapatti. There was no spice or masala and I didn't like the food at all.

I got very close to Shri Jamnalal Bajaj's family. His daughter Om and son Ramkrishna would come to visit me often. Although I came from a middle class background, we always had a servant. I found it so difficult to wash the thick khaddar saris, and often young Ramkrishna and Om helped me wash my clothes! One day Om and I went to Nagpur for an outing. Shri Jamnalal Bajaj had a house there, and both of us went there for dinner. One of the most memorable treats was when we went to the local photo shop and had our black and white photographs taken! Kaka Saheb Kalelkar was an eminent freedom fighter and a supporter of Gandhiji's movement. He happened to come from Belgundi, Tendulkar's village and was also, co-incidentally, one of my father's closest friends. Kaka Saheb Kalelkar would welcome me to his home and if it was late he would request someone to escort me back to the ashram. Once he asked Shri Jamnalal's older son, Kamalnayan to escort me home. Kamalnayan dropped me by cycle to Wardha and very sweetly, in his charming way and with a twinkle in his eye, said, "Why didn't you come earlier! I just got married. If I had met you I would have married you instead." My friendship with the Bajaj family was to last a lifetime.

This was just the first of many jottings that I found in my mother's papers. She had always wanted to be able to string all the incidents of her life into a book. Much of what I describe below comes from her writings, but I have also used other documents and discussions and conversations to piece together my parents' story.

Belgaum

Central Maharashtra gets very hot in summer and my mother Indumati Gunaji pined for Belgaum, which was densely forested and at a height of 2500 feet above sea level. Indumati had been away for a long time, she had spent two years in Pune, studying, and then in Wardha. She now longed to go home. She'd worked as Rector of the Mahila Ashram in Wardha where she had got to know the dynamic Mridula Sarabhai, Vikram Sarabhai's elder sister from Ahmedabad. When Mridula heard that Indumati was planning to return to Belgaum, she requested her to do a small assignment which involved the collection of data on the employment of children by beedi factories situated in towns such as Nipani and Sankeshwar, both fairly close to Belgaum. On one of her trips to Belgaum, my mother completed her study and wrote an article on the pathetic working conditions of women and children in the beedi factories. She then began asking her friends for suggestions about where she could publish it. Anuradha, her younger sister, told her about a local weekly Marathi newspaper called *Warta News*. The newspaper, she said, was fairly liberal in its views and often published articles that were strongly worded, with anti-establishment points of view. The newspaper had recently been started by a certain gentleman named Tendulkar, who had returned from Germany a short while ago.

A young Indumati

In fact, Dr A G Tendulkar was the talk of the town, especially with his brand new red convertible Mercedes which had recently rolled through the main street. Everyone stopped to stare at the spectacle of his car whizzing past. Little children ran behind it. No one in Belgaum had ever seen such a big car before! That too, the newest model, and a convertible! Anuradha seemed to have all the latest news about him, and informed Indumati that he was married to a famous German woman who had stayed behind in Berlin. Indumati found this gossip about Tendulkar intriguing, though she wasn't surprised that this new, colourful personality was the talk of the town and had set tongues wagging. Anuradha told her that Tendulkar had a doctoral degree from Berlin, and that he had returned to India because he wanted to start some kind of industry here. There was something about this larger-than-life personality, his Mercedes, his fearlessness, that touched Indumati's fancy. She half-believed what she heard about him, and half-listened to that something at the back of her mind that warned her to stay away from him.

Indumati tried to contact all the local newspapers to place her article but received no encouragement from anyone. The tobacco lobby was a powerful one and no newspaper was willing to openly criticise their employment policies.

"The only paper that will publish your piece is the *Warta News,*" said Anuradha to Indumati. "I know the sub-editor, let's give the article to him. We don't have to meet Tendulkar, we can go when he is not in the office. I will ask the sub-editor for a suitable time. We will go at a time when his big car is not parked outside the office." Indumati had to make a decision. She could choose to have her article published in a liberal newspaper whose publisher was willing to accept articles criticising tobacco business houses, or she could choose not to be published at all.

The next day, the two sisters strolled up and down the road in front of the *Warta News* office, checking whether Tendulkar's Mercedes was parked there. It was a little after 11 in the morning. Since they didn't see the car, they decided to go to the office to hand in the article to the sub-editor before Tendulkar arrived. They entered the building and gingerly approached the narrow staircase. They climbed up the first floor to the *Warta News* office and knocked on the door. There was no reply. Impatiently, they knocked again, and a few seconds later, to their complete surprise, Tendulkar opened the door.

The sisters stood speechless. They hadn't bargained for this! Indumati couldn't take her eyes off Tendulkar. Everything about him – from his thick, black hair to his elegantly tailored clothes – exuded a warm, confident appeal. He was tall and good looking. Indumati found herself blushing. She was aware of Tendulkar's sharp scrutiny, checking her out from head to toe. He courteously invited them into his crowded newspaper office and arranged for chairs for them to sit.

"Do please come in, I am Dr Tendulkar," he said, as he offered his hand to both of them, and then, politely, "How can I help you?"

Anuradha greeted him with a quick Namaste in the traditional Indian way, but Indumati shook the hand that he had proffered to her saying, "Dr Tendulkar, I have written an article that I would like you to publish in your newspaper."

Once seated at his table cluttered with local publications, he turned to them and said, "But first, you must tell me what I can offer you to drink. Would you like some tea or coffee?"

"Thank you, Dr Tendulkar. Just a glass of water would be fine. My name is Indumati Gunaji and this is my sister Anuradha. I was working in Gandhiji's Mahila Ashram until recently, and I was asked to write a report on the employment terms for women in the beedi factories. This article is based on the research I did for that report."

She handed over the article, somewhat hesitant and unsure of his reaction. Would he accept it or not? He glanced through it.

"Very interesting. I was aware that the beedi manufacturers needed women and young children to roll beedis, since they have slim fingers, but I had no idea about the kind of exploitation that exists in this industry," he said.

The conversation started off with the beedi manufacturers and soon moved into the realm of local politics, until they finally started to discuss the Indian freedom movement and developments in Europe and America. Indumati lapped up all the information that Tendulkar so disarmingly shared with her. Despite her earlier reservations, she was totally mesmerized by him. Anuradha had been put at ease by his initial welcome but soon became restless and bored with the conversation. She was not interested in politics, and wanted, more than anything, to leave. She was a little unnerved by the manner in which Tendulkar commanded Indumati's full attention.

I think my aunt Anuradha felt an instinctive need to protect Indumati. She had always claimed that her older sister could not take care of herself as she was a die-hard romantic. Anuradha actually tried to pinch Indumati under the table in an attempt to divert her attention from Tendulkar. But Indumati merely pushed her hand away. She tried to glare at her, but Indumati chose not to respond. Anuradha knew her sister well, she saw that something deep within her had warmed to the bold, raw energy of this man, and she was captivated, unable to resist his charm. "What could I do, I could see that both of them had fallen for each other!"

The sisters finally accepted Tendulkar's offer of tea and biscuits. They listened attentively to his views on British Rule and the workers of the Indian National Congress. Tendulkar strongly believed that the entire freedom movement should have been handled differently. He was critical of the impact of the 'Quit India' movement initiated by the Congress party on the poor farmer or villager. He felt strongly that the lives of the marginalized farmers would not improve even if India were to get freedom from the British. "I have returned to India after almost eight years and the situation in the world outside has changed substantially. But sometimes I wonder how India will rule itself once the British actually do leave. What kind of leadership and ideology will we adopt that can unite such disparate regions?"

Indumati felt that his views were well thought out, and agreed with him at various points in the conversation, especially on his observation that the Civil Disobedience movement was actually a rehashed, revised version of the Gandhian passive resistance movement.

"It's the same people all along," he said. "I have observed Gandhi, Nehru and other leaders when they've addressed large crowds, and even on a more personal level. Gandhi's personality has a huge influence on the masses. He's certainly a very impressive figure. But I'm almost restless to see where India is headed today."

Indumati shifted uneasily. Her initial attraction was being slowly replaced by a kind of exasperation. She didn't like the manner in which he spoke about the Congress leaders. She would not accept any criticism of them.

"Dr Tendulkar," she said. "What has brought you back to India? If you have so little confidence in Indians, maybe you should have stayed back in Germany. Gandhiji has led nationwide campaigns in order to alleviate poverty, to demand the equal treatment of women, to build religious and ethnic amity, to end untouchability, and to increase our economic self-reliance. Above all, he has been working zealously so that we may achieve Swaraj, independence from foreign domination. He has dedicated his life to this cause."

"No, Miss Indumati, don't misunderstand me," he said. "I respect Gandhiji and his dedication to the freedom struggle. I look at the Indian villager and my heart goes out to him, he may be hungry but he is still proud, he may be fatalistic but he is still hard-working, he is possibly the most pure-blooded person in the world. He is full of possibilities and I think he is the only hope for the future of India. Gandhiji and the Indian Congress Committee are the only leaders that we have today in our fight against the British. I believe with Gandhiji that the real power of India is in its masses. But when the British are no longer the rulers will our Indian leaders be able to address the huge problems that our country faces?" Tendulkar spoke straight from the heart. He then got up from his chair and started pacing the room, chain-smoking all the time and commenting about day to day politics, Indian customs and rituals. Indumati could not help but notice his hands and his artistic, tapering fingers as he absently pushed his hair off his forehead every now and then.

"What have you done, Mr Tendulkar, since you came to India?" Indumati flared up. "You are in no position to criticise or condemn the actions of our leaders. At least we try, we put up a fight. What have you done? You do nothing but criticise. Which is worse, do you think? Don't talk about our Indian gods in that manner, why should the gods laugh at us? It is the British who are laughing at us. We are so many of us, and yet, we can never come to any consensus about anything! That is why the British have ruled our country for so long, because each Indian wants to criticise the very people who are giving up their lives for the country!" Indumati was trembling as she spoke. She had never articulated her thoughts so clearly. Tendulkar stood stock-still, somewhat taken aback by what she had said. It was true that he had done nothing for his motherland, he thought. By now, Anuradha was becoming impatient. She insisted that they both leave, she told Tendulkar she needed to get home, and soon after, they said goodbye and left.

I learnt much of this from my aunt, Anuradha and from my parents' accounts of this encounter. My mother's entry in her journal describes at length her first impressions of my father:

Tendulkar was a real charmer! Till then I had only come across upright middle class Maharashtrian men terse in their mode of speech and reticent in their manner. Meeting Ganpat who would stand every time I entered and kiss my hand and look at me as though he had seen a vision took my breath away! I had never met anyone like him and was tremendously impressed by his vast knowledge and qualifications. In fact just a few days before meeting him, my neighbour Dr Kokatnoor who had come from the United States and now lived in Tilakwadi had suggested to me that he would introduce me to him. He said, 'Indu let me introduce Dr Tendulkar to you. I feel that you both will make a good match!'

I had only seen this Dr Tendulkar once before and that was when I had accompanied Gangadhar Rao Deshpande to the railway station to go to Jabalpur, and we were waiting on the platform for the train. Dr Tendulkar came up to pay his respects to Deshpandeji. Gangadhar Rao for some strange reason did not even introduce us to each other. We only looked at each other and Gangadhar Rao told me later that he had purposely not introduced me because Dr Tendulkar had lived many years in Europe and he had heard that he was married to a German woman! Well, when I look back I realize that if you are destined to meet it happens anyway.

After our encounter in his office Dr Tendulkar and I gradually started meeting more often, and we fell in love with each other. He told me about his early life. Tendulkar and his three brothers were born in a small village called Belgundi which was just 15 kilometres away from Belgaum city. Ganpat Tendulkar had indeed had an interesting life. Unfortunately both his parents passed away when he was quite young and he and his brothers were brought up by their maternal grandmother in a small town in Goa. But fortunately for him, his father had had the foresight back in 1910 to insist that the four sons study in an English medium school rather than the local school. I really believe that this made a lot of difference to the opportunities that the boys got later. As the four sons had no financial backing, parental or otherwise, they would earn a little money by singing bhajans and by chanting Sanskrit slokas at various temples near the area where they lived. Ganpat had a flair for languages and spoke fluent Sanskrit as well. Apparently he could not take his school-leaving certificate exam in Vengurla as he was underage. His brother Purshottam who was about four years older than him was scheduled to do the exam with him, but Ganpat decided to go to Sabarmati and take the exam from there. This indeed was a feat in its own right because he undertook the entire journey from Vengurla to Sabarmati on foot!

Several of India's renowned scholars and college professors had taken up residence in Sabarmati ashram in protest against the British rule. While still at Sabarmati on Bapuji's birthday in 1921 Ganpat was given the opportunity to address the large gathering that had assembled there. He spoke about Gandhiji's life for one hour, in Sanskrit! I remember him recounting that while rendering the speech he got stuck midway when Bapuji suddenly exclaimed in appreciation, and that somehow broke his fear and gave him the confidence to complete his speech.

This impressed the august gathering and Ganpat later stayed on at the ashram and worked as Sardar Vallabhbhai Patel's personal secretary. Vallabhbhai Patel and Tendulkar had a long relationship. Congress leaders such as Motilal Nehru and Topiwalla were impressed with his intelligence and felt that with the proper exposure and education, he would be a great asset to the nation. They decided to send him to the UK to appear for the Indian Civil Service examination. His very close friend S K Patil who was roughly the same age as him and belonged to the same community of Kudaldeshkar Brahmins, had been sent to London on a Topiwalla scholarship to complete a course in journalism. Ganpat was also fortunate enough to be given a Topiwalla scholarship.

Ganpat, who had never even been to a big city, was to set sail for London in 1923. Soon after he boarded the ship, he found that the cabin boys and waiters were mainly from Goa, and Ganpat's fluency in Konkani, their language, endeared him to them. They took turns during the three week journey and would go to his room and educate him on the ways of the western world – something he knew nothing about and had never come across in his life in Belgaum, Goa, Vengurla or Sabarmati. The waiters taught him how to do what are today considered elementary things like tying one's shoelaces, they showed him how a necktie was to be worn, and how to eat with a knife and fork. Most importantly, they helped him brush up his English.

I could not get Tendulkar out of my mind after meeting him at the newspaper office. I had never met anyone like him before. I replayed the conversation several times in my mind, convincing myself that I had said the right things. We'd parted fairly amicably in the end, and I wondered why there was no response from him about my article. Finally, three days later, a young boy came running across the garden and into the house looking for me. "Indumati, Bai, I have a note for you! The Sahib with the big car is waiting for you! Here, take it!" he handed me a piece of paper, completely out of breath. I read:

My dear Miss Gunaji,
I would like to meet and continue our discussion about the article you had submitted for publication. I am waiting outside

your house. If it is convenient for you, I would be happy to meet you.

Yours very sincerely,
Ganpat Tendulkar

I read my mother's journal long after she had died. By that time, I was familiar with many of the stories I found in it. My mother had described to me in detail how their romance had built up, how she'd felt on getting this note from my father, and what happened after that.

Indu was excited at the prospect of meeting Tendulkar again, yet the boldness of his actions made her hesitate. She wondered if it would be proper to meet him again, asked herself what it would lead to. She went to her room and looked at her reflection in the mirror. Her cheeks were burning and her heart raced. She had been unable to sleep since their first encounter, and now she couldn't help but wonder whether she had been too rude to him. Just then, her mother entered the room.

"Mother I am just going out for a little while to meet Dr Tendulkar, the editor of *Warta News*," she said nervously. "He is waiting for me in his car. He wants to discuss the article that I had submitted a few days ago."

Her mother nodded her approval reluctantly. Ever since Indumati had joined the Congress party, her mother had been unsure of her daughter's reactions to her advice. In a way, Indumati had stopped seeking her mother's approval or permission for most things. Indumati saw that Anuradha was standing behind their mother, mouthing the words, "Don't go".

"I am going then," Indumati said. She knew Anuradha would reprimand her later when they were alone. She would demand to know how Indumati had the gumption to go and meet a man unknown to her parents. And that too, a married man! Indumati walked slowly towards the car. Tendulkar almost sprang out to meet her.

"Indumati," he said breathlessly, "I am so glad that you came."

"Hello Dr.Tendulkar, what is it you want to discuss with me?" Indumati asked with cool composure.

"I wanted to discuss your article with you. There are many aspects that you have not considered," he said, leaning on the side of his red Mercedes. He looked stunningly handsome in his casual half-sleeved shirt and his crisply ironed trousers. His shoes were polished to perfection and his silver cigarette case that rested in his well-manicured hands revealed traces of his European lifestyle.

"May I invite you for a short drive? Maybe you could show me the 'Congress well' built especially for the All India Congress meet in 1924," he said.

He opened the door of his car for her and Indumati got in. She loved the feel of the plush German upholstery. She had never seen anything like this before and was delighted by the smell of the leather and the tobacco that lingered inside. The sincerity of his request to be shown the Congress well was what made her decide to get into the car. She guided Tendulkar to the site. It was just a few minutes drive away.

"I have gone through your article and would like you to make some changes," he said, matter-of-factly as they drove. "I would like you to compare the wages that these tobacco factories are actually paying the women versus what they are paying the young children. I must say I found your article fascinating and informative. I had not realized that this was the level of exploitation of child labour in India today."

"When will the article be published, Dr Tendulkar?" she asked.

"This Monday or, latest, by Tuesday," he replied. "But tell me, Indumati, tell me more about the Congress well close by, the historical site where the 39th Indian National Congress was organized. I have heard that there was a Khadi and Village Industries exhibition too and it was one of the few sessions with Mahatma Gandhi as President. Were you a part of it?"

"I was only 12 years old then and had registered as a volunteer to the Congress. I remember every incident as though it happened yesterday," Indumati replied.

"What were the duties assigned to such a young girl?" Tendulkar asked somewhat amused at the idea of a young Indumati volunteering for the Congress.

"I was assigned the duty of serving water to all the delegates and participants. It was back-breaking work but I got to see national leaders like Vallabhbhai Patel, Kaka Saheb Kalelkar... and many other eminent Congress workers. I remember Shaukat Ali and Mohammed Ali moving around. How good-looking they were – and at that time I had never seen men so tall! I used to join them in their morning rounds which were known as prabhat pheris. The leaders would lead with a green flag and we would follow, singing patriotic songs with them. The session was dynamic and it enthused everyone who witnessed it. It made them committed workers for freedom."

Tendulkar smiled at Indumati's enthusiasm, and listened intently to every word she spoke. She showed him the Congress well and the few other sites that marked the historic occasion. "The compound for the meeting was huge and the entrance to the compound was decorated in the style of the ancient stone temple at Hampi, which was built at the time of the Vijaynagar empire," she told him. Seeing that he was interested, she continued. "I still remember Gangadhar Rao Deshpande and Mr Hardikar, they were the two people in charge of the arrangements. You could see them every morning during the session riding on horseback around the 85-acre compound designated for the Congress."

This rang a bell for Tendulkar and he asked. "Wasn't it here that Gandhi spoke of incorporating what were to become the two symbolic elements in his leadership? One was the hand-operated spinning wheel which he felt could be a sacred instrument in bringing about political, economic, and social consciousness among people. The other of course being the idea of non-violence as a powerful weapon to fight repression and the British aggression."

Indumati smiled to herself. Of course she was aware of this, but she loved hearing about these important symbols again from Tendulkar. There was something about the way he articulated things, how he enunciated each syllable, that she found extremely attractive.

"Yes, you are quite right," she said. "This event became the turning point of my life. It was here that I heard Gandhi expound his philosophy of non-violence and outline his approach to strengthening the party from the grassroots and up."

Indumati and Tendulkar spent the entire afternoon together and she marvelled at how he shared her enthusiasm and her love for India. They were both aware of a strong connection between them: their desire to free their country from the British. Yet, they were also conscious of the enormous differences in their background and experience.

Tendulkar was an experienced man and as they talked, he took her right hand and held it between his, as though he were about to read the lines on her palm. Instead he drew her palm towards his lips and kissed it lightly.

"Dr Tendulkar, what are you doing?" she gasped. She drew her hand away, although somewhat reluctantly. His touch had been reassuring and warm. There was nothing cheap or brash in what he had done. But she hadn't expected him to make such a bold gesture, and the stolen kiss caught her completely by surprise.

"Nothing, Indumati," he said unabashedly with a twinkle in his eye. "I am merely saluting the most beautiful freedom fighter that I have ever come across."

At a loss for anything to say, she coughed, and that broke the tension of the moment and they both burst into laughter. Indumati blushed. Here she was supposed to be the mature, independent, freedom fighter, and yet, in front of him, she felt like a young girl.

Tendulkar smiled at her and said, "I would like to talk to you more about the Congress party and how I can support them. There is so much that I want to talk to you about. I have not forgotten the words you said to me, when we first met, about my criticism of the Congress party. You were right and I realize that the time has come for me to translate the love I have for my country into actions and deeds. I have returned to my homeland India as a stranger, after having lived the most formative years of my life in Germany." She was surprised that her words had had such a great impact on this well-travelled man, and that he wanted her to guide him. He was able to evoke a strong reaction in her. She felt morally bound to reintroduce him to India.

It was now evening and the sun was setting. The sky was ablaze with colour and there was a chill in the air. "Dr. Tendulkar, I must go home," Indumati said, not really wanting their conversation to end, but fully confident that she would meet him again and they would talk more about their future, India's future. "My family will be wondering where I have gone," she said.

Tendulkar drove her home. Neither of them spoke and the short distance was covered in minutes. Tendulkar parked the car outside Indumati's house.

"Please Indumati," he said, turning to face her. "If you are free tomorrow afternoon around four, please do come to my office. We can go through the changes that have to be made in your article. Once the changes are made we will give the article for printing immediately."

"Yes, I will come, Dr. Tendulkar," she replied, and went inside.

The meeting with Tendulkar had been too quick for anyone to really notice anything. Even her mother who had been busy cooking the evening meal hadn't missed her. Only Anuradha, who followed Indumati to her room, knew that something was up.

"What did he say Indumati?"

"None of your business, Anuradha. You won't understand anyway! Tendulkar is too sophisticated for simple people like you to understand!" Indumati did not want to diminish the impact of Tendulkar's words by allowing Anuradha to scrutinize them.

"Indumati, will you be meeting him again?" Anuradha persisted.

"Yes!" she retorted impatiently. "He asked me to meet him tomorrow in his office and I will be going alone this time."

Anuradha stuck her tongue out at her sister and rushed out of the room.

Indumati's father was the first to see the article a few days later, when it was published. He came home from his evening walk with a copy of *Warta News*, handed it to Indumati and complimented her on the piece. Although a lawyer by training, he had been associated with the town planning, and, on his own initiative, had planted tamarind saplings on the roads in the town. With five sons and two daughters, he had found managing the household difficult. Indumati's father did not believe in the dowry system, which though frowned upon, was an accepted custom in Brahmin wedding alliances. Money did not change hands officially, but there was always the issue of wedding presents, property and financial benefits. He did not agree with this custom of giving gifts, on principle. He was anxious that both his daughters find suitable husbands and settle down. Particularly Indumati, who was already 26. But at the mention of marriage, Indumati publicly announced that for her, her country came first. Her political activities had taken over her life and she had started wearing homespun cotton, which was the symbol of the Congress party.

Tendulkar teased her a few days later, when she went to thank him for publishing the article. "Indumati, I have been meaning to ask you a question for several days. Do you remember the day that you came to the office to meet me the first time? I happened to look out of the window and saw both you and your sister walk up and down several times before coming up. Were you hiding from someone?"

Indumati started laughing, So they had both been watched that day!

"No, No," he said. "I am asking you because just the other day, the British Divisional Commissioner Major Rogers called me to his office. They have been keeping track of my activities in Belgaum since I have lived in Germany for so many years. Apparently, he got wind of some rumour that I have a secret device embedded in my watch! He was told that through this contraption I could actually transmit wireless messages straight to Berlin! Anyway, I took off the gold Omega that had been given to me as a present and left it with him. Such strange rumours are being spread about me. I thought maybe you had heard some such fantastic tale and therefore both of you were extra careful that no one should see you enter."

"No, No, please don't think that," Indumati replied. "In fact, Anuradha and I were a bit diffident about meeting you as we had heard flattering things about you. We were simply not sure how you would receive us." She smiled to herself, because the way he had received her, and she him, seemed too significant to be a trifle. She thought that she would always measure her life as "before" and "after" the meeting with Tendulkar.

A few days later, Indumati received a message from Tendulkar asking her if she could be ready within an hour, as he wanted to take her for a drive to Belgundi, the village in which he had lived as a child. It was a 15 km distance from Belgaum. Indumati was thrilled. She sent a message through Ramu, the gardener boy, telling him that she would be waiting. Anuradha walked in as she was getting ready. When Anuradha saw her sifting through the saris in her cupboard, she understood that she was going to meet Tendulkar.

"Akka, please don't go out with him," she said in a cautionary tone. "You will only get into trouble."

Indumati gave her a look. "What is wrong if I meet him?" she said. "We are friends. It's not like I'm running away with him. I'm not doing anything wrong."

"Akka, you don't realize it, but people will start talking about you, and that will upset our parents," said Anuradha.

"No one will see us," said Indumati as she pinned a string of fresh jasmine flowers to her hair.

Anuradha gave her a disapproving look, but Indumati returned it with a charming smile. "I will be back by evening," she said. "I promise."

Tendulkar was waiting a little distance away from the house. Indumati, her heart beating faster than normal, approached him slowly and folded her hands in a Namaste. He greeted her with a look that told her he was more than relieved she had decided to come. It would not have surprised him had she declined his invitation, as the warnings her sister had given her were commonly held views among many people. But Tendulkar had wagered that Indumati was not the kind of person to allow her every moment to be dictated by common norms. Her hurried steps towards him, with wisps of her dark hair escaping from her long braid and dancing around her face, filled him with joy. Before long, they were on their way to the little village in his red Mercedes.

After some small talk, Tendulkar said, "The other day, Major Rogers, the British Divisional Commissioner, dropped in to see me. He had noticed that I had started hoisting the tricolour, 'Free India' flag from the rooftop of our office building. He threatened to take action against me if I didn't take down the flag."

"That sounds serious," said Indumati.

"Yes, he was quite the serious fellow. So I said, 'Major Rogers, I shall give immediate instructions to my servant Babu to get the flag down!' In the meantime we took a seat in the lounge. 'Babu!' I called, knowing Babu was right outside the door, 'Go at once to get the flag down!' Instantly, almost out of nowhere, Babu emerged with a bottle of Scotch and two glasses!"

Indumati laughed. She found the whole scene quite amusing.

"I didn't have to try very hard to persuade Major Rogers to join me for a drink. He's a nice fellow. He went on to tell me how much he had begun to enjoy Indian curry, and was almost apologetic about ordering me to bring down the flag."

"So Babu did take it down in the end?"

"Yes, Major Rogers said he was afraid that if he permitted me, then it would become a precedent for everyone else." They drove for a while in silence, both of them aware of the serious implications of this otherwise amusing incident.

Tendulkar had planned this excursion and was excited about showing Indumati picturesque locations around Belgundi – he showed her the small temple under the banyan tree at the entrance and the hillock, which was on land that he had recently purchased. They climbed to the top of the grassy knoll. "One day Indumati, I will build a huge house with full length glass windows on top of this hillock," he said, gasping for breath as they had walked up very quickly. "It will be a beautiful house. I will design it in such a manner that when you stand in the centre you will be able to see a 360 degree panoramic view!"

Indumati smiled. "You are a dreamer, but I can just imagine it. It will be beautiful."

They spent several minutes under the only tree on the hillock, the Jamun tree, enjoying the fresh air and breeze that in spite of the intense afternoon sun, managed to cool the area. Indumati enjoyed being in his company. He made her feel special.

Later they went down to the village and sat with the villagers for several hours. Indumati was impressed by the contact he had with his old village, after many years abroad. Tendulkar in turn was impressed by the skilful manner in which Indumati managed to assemble the village women, encouraging them to discuss their problems with her. She saw him watching her with a smile.

"This is my duty," she said, almost apologetically, but knowing that he understood and approved of her genuine interest in the plight of the village women.

They left the village, and as they pulled into Belgaum, Tendulkar invited Indumati to his home. He was a little surprised when she accepted, but for Indumati, time seemed to have come to a standstill. The age difference between them was eight years, but he seemed to be so much more mature, suave and cultured than any other man she had met. Tendulkar's servant was waiting for him, his evening tray drawn out with his regular bottle of scotch whisky and soda, and rushed to make a cup of tea for the guest. Tendulkar as was his habit, settled down to his evening drink of whisky.

"I know you are not accustomed to alcohol being drunk," he said. "I therefore hope you don't mind my having a drink?"

"I have actually never seen alcohol before," admitted Indumati. "My father is very religious and would never encourage my brothers." She looked at Tendulkar demurely, then mustered the courage to say, "I believe in Germany all women drink. Especially when their husbands come home each evening. So if you don't mind I wouldn't mind tasting some!"

Tendulkar looked at her and smiled. "No, no this is a very tricky thing, this drinking of whisky. I seriously don't think you are ready for this Indu," he said. "You are quite too innocent."

Indumati was secretly thrilled by his refusal. Although she had offered to join him, it would have been difficult for her to keep up the farce if he had allowed her to drink.

Tendulkar took a long draw on his cigarette. Then he got up and started pacing up and down with his hands in his pockets, talking all the while. Indumati sat spellbound, watching him sip his whisky and smoke his cigarettes one after the other. She had never seen anyone smoke or drink, and never dreamed of it being done so casually.

She was fascinated as she listened to him talk about Europe, Germany, and Paris. Secretly she also thirsted to travel and see foreign countries. She loved the way he expressed himself and articulated things, and listened as he described his experiences in Germany and the things he had seen and witnessed on his many travels, and she quite forgot that she had to go back home. Here was a whole new world opening up to her that was unlike anything she had seen before. There was something about Tendulkar that was so different and unknown, and yet, so appealing that she couldn't resist. She had never experienced this sort of fascination for a man before. Tendulkar had a rare charisma that made her forget her family and friends.

The magic of the moment was unceremoniously interrupted when Indumati's mother and brother stormed into Tendulkar's house. Indumati had been out since morning, and now it was evening and her mother was worried. Her younger brother Bal had run into a friend who informed him that he had just seen Indumati walk into the house of the "foreigner". When Bal told their mother about Indumati's whereabouts, she was so disturbed that she forced him to accompany her to Tendulkar's house.

Tendulkar stood up to welcome her, but Indumati's mother's eyes were fixed on her daughter. As Indumati approached, her mother rushed to her, gripped her shoulders and said, "Where have you been?" She was angry, but she composed herself, faced Tendulkar and responded to his Namaste. Tendulkar spoke to her in Marathi, asking her to sit down. She smiled politely and covered her anger with an apology. "Thank you, but I have to go home with Indumati. Her father will be wondering where we are. Namaste!"

Indumati followed her mother meekly out of the room. Tendulkar accompanied them out of the house, and offered to drive them home, but Indumati's mother refused. Indu knew how her mind worked – she was not going to let Tendulkar feel like he could make up for his gross misdemeanour of taking her daughter away from her by offering her a ride in his fancy car. She could tell that her brother Bal thought differently. He would have preferred the ride home in the plush Mercedes, To his mother's dismay, Bal shook hands with Tendulkar, but quickly stopped the smile spreading across his face when, from the corner of his eye, he saw the dark look his mother gave him. Bal, similar to his sister, was clearly smitten by Tendulkar's magnetism and his unruffled poise.

Once they reached home, Indumati unleashed her anger at her mother. "How dare you come and humiliate me?" she said. "I am not 16, and you know that I am perfectly capable of handling such situations. Please keep in mind that I am educated and have lived all by myself in the city. Why do you doubt that I can look after myself? Why did you have to follow me?"

"Was it necessary to go to this man's house? No decent girl would have gone to a man's house unchaperoned! What has gotten into you? Who will marry you now?" her mother burst out, unable to repress all the fears she had kept inside her for so many days, ever since she first heard of her daughter's meeting with Tendulkar.

"I will look after myself. You don't have to worry about me," Indumati retorted.

It was only when Indumati's father entered the room and saw the two of them arguing that they both calmed down. He shook his head quietly and retreated to his writing den. He was truly disturbed by what was going on, but sensed that this was not the time for him to say anything or get involved. Over the next few days, the women in the house slowly fell into a kind of pattern. Indumati tried not to cross her mother's or her sister's path while her mother, and to a lesser degree Anuradha, pretended not to notice that she was going out to meet Tendulkar.

During one of their meetings, Tendulkar asked Indumati how she came to be so passionately involved in the freedom struggle, since no one else in her family seemed to share her sentiments. Tendulkar was excited about this similarity in their pasts. "I had lived in the Sabarmati ashram before I left for Germany and know how difficult life can be in the ashram, at least until you get accustomed to it. Did it suit you to live there?" he asked.

"I was there for almost a year and I could not bear the heat in Nagpur and so I returned to Belgaum," she smiled. "Besides,

Bapuji would often tell us we must go to the villages and work. So I decided that I would do service in the villages near Belgaum. I had spent several years away from home when I was in college in Pune, and I longed to be back in my father's house."

It was in conversations like this that Indumati and Tendulkar got to know each other. They loved sharing their thoughts about their lives and concerns. The days drifted into weeks and the romance between them blossomed as they fell into a routine of spending as much time together as possible. Every evening at six, Tendulkar would wait outside Indumati's house and they would go for a drive, often to the nearby villages where they would talk to the villagers about Gandhiji and the freedom struggle. Tendulkar became more and more enamoured of Indumati's beliefs and causes. It was a new experience for him, discovering India through her eyes. He was simultaneously developing a taste for Indian politics. He was also aware that unless he shared her passion for service at the grassroots level, as Gandhiji had advocated, Indumati would be less inclined to spend time with him.

Initially, as Anuradha had warned, Indumati was embarrassed to be seen in public with Tendulkar. Belgaum in the early 1940s was a very conservative town. She became aware that rumours had begun to spread about their relationship. One day, when she returned from their evening drive, her father called her to his room where he devoted most of his time to writing and to practising naturopathy, after having given up his law practice several years earlier.

"Indu, you are meeting Tendulkar every day," he said. "What are your plans regarding him?" He asked the question without looking up from his writing. He was sitting cross-legged on the floor, near the low desk, and the room contained several steel cupboards which were full of books and notes that he had written. The black stone floor was covered by a straw mat on which were strewn a few cushions. When she sat down next to him, she noticed that her mother was there too, seated in one corner of the room, saying prayers by counting her prayer beads. It seemed that her mother had been crying and that her father's calling her in to talk to her must have been prompted by her mother's concern for her.

"Oh father, I am merely helping Tendulkar plan his new house in the village of Belgundi where he was born. He has purchased some land there. We have also been visiting the nearby villages and explaining Gandhiji's principles of non-violence and civil disobedience to the villagers. We have told them that they must not support the British officers in anything, even if means that they have to go to prison."

Indumati's father looked up at her and put aside his writing. She was his favourite child. He had encouraged her to study and go to college at a time when very few girls opted for education beyond compulsory school. He knew that she had grown into a clear minded, strong, and opinionated woman. He had not said a word when she became active in the freedom struggle, nor when she joined the Congress party. Not even when she took part in rallies and protests for which she could have easily been arrested. He also knew that he had no control over her or the outcome of her friendship with Tendulkar. Still, this time he felt he must say something, at least offer his opinion to her.

"Indu," he said quietly, but his voice was firm. "People are talking and they are saying nasty things about you. They are saying that you are having an affair with this Tendulkar. I have heard that he has a wife in Germany?"

Indumati was embarrassed. She could not stop the tears from rolling down her cheeks. It took her a few moments before she could trust her voice to be steady enough to respond.

"Yes, father, he is married. To a very famous German writer called Thea von Harbou. But father, Germany is at war with the world and no German is allowed to be married to a foreigner. She is many years older than him, and she has told him that she will not get in the way of his marrying an Indian." Indumati felt her cheeks flush as she recalled the thrill she had felt when

Tendulkar had told her this himself. He had been very open with her about his relationship with Thea von Harbou, and how the situation in Germany had interfered with his ability to stay there as her husband.

"Indu, this is a very serious issue," her father continued. "You know I respect your independence. But you also know that your actions affect the entire family. Your conduct and reputation will also impact the marriage prospects of your younger sister. I will not be able to arrange a suitable match for Anuradha if this continues. I'm asking you to stop meeting Tendulkar."

Indumati was in a dilemma. For the first time in her life she had met someone who shared her dreams. He was also handsome, well educated, and had a vision of doing something for India. Yes he was married. But he had explained to her that though he was considered married to Thea von Harbou, it was not an official marriage, as in Berlin under the Nazi regime, no German was allowed to marry a foreigner. Tendulkar had explained to her that Thea von Harbou was 17 years older than him and had encouraged him to go back to India and settle down with an Indian woman and start a family. Tendulkar told her several times that he now felt the need to settle down and have a family and children. "Thea knows that she can never come to India, not now, at least not till the war is over."

My mother writes:

> The next evening, Tendulkar must have noticed that I was quieter than usual. He sensed something was amiss. 'What is it, Indu? What has upset you today?' he asked.
>
> "'My father spoke to me. He says that people are saying nasty things about me because I spend so much time with you. Everyone knows that you have a German wife."
>
> I felt a mixture of anger and confusion and couldn't stop my tears from falling. "I cannot let my father down. I don't know what to do!"
>
> Tendulkar gently lifted my chin with his finger and looked

into my eyes. 'Indu, you know that I have already informed Thea that I have met you. However, the whole world is going through difficult times. It is difficult for me to offer to marry you at this stage.'

He held my gaze and I could feel his intensity.

'But I know one thing, and that is that I cannot live without you. You have become the most important person in my life. If a day passes and I do not meet you, I can think of nothing else but what you must be doing.'

I wept as we embraced, I could not imagine going back to a life without him, but the world seemed to conspire against us. First, it was the political situation in the world, and now my family. Why couldn't the world see Tendulkar the way I saw him?

As we parted that evening, I made Tendulkar promise that he would not try to contact me any more. It broke my heart to ask for this, but I did not want to hurt father. Tendulkar reassured me that he would always be waiting for me. If ever I needed him, I should just send a message and he would be there for me. On my way home, I suddenly felt the urge to visit the Shiva temple where the Shiva Lingam was the centre piece. I had not been to the temple for several weeks, yet the cold black stone under my feet, the fragrant and familiar smell of burning joss sticks and the warmth of the glow of candle-lit lamps calmed me a little. These were the sensations and smells I was accustomed to. I was in time for the evening aarti when the pandit, along with devotees, sang songs in praise of God. As this was happening, the priests were passing around a small flame in front of the deity. Some devotees rang bells and others blew the conch. I stood in front of the altar and prayed for guidance in this troubled and confused time, for a better relationship with my parents, and for a way out of this terrible situation. Having shared my problems with my favourite deity, I returned home in a much better mood.

In the days that followed, time seemed to drag endlessly. I missed Tendulkar, our meetings had always been exhilarating, and now the minutes dragged as I realized the sacrifice I had to make. I was moody, didn't eat properly and generally spent my time moping around the house. One evening, the day before I was to leave for Bihar on Congress party work, I returned home and immediately sensed something was wrong. Mother was lighting the oil lamps in the house. My younger brothers Bal and Rama were waiting for me.

"Here she comes," Rama said. Then he blurted out in anger,

"Do you know that because of you, the British Army officers returned our applications and told us we could not join the British army? All because of you!"

"Why, what have I done?" I asked, more alarmed by his hostility than by the accusations he had made.

"What is it that you have done?" Bal sneered, his lips curling into a snarl. "The British army has found out that you are a Congress worker, and therefore, we are no longer on the merit list."

"Why was it necessary for you to join the freedom struggle?" Rama asked angrily. "Are there not enough other people in India to carry out the fight against the British?"

"Each one of us has to fight against the British," I retorted. "It is our fundamental right as Indians to be independent."

"Akka, you have spoilt our chances for a glorious career in the army," Bal said sullenly.

"Bal, you are so naïve!" I said with exasperation. "Don't you realize that until we get Independence, you will be fighting for the 'British' army, not the 'Indian' army? Why can't you apply for a career somewhere else? Look at both of you – you are still so young, why don't you educate yourselves?"

Just then our parents entered the room. "They are not like your older brothers," mother announced. "Both Bal and Rama do not want to study any further. That is why they want to join the army," she said with finality. I thought for a few minutes, then said,

"All right, if it will help both of you, I will resign from the Congress party."

Instead of cheering with relief, as I had expected my brother to do, Rama retorted arrogantly,

"It's no use now. The damage has been done. I made enquiries today through my friend who works in the Army recruitment office. He told me that even if you resign from the Congress party, we will always be suspect because of your track record."

I felt terrible. I looked at my father who had joined them, but had not said anything.

"I am sorry, Rama and Bal. My intention was in no way to spoil your career prospects or your futures. When I joined the freedom struggle, I had no idea that it would affect anyone else's life. I do not know what to do anymore," I said quietly and then left the room, leaving my brothers still grumbling. My father told the boys to calm down, reassuring them that things would be all right and would sort themselves out. He knew that I was upset and contrite, and he didn't want to aggravate the situation further. That night I went to sleep upset and hungry. I was totally isolated in my family.

Early the next morning, I made my way to the railway station to confirm my reservation to Bihar. I made arrangements to leave my luggage in the waiting room, and since it was still a few hours before my scheduled departure, I started walking back home. Lost in my own thoughts, I did not notice Tendulkar driving by. But he must have seen me as he immediately stopped the car, got out and walked towards me. I saw his tall, familiar frame, my heart skipped a beat. Then the enormity of what had transpired during the last 24 hours suddenly made me feel weary. I unburdened my heart to the ever solicitous ears of my friend and love.

"Why is all this happening to me?" I asked. "Why do you always appear from nowhere when I need you most? Were you following me?"

Tendulkar replied seriously, "No Indumati, I was not following you, but believe me that if it helped the situation I would have done! We are fated to be together, Indumati. This is our world, this is our reality, and this is about you and me. Our life has to have a new beginning, a beginning in Free India. The time to be scared of our own shadows has gone. You are an adult, what can anyone say to you? Come, Indu, let us discuss what we can do."

I had become familiar with Tendulkar's European mannerisms and way of speech, and had total confidence in his words. We drove to his house, and as soon as we entered, Tendulkar embraced me passionately. This was the first time I surrendered completely to him. Tendulkar, an experienced lover, had to reassure me over and over again that he would always be by my side, no matter what. The pain of our separation during the last few weeks dissolved as we renewed our pledge to each other.

That evening, I realized that I could no longer live without him. He drove me back to the train station in time to retrieve my luggage and board my train. I passed through the nearly deserted station where the porters were already forming groups for playing cards or eating food. Their work for the day was done, as this was the last train out that night. I was a little tense and wondered whether anyone from my family had seen him drive away. I felt nervous and uncomfortable when I saw my brother Bal waiting for me on the platform. I approached him diffidently not knowing what message he had brought for me. The moment he saw me, he threw the cigarette he was smoking on the ground and stubbed it out with his foot.

He walked up to me and he sullenly handed me a package. "Mother asked me to give you this. She has packed you some clothes and some food, for your journey. She wants you to write to her once you reach Ramgarh."

I took the package and thanked Bal, and apologized to him for what had happened. And then, I said, "Bal, I have an idea – why don't you join the Quit India movement instead?"

"No Akka," he said with a sarcastic chuckle. "Please! let me decide what I want to do by myself. I don't need you to tell me what I should do anymore." In his words I heard the echo of my own plea to my father.

"Have a safe journey," Bal waved his hand and got off the carriage as he heard the railway guard blow his whistle. I watched him walk away from the platform. I was sure he had guessed where I had been all day. Perhaps he had seen Tendulkar dropping me at the railway station. If he had, I knew that Bal would probably tell father, but somehow it just didn't seem to matter anymore.

Tendulkar and Thea

My father often spoke of Thea von Harbou with great affection. I remember these conversations vividly. Meeting her in Berlin in 1933 had been a watershed in his life. I was very curious about how they had met – their backgrounds were so different, what could have brought them together? Thea von Harbou was a renowned writer and had successfully published numerous books and screenplays and had worked for most of the well known German film directors. What could they have had in common? My father told me the political situation in Germany at the time contributed a great deal to bringing them together. He was at Berlin University, working on his PhD. He had been a journalist with a couple of German newspapers such as *Tageblatt* and *Weltbühne*. When the Fascists took over, he had to give this up and he focused then on his research. Meanwhile, Thea was just coming out of a long, turbulent and embittered relationship with her then husband, the film maker Fritz Lang.

But how did their paths actually cross, where did they find each other? My father told me very little of this – or perhaps I did not ask enough questions. That's often the way with family histories. Now when I look back, I regret that I did not push him to tell me more, or even speak to my uncles who were there with him. All of them had lived through the Weimar Republic and the Third Reich, and it would have been wonderful to listen to their memories

Thea von Harbou with Tendulkar

of the time. I knew that Thea was fascinated by India, and had been even as a young girl, and that she had actually written and published a novel, *Das Indisch Grabmal*. Perhaps it was this interest that brought them together. My father was a young student at the time – there was a great difference in their ages – and he was educated, good looking, well spoken and deeply committed to an independent India, free of British rule. Perhaps it was this she found appealing, despite the difference of 17 years in their ages. He had just returned from his trip to India where he had followed the Indian Congress party for almost a year and he spoke about his fellow Indians with enthusiasm and zeal. Perhaps his energy and intensity touched something in her.

When I cast my mind back to what I had heard as a child, stray sentences surface in my mind: "she loved India", or the thing my mother often said to me: "I promised Thea that if I had a daughter, I would name her Thea." My father's younger brother, my uncle Shripad often told us that "Thea would make us call her Tai which means older sister in Marathi and she loved us all like her own family." He said that she had a dream that one day she would visit India.

It is pointless to think this now, but I so often regret that I did not begin work on this book earlier, when the main players of this drama were still around. When, at last, I did begin work, I had to search deep in my memory, and go back to the small notes, to letters, to diaries and impressions that I had carried in my head for all these years. I also felt hesitant because I am not a student of history or of cinema: how, I wondered, could I deal with this amazing story that was so caught up with the histories of India and Germany? How do it justice? And there was another thing: as I began to read about Thea von Harbou, I came across references to her being part of the Nazi party. Did I really want to go there? I was confused. How could this woman who my father had loved and married have been part of the Nazi party? I almost did not want to know. The dilemma stayed with me.

One day, at the Jaipur Literature Festival, I met Thomas Keneally, the author of *Schindler's List* and when I spoke to him about this story and my frustrations, he said, "Continue writing and you will be guided by the spirits of your loved ones."

And that, I think, is what happened. One day, out of nowhere, I was consumed by a desire to visit Berlin. It was odd, I'd been to Germany many times, but somehow I had never visited Berlin. I had friends and relatives in Duisburg, Aachen, Frankfurt but knew no one in Berlin. I really don't know where the thought came from, but it took hold of me powerfully, and it soon became my mission to go there. Uppermost in my mind was the desire to visit the grave of Thea von Harbou.

I had no idea how I would do it, or even how I would find the grave, but I realized we're living in the twenty-first century so I did what all of us do when we're looking for something, I

Ayi Ganpat Tendulkar

googled. Thea von Harbou's name threw up a portal on her, it was dedicated to her films and books. Suddenly interesting articles, interviews, photographs began to fill my laptop screen! The portal was hosted by three people – Dr Lothar Gunther, Herr Kleiner and Andre Kagelman. I decided to write to them.

> My name is Laxmi Dhaul and I am the daughter of Dr Ayi Tendulkar. My father was married to Thea von Harbou. He passed away in 1975 in India. I was too young then to ask him much about his experiences in Germany but often heard people in the family talk about Thea von Harbou. I am currently working on a book which recounts the saga of my parents' lives, and I have relied heavily on my mother's journal. She was called Indumati Tendulkar. She passed away a few months ago at the age of 94 and I just can't stop the story from coming out of me….My parents were married in Gandhiji's (Bapuji's) ashram in 1945 after being imprisoned by the British and their story is a real saga. Apparently when they wanted to marry, Gandhiji imposed some conditions on them – he insisted that Tendulkar get Thea von Harbou to write to him that she did not object to their marriage. My mother also stayed with Thea von Harbou for a year in 1952 and promised her that if she had a daughter she would name her Thea. The story I am writing covers the entire spectrum from Bapu to Berlin. It also describes my father's early life. I have been attempting to read your comments and fascinating research on Thea von Harbou but unfortunately I do not have German….

Less than two days later, Dr Gunther wrote back:

> Dear Laxmi Dhaul,
>
> I was more than surprised to hear from you as daughter of Dr Ayi Ganpat Tendulkar. Thank you very much for all the information. Naturally, I and my two partners who do research on Thea von Harbou would like to hear more from you as well as read your writings on this subject. You may get more information from our blogspot: http://thea-von-harbou.blogspot.com. Please do let us know when you plan to come to Germany, and which

places you are likely to visit. My partners are in Cologne and in Kassel and I live in Berlin. From where did you get my address? Anyhow, I am also looking forward to cooperate with you and if possible to meet you in Berlin.

　　With greetings from Germany

　　L. Günther

I visited Berlin shortly after and was happy to meet Dr Gunther who was personally handling the Indian component of Thea von Harbou's portal. He came to see me and presented me with a book he had written on Indians in Berlin titled *Der Indien in Berlin*. He had made several references in this book to my father. The book contained interesting information for me – a copy of Papa's application for permission to do a PhD degree, a handwritten biographical note, the first page of his PhD dissertation and more.

"We never knew what happened to Dr Tendulkar after he left Berlin," Dr Gunther told me when we began talking. I told him that once my father had reached India he had barely managed to settle down and start a newspaper in Belgaum before the war started. He was then a political detenue and was imprisoned for almost five years after that. "Frau Guttman, Thea von Harbou's secretary, told us a lot about your father," said Dr Gunther.

I learnt that Dr Gunther shared my fascination for Thea von Harbou's life and had come across her name while doing research on the life of Subhash Chandra Bose. Subhash Chandra Bose, freedom fighter and founder of the Indian National Army lived in Berlin from 1941–1942 and had evaded imprisonment by the British in India. He had made his way to Berlin to appeal to Hitler for support against the British. It was during this time that Thea von Harbou helped many Indians who were in Berlin then and was very supportive also of Subhash Chandra Bose. This was completely unknown to me as nobody had mentioned it in my family. My uncle Shripad who stayed back in Berlin during the war had mentioned Bose's name and the names of other Indians but not much more, and I did not, for example, know that Thea von Harbou was actually with Subhash Chandra Bose in 1942 when he made his famous "Azad Hind" radio broadcast from Berlin!

Dr Gunther went with me to Thea von Harbou's grave at Grab-Charlottenburg-Wilmersdorf-Heerstraße. It was in a beautiful wooded park spread over several acres, with trees, flowers and ornamental plants surrounding a natural lake. I was told that this was the graveyard for celebrities and Thea von Harbou's grave was chosen as a revered and 'honoured' one by the city of Berlin. I was happy to put a few flowers and whisper some prayers. Both my parents had told me several times that she was a wonderful person and had helped and loved not only my father but all the Indians that she came across.

I was convinced now that some unseen hand had led me to Berlin and had guided me towards Dr Lothar Guenther. Listening to him, I realized that a whole new vista had opened up and it was amazing that he had been collecting material over the years purely out of interest. I also showed Dr Gunther the paper where my father had jotted down a chronology of the milestones in his life. This, particularly the dates, helped Dr Gunther to trace several of my father's articles (written in impeccable German!) in *Der Berliner Tageblatt*, the German daily. He was impressed by Papa's command of the German language and even translated the articles and sent them to me. I've put some of these at the end of this book as I feel they help to give a flavour of the political and social scenarios of India in 1930–1931 even though they were written primarily for a German readership.

Dr Guenther sent me a chapter from the book, *The Women of the Nazis (Die Frauen der Nazis)* written by A M Sigmund in German. The book had a chapter on Thea von Harbou which he very kindly translated for me. It was fascinating to read and gave me a wonderful insight into Thea von Harbou's life. In the book, the account of her meeting my father did not differ very much from what I had heard except that I had been told that they met

The book cover of *Die Frauen der Nazis*

at Thea's house and not Conrad Molo's apartment (as the book described). I produce below a translated excerpt from the book about Thea's meeting with my father.

On the 12th of January 1933 Thea von Harbou visited the studio of Conrad von Molo, a friend, who had done the cutting of the film. There she met – according to her own reports – the handsome and sympathetic Indian Ayi Tendulkar and both had a lively discussion. The young man, a follower of Gandhi, was studying in Germany and was also the expert for Indian questions for the members of the political journal *Weltbühne*. They talked about the West's fascination with the Orient and about the freedom struggle of Indians against the English and they made friends, a friendship that quickly turned into love. The close relationship between the 42-year old lady and the 25-year old Indian was against any convention and attracted attention even among the liberal film circles of Berlin. When the wealthy and generous author purchased for her young lover a car and a lot of gifts, people reacted with mockery: "It was probably genuine love", described an intimate friend, "but personally as a friend of Fritz Lang I disapproved of this unusual story because Ayi was much younger than Thea von Harbou.

In fact my father had mentioned Conrad von Molo's name several times. I believe they stayed in touch with each other even after the World War II. Conrad von Molo was a film director and had worked closely with Fritz Lang and Thea von Harbou on several projects. I remember being told that Thea von Harbou had come across an article written by my father on India and was curious to meet him. Conrad told them both about the other and Thea invited my father to her house. After I read Sigmund's account, I realized it was very similar to what my father had told me – at the time I had not paid much attention to his story, but now, as I thought back, the details came to me. Here is what he had described:

On the evening in question, my father said he found himself outside Thea's house. Nervously, he rang the doorbell, wondering how he had allowed himself to get talked into coming to this place. He had come straight from work and couldn't entirely explain what he was doing there. Nor could he possibly conceive of what he might say to her. He waited patiently until the door was opened. A middle-aged woman stood in front of him, dressed in black. Tendulkar was a bit confused. This wasn't what he had imagined Thea would look like.

"Frau Harbou, I am Ayi Tendulkar," he said.

He extended his hand to greet her, but instead of a reciprocal gesture, the woman asked him to enter the drawing room. It held a collection of carpets, rugs, masks, wall hangings and figurines from all over the world. He turned around as if to make polite conversation about the artifacts when the woman spoke.

"Please do sit down. Frau Harbou will join you shortly. I am her secretary. She is expecting you."

Tendulkar felt a little foolish at having mistaken this middle-aged secretary for the renownedly beautiful Thea. He sat down, a little intimidated by the plush interiors. The walls were lined with art. There was an abstract painting by the Austrian painter Egon Schiele. The room was warm and sensual, the windows draped with heavy silk curtains. Cushions of embroidered silk were strewn upon the sofa. There were Japanese masks, Siamese temple flags and Chinese sacramental vessels, a grand piano and an expanse of book shelves. A huge Tibetan carpet replete with fiery dragons and cryptic symbols hung on the wall facing him. From a distant kitchen the aroma of hot, freshly baked cake wafted through the entire drawing room, whetting his appetite.

Tendulkar was lost in his observations when Thea entered. She wore a blue dress that ended at her knees. It was a crisp shade that brought out the light-blue colour of her eyes. A small black terrier followed her every move and then went straight to Tendulkar, sniffing him suspiciously. Tendulkar stood up immediately. Thea stretched out her arms and surprised him with a warm, friendly hug.

"Herr Tendulkar, I feel like I already know you through your many articles on India. Welcome to my home, and thank you for the honour," she said.

They sat down on easy chairs facing each other. Tendulkar felt a little out of place. He became conscious of his frayed collar and his general dishevelled look. Sensing his discomfort, Thea made a lot of small talk until finally, they slipped into conversation and even the black terrier decided that the guest was harmless and started to ignore him.

"Conrad has been telling me a lot about you. He really values your friendship," said Thea. "He's also been telling me about the current developments in India and I must say I'm fascinated by all he tells me. India, the sleeping giant, finally awakens. It is no longer the mystical land of snakes and magicians. I'm very interested in hearing about Mahatma Gandhi. I know you must think that we Germans are hard-hearted and only believe in force. But that isn't true. There are many of us who want peace and harmony, who respect Gandhi's philosophy of non-violence. We are prepared to learn from the East, if we can. Tell me, Herr Tendulkar, have you met or interviewed Gandhi?"

Tendulkar was impressed with Thea's impeccable English, although her German accent was quite strong. He had expected her to be older, but she appeared to be in her mid-forties and her enthusiasm was infectious. He had never met anyone quite like her. She had a feminine charm that he was drawn to, yet she was emphatic in her views and thoughts. Her steel-blue eyes soaked in everything, every tiny detail, and he could sense her nervous energy. He was seduced by her elegance and her aura.

"It's a long story, Frau Harbou. I'm surprised that you're even interested in hearing it," he said.

"Of course I'm interested. It has been my wish to visit your country one day. I've been so fascinated with India, ever since I was a girl. But I must insist that you do not call me Frau Harbou. Call me Thea, like your friend Conrad does," she said. Thea was 17 years older than Tendulkar, but when they both looked at each other, it was as though any difference in their age and background had dissolved.

"Thea, it will be my honour to call you that. Please call me Ayi. My first name is actually Ganpat, but Germans find it too strange."

Though initially Thea had seemed a little distant, she now appeared warm and affectionate. She spoke very little about herself, never mentioned how successful her career as a scriptwriter had been. She seemed like the perfect hostess, domestic, maternal, sophisticated, and sensitive. The maid brought in tea and an assortment of cakes and sandwiches. His hands trembled as he drank his tea. She watched him intently, and realizing he was

Scenes from *Das Indische Grabmal* (The Indian tomb)

hungry, she piled pastries and sandwiches on his plate while eating very little herself. Tendulkar told her about his experience in Sabarmati ashram as a young boy and the impact that Gandhi had on the freedom movement.

"Tell me more Ayi. How on earth have you managed to survive for so long in a country so far removed from your dear India?" she asked.

Tendulkar told her about his time as a student at Gottingen University where he studied during the day and worked in a factory at night. It was a Herculean task working on a PhD while also holding a job. From what he told her, he was fluent in both German and French. His manners, too, were impeccable. He didn't seem like a foreigner, and wasn't clumsy or star-struck around her as most people were.

She was surprised by how suavely he carried himself and the elegance with which he spoke. She was drawn to him, he was handsome though not in the Germanic way that she was accustomed to. All in all there was something very sincere about him. She told him she recognized his ambition, his deeply rooted desire to achieve something in his life. She invited him to stay for dinner during which he continued talking about his university days.

"Initially, Professor Schubring helped me out. He later became my father-in-law," Tendulkar noticed Thea's eyebrows lift at this and quickly explained. "His daughter and I were both students in the same class, and we were married for a while."

"Were married?" Thea inquired, with a bluntness that Tendulkar found attractive.

"Yes, Thea, were," he continued. "Her father, Professor Schubring was a wonderful teacher to me and gave me tremendous support." Time passed quickly for the two of them. She had made him feel so at ease, listening and making him share his experiences. Even her dog, Pumpernickel, lay curled on his lap, fast asleep.

Now it was Thea's turn to talk. She told him everything she could about her life, about her first husband Rudolph Kleine Rogge and her impending divorce from Fritz Lang. She talked about the failed relationship openly. Though they had separated, they continued to work together when they had to. Thea modestly described some of the films on which they had worked together as a team. After dinner, they sat down to dessert and coffee. Thea told him about her fascination for stories about exotic lands and about the novel she had written when she was very young, titled *Der Indische Grabmal*.

"Germans love to hear about exotic things like maharajas and slave dancers, the Indian rope trick, and magic. My novel provided them with all of this. Needless to say, it was an instant success. In fact, a film producer even wanted to make a movie out of it. I was asked to adapt the novel into a film script. The rest, as they say, is history. I had found my vocation as a script writer, and my interest only grew with time," she said. "So, what do you do besides writing for a newspaper?" she asked, shifting the focus onto him once again. They had switched from English to German.

"At the moment, I'm preparing to enrol for a doctorate programme at the Friedrich-Wilhems-Universtat in Berlin. I'm hoping to focus on mathematics and applied philosophy," he replied. "My dissertation is on the Indian mortality rate," he continued. "In the evenings, I am head of the Indian Bureau in the *Berliner Tageblatt*. I have to make myself available to other journalists for any queries on the political situation in India, especially with reference to British rule, and Gandhi's attempts to free India. The newspaper sent me to India in March 1931 to report on developments there. I got back in December. I've also been to South America on work. I just returned, in fact, from Argentina a few months ago."

Thea von Harbou smiled, "Yes I know, I have a secret to share with you. See this," and she opened a folder that was kept on the shelf. It was full of neatly filed cuttings of his articles in *Berliner Tageblatt*. "I enjoyed reading the stories you wrote from India in the *Berliner Tageblatt* and I have saved three out of four of them." Tendulkar was a little surprised as he opened the folder gingerly and saw the headings. He was pleased to see that she had taken the trouble to keep these. But it was, by that time, quite late and he had to leave. They bade each other goodnight and Tendulkar made his way to his car, realizing he was completely captivated by this woman who was 17 years his senior. She made him feel special. Until this evening, he had been convinced that he had mapped out the course of his life and would return to India sooner or later. Suddenly, none of that seemed to matter. What he was excited about was Thea's request that he meet her at the film studio at Babelsberg the next morning. He was already anticipating this next encounter, wondering what time would be appropriate to get there.

A few weeks after this successful evening, Thea left on an official film-promotion tour. She travelled all over Germany, made stops in several cities, and was gone for weeks. Tendulkar missed her badly and decided to make sure there were always flowers to greet her in every hotel room she was scheduled to stay in. She rang him up the first time she received the flowers. By the time it had happened six times, she was completely overwhelmed. His kindness and attention left her speechless.

Berlin

Tendulkar met Thea in January 1933, just a few days before Hitler was sworn in as Chancellor of Germany. Hitler's rise to power heralded the end of the Weimar era. The 14 years of the Weimar era were also marked by explosive intellectual productivity. Germany was the centre of the performing arts, cinema, art and architecture in Europe. It was during these years that Thea von Harbou and Fritz Lang had made their mark in the largest film studio in Berlin known as Universum Film AG (UFA), producing several black and white films that are even today considered classics, such as *Dr Mabuse* (1922), and *Metropolis* (1926). Based on the novel written by Thea, *Metropolis* was a sci-fi movie based on a mechanized city of the future. In it, futuristic and fantastic images provided the backdrop for a story about the battle between good and evil.

I still remember the gleam in my father's eye when he spoke about how wonderful Berlin used to be in those days – he would call it the centre of the western world, a vortex of creativity, a leader in innovation in the field of films, the visual arts, architecture, theatre, and music. Being a student and a journalist allowed him to be at the heart of much that was going on in Berlin. He spoke about his impressions of the Berlin Olympics in 1936 and how India had won the gold medal in Hockey, he told me about the developments in steel and other industry

and how that had been his trigger to want to start industry in India, and often he told me about the decadent lifestyle of the rich in Berlin.

Soon after Papa and Thea met, the political situation in Germany changed drastically. Hitler was sworn in as Chancellor and the government clamped down on the opposition. In his book, *Weimar Germany: The Republic of the Reasonable* Paul Bookbinder writes:

> The Weimar republic soon came to an end after the passage of the Enabling Act of 1933 by Hitler which empowered the cabinet to legislate without the approval of Reichstag or the President, and to enact laws that were contrary to the constitution. This was intended to forestall any action against the government by the Communists. Hitler used the provisions of the Enabling Act to pre-empt possible opposition to his dictatorship from other sources, in which he was mostly successful.

Shortly after, in September 1935 Germany announced the Nurnberg Laws – these particularly affected foreigners who lived in Germany whether they were students or professionals. They

Yeshwant Tendulkar, Thea von Harbou, Karin, and Tendulkar

were put under tremendous scrutiny and had to apply for special permission to pursue their education in schools and colleges.

The Nurnberg laws were introduced at the Annual Nurenberg Rally of the Nazi Party. The 'Law for Protection of German Blood and German Honour', prohibited marriages and extramarital intercourse between Jews and Germans and forbade the employment of German females under 45 in Jewish households. The Reich Citizenship Law declared those not of German blood to be Staatsangehörige (state subjects), while those, classified as "Aryans", were Reichsbürger (citizens of the Reich). The laws were primarily directed at Jews who were considered to be non Aryans. But with time, and in particular during the war, the common people in Germany thought or were made to think that foreigners like Slavic or coloured people also did not come under the rubric of 'Aryan'. Germans were advised to avoid marrying foreigners at that time, and were under scrutiny and observation even if they befriended foreigners.

I remember being told that due to these laws Thea von Harbou and my father could not get married officially but had a secret Indian-style wedding ceremony. This is also mentioned in several books written about her. It must have been very private and they must have exchanged rings and perhaps garlands and I am sure my father would have conducted a small Hindu puja for the occasion!

A M Sigmund speaks of Thea and Tendulkar's life together thus: "Thea always went alone, unaccompanied to the many receptions thrown in honour of the successful film team (Thea von Harbou and Fritz Lang). Her Indian partner in life, with whom she shared a flat in the Gelfertstrasse of Berlin, did not appear on these occasions. Generally, he also remained in the background." I am quite sure that my father was working on his PhD thesis at that time and must have been busy studying. Sigmund's explanation, though, was different. She wrote: "According to racial laws of the Third Empire, Indians were considered to be Aryans, but in spite of that, her relationship with Dr Tendulkar was nevertheless not approved by NS-circles. Thea von Harbou took that into account and lived secluded with her lover."

It was also interesting to read about Thea 's marriage to Fritz Lang in Sigmund's book. She mentions that the marriage between Lang-Harbou was only "on paper" for several years. Apparently, according to her, tensions began early and within the first year there were insurmountable differences, and she quotes Thea as having said "We were married for eleven years, because we found no time in ten years to get divorced." In spite of that, Thea was upset when Fritz Lang got involved in 1928 with Gerda Maurus, the star actress of their jointly directed films such as *Spione* and *Die Frau im Mond*. Thea also suffered from heart convulsions but kept silent about these and the three continued to interact with one another. Sigmund quotes a friend of the couple who described the situation thus "At that time Thea was middle-aged. She was cultivated and educated and maintained a reserve. She had inspired

Fritz Lang and was obviously cleverer than he was, but was not treated very well by him and found him difficult to cope with. Once Gerda Marcus entered the scene the couple began to live separate lives."

Despite all this, however, they remained in touch professionally and worked together. Apparently, Fritz Lang's several affairs did not affect their working relationship. Indeed, they travelled together to England, Vienna and Istanbul to promote his films.

> Everything changed with the entry of Ayi Tendulkar into Thea's life. In 1933 Fritz Lang was together with Lily Latte. But he did not grant his wife the same freedom that he sought for himself. On the contrary, he considered her relationship with the young Indian an assault on his male honour. When Thea finally separated from him in spring 1933, he reacted with indignation and offended pride. 'He was enraged about the fact that Thea had left him.' wrote Conrad von Molo. Altogether, it was a break leaving no space for further cooperation. With the film *Das Testament des Dr Mabuse* both ended their marriage and their common career and they brought to an end an important chapter in film history after producing nine great common productions." (Sigmund)

It was through my father's stories that I really began to understand Thea as a person. They had both met at a very difficult time, everyday life in Germany was changing in a way nobody had expected. Reading Sigmund's comment about Thea going unaccompanied to film releases reminded me that Papa had once mentioned that when he began to live with Thea, he was busy studying and it created too much controversy for both of them to be seen in public together as Thea was considered a celebrity in Germany and was often in the press. So they didn't go out together much, but they did entertain often at home. Thea was a gracious hostess and loved entertaining her close friends. I am told that Thea was an avid Bridge player and Papa too loved the game. Thea's Bridge parties were well attended. I remember being told that it was at one such party at Thea's house that Papa actually met Fritz Lang. This is the story I remembered him telling me.

My father told me that Thea spent several weeks planning the Bridge party. She paid careful attention to the guest list, making sure that she included friends and colleagues from the film industry as well as a group of intellectuals and professionals. She invited all her Jewish friends, as she was always known to do, offering them a helping hand in these terrible times. She served dinner first, and after everyone had eaten the game of Bridge began. Not everyone played and those who weren't thus engaged, chatted over drinks.

Tendulkar noticed Fritz Lang looking watchfully at him several times from across the room. He had brought along his friend Lily Latte, who remained at his side. Up until now, Lang hadn't really mingled with the Indians in Berlin. Tendulkar wondered privately if Lang's view of Indians would be limited to his knowledge of the characters he depicted in his film scripts. They were all yogis or maharajas or beggars, quite unlike Tendulkar who wore his elegant trademark white suit.

Throughout the evening, Tendulkar and Thea exchanged glances, even while they were in conversation with other people. Fritz Lang noticed this obvious and deliberate display of intimacy. At some point, Lang approached Tendulkar, "So, you are Tendulkar," he said, stretching out his hand in a what my father described as a "condescending handshake". He smiled, but a steel-cold gaze in his one good eye revealed his otherwise well-concealed hostility. "I've read your articles on India and Gandhi in the newspaper, Herr Tendulkar," he continued, looking at Tendulkar through his monocle and puffing on his cigar. Tendulkar sensed that Lang was trying to probe him, perhaps to find out what it was about this complete stranger that so fascinated his ex-wife. My father knew though – a discovery he had made over the last few weeks – that for all her sophistication and aristocratic breeding, Thea was a diehard romantic. That, coupled with her almost impulsive attitude towards life, made her quite unpredictable.

"Is it true, Herr Tendulkar, that the *Berliner Tageblatt* is changing hands?" Lang asked. Tendulkar wasn't paying much attention – for a moment, his attention was on the political history unfolding around them. But he was also aware of Lang's scrupulous observation of every nuance of his speech and gesture. Lang continued, "Do you know, Herr Tendulkar, that when Thea and I met, in 1917, we worked together on the adaptation of her novel, *Das Indische Grabmal*? We were both enchanted by your country, or rather with what we thought India was all about. We were even a little fixated, I would say. My good friend Joy May produced the film and he asked me to help with the writing and with organizing the production, but to my great disappointment, he directed it himself!"

"Yes, Herr Lang," Tendulkar replied in impeccable German, "I have read the novel and also seen the film. It is indeed very imaginative, and quite fantastical. India is very different from what you have depicted. At this moment, Indians from every walk of life are joining in the Civil Disobedience movement against the British. It's been a truly successful endeavour. At one point, Britain responded by imprisoning over 60,000 Indians in a single day."

"Quite so," said Lang. "I heard about the incident, and then the Viceroy, Lord Irwin, was it? Yes, Lord Irwin, he called Gandhi for talks. A pact was signed and Gandhi was invited to some conference and left for London. We saw in the newspapers that he even visited the Queen of England wearing nothing but a strip of cotton around his waist and a wrap around his shoulders." Lang chuckled and puffed away on his cigar. "What a change! For a man who studied law, and who must have worn European clothes for so many years."

"Herr Lang, you may not be aware of this, but immediately after he returned from England, Gandhi was arrested without a trial. The government wanted to isolate him from his followers."

"Yes, I read about that. And now he is fighting for the marginalized farmer, but what do you call them again in India?" Lang asked, trying to recall the word he had read somewhere. Despite everything Tendulkar had heard about Lang, and his earlier reservations, he found himself warming to him. He felt a kind of camaraderie with him as the ice gradually melted between them.

"Gandhi is on a mission to improve the lives of the untouchables," said Tendulkar. "He calls them harijans, children of God. On the eighth of May, this year, Gandhi began a 21-day fast, to make his case against the exploitation of these harijans."

"Quite a wonderful man, this little man, Gandhi!" Lang chuckled. Just as he turned around, he saw Thea approaching them.

Tendulkar turned to greet her. Thea was amused at the spectacle of the two men engaged in deep conversation. She had been curious to hear what they had to say to one another. She had been watching Lang very carefully. She knew him well, and had expected an outburst, or some kind of negative reaction from him when he met Tendulkar. She was relieved, but also surprised at the ease with which they seemed to converse. The amicable atmosphere between the two men was partly due to how taken aback Lang was at the favourable impression young Tendulkar made on him. He had not expected Tendulkar to be an intellectual and a scholar. He had only heard about his work at the newspaper. There was something about the young man that he liked, something about his straightforwardness and honesty that had disarmed Lang, who was known for being temperamental and arrogant.

Soon afterwards, the dinner party wound up and guests began to leave. It was then that Lang casually went up to Tendulkar, and in a return to his habitual harshness, pronounced, "Hitler personally does not like Indians. On the contrary, he admires British rule. He likes how they control the Indian masses, and how they've kept the race clean. He has never considered Indians equal to the white race."

"I will tell you a secret, Herr Tendulkar," Fritz Lang continued, almost sarcastically. "This is something even Thea does not know… I am toying with the idea of leaving Germany, at least until the current political rule changes. I do not have any sympathy for what has been happening in Germany." Tendulkar realized that Lang was somehow using him to inform Thea that he would be leaving Berlin soon.

According to various biographies written on Thea, she was home-schooled after the age of 14 when she had left the Secondary School for Girls, Luisenstift, at Radebeul near Dresden. She didn't like the school or their methods of teaching. After she left this school she was educated by her mother and grandmother. In time, Thea became fluent in English and French as well as in arts and music. She was fascinated by Tendulkar's aptitude for mathematics, yet she would often tell him that he should go back to India and start an industry. "A Doctorate in mathematics will be of no use to you," she would say. "Steel, cement, power, these are the things that India will need once the British leave the country. These are the things that Germany is proud to contribute to the world." It was on her insistence that he enrolled in Berlin University for a postgraduate degree in Mechanical Engineering.

Thea was responsible too for Tendulkar inviting his younger brother Yeshwant to study in Germany. Tendulkar had left home when Yeshwant was just 12, and it was only during his most recent trip to India that the two of them had been able to spend time together. Their mother had died soon after she had given birth to Yeshwant, and he had been brought up by their maternal grandmother. Yeshwant was barely 20 and naturally, Tendulkar was concerned about how he would adapt to German culture, having never left India before.

Thea was apparently a bit surprised at this concern – perhaps because she'd seen the ease with which my father had taken to the German lifestyle. Father would often explain to me that he was able to make the transition from India to the European lifestyle whilst he was still young, easily. He said, "When I first went to Europe, I had just about turned 18. I didn't even know how to tie my shoelaces! My experience in India had been very traditional and focused on smaller towns. I had very little exposure to living in large cities, least of all living on my own in the West. The first time I travelled by ship from Mumbai to London, the Indian stewards – who were mainly from Goa – befriended me since I spoke their language fluently. It took me quite a bit of time to adapt to the way of life in Germany."

Tendulkar did not want his brother's arrival to inconvenience Thea in any way. He assured her that once Yeshwant learnt a little German, he would help him get a part-time job and move into an apartment close to them. But Thea wouldn't hear of it. "Let him live here and really settle down. Later we can find him a place to live. It's not easy to get jobs these days. You know the state the economy is in. Also the SA guards will be very suspicious of him," she said.

Yeshwant arrived a few weeks later. He was tall – over six feet and with a shock of black hair brushed straight back from his forehead. He seemed simple, affable, in awe, almost, of his brother's relationship with Thea. He had never encountered anyone as elegant and sophisticated as his German hostess, and for a few days he found himself quite tongue-tied around her.

Yeshwant, who later came to live in Mumbai, would describe to me the manner in which Thea took him under her wing. Thea wanted to show him the whole of Berlin, the Brandenburg Gate, the Tiergarten, the river, the Opera House, the Berlin that she loved and that she wanted to share with him. Yeshwant was wide-eyed and awe-struck. He had never seen such beautiful buildings, or such broad roads. He was fascinated by the cars on the roads. His older brother sensed that he needed more time to adjust to this new environment and suggested that they stay indoors for a few days during which he could familiarise himself with the language and the climate. But Thea took him shopping, kitting

Tendulkar and Thea von Harbou in Berlin

him out with shirts, jackets and shoes. Yeshwant was overwhelmed and touched by her generosity and warmth.

For a long time he addressed to her as Mrs Harbou, but Thea didn't like that.

"Why don't you call me Thea?" she asked.

Yeshwant was apologetic. "I'm not used to addressing someone older by their first name. I even call my brother Dada," he said sheepishly.

"Tell me, Yeshwant, if I had been your elder sister, how would you have addressed me?" Thea asked.

"Mrs Harbou," he said. "I would have called you Tai."

"Then that is what you will call me henceforth, Tai," said Thea.

Yeshwant was touched. And before long, Thea became extremely fond of him and the two became close. Yeshwant enrolled in German classes. He was quite the loner and loved walking the streets of Berlin. He didn't make friends too easily, and was rather intimidated by women. Once, a younger sister of one of Thea's secretaries took a fancy to him and asked him out for a movie. That evening Thea and Tendulkar were surprised when Yeshwant returned home earlier than they expected. He burst into the house and declared, "She tried to kiss me!" They could hardly contain their laughter. Yeshwant refused to go out on any more dates. He confessed to Thea one day, that when he returned to India, he would marry a simple Hindu girl.

Yeshwant was very disturbed by the way in which Nazi propaganda was gaining ground. He failed to understand the targeting of the Jews. One day, he broached the subject with his brother. "In India, we are told that the Aryans invaded India and that they forced the dark-skinned inhabitants to travel further south. Are we not the same Aryans as the Germans? I keep hearing them use the word Aryan. Who are they referring to?"

"The Nazis refer to their Indo-Aryan roots when they feel they needed a scientific cover to their plan of establishing a

superior 'Nordic' race," said Tendulkar. "The term 'Aryan' used in Berlin is used exclusively for white-skinned Germans, to distinguish them from foreigners and from other communities. In their racial philosophy, the Nazis do not refer to Indo-Aryans who had mixed with the native, coloured people in India. They are looking to create a mythological picture of blond Nordic ancestors whom they refer to as Aryans."

Thea sat knitting while listening to the conversation between the two brothers. She suddenly interjected. "Yes, Yes, that is true. The Germans too have their epic stories known as the "Nibelungenlied", the national epics of the Germans. We made a movie on the Nibelungen in 1924 as we wanted the German heroes of the past to become icons and recreate national pride in the Germans. I studied over twenty different editions of this saga and finally when it was time to make a script based on it, we settled on a mixture of heroic adventures to rekindle national pride. The most popular German saga from the Nibelungen epics is one where their principal hero, Siegfried, who was blond with blue eyes, kills the dragon. He was made to exemplify the Nordic race. He came from the mythological Nibelungen people or tribe."

A A Sigmund describes how Thea worked out a detailed script and fixed every camera position for this film. She divided her script into pictures, gave detailed instructions on every single shot and for settings to be made in epic width. In the Babelsberg studios, they hurriedly constructed the sets which included medieval lanes of small towns, a landscape of the Rhine river, a dark German fairy forest, a mystical cathedral, the fortress of Attila, and most importantly a gigantic dragon that came to life with the help of 24 men! Fritz Lang asked for strict styling and standards and directed in a meticulous and dictatorial way. The hero, Siegfried, was depicted as a "typical north German character" who appeared noble and radiant in contrast to the Huns exemplified by Attila the Hun who was dark with rough and coarse features.

The production of this very expensive film went on for two years (*Part 1 – Siegfried; Part 2 – Kriemhild's Revenge*). The scenes were repeated nearly a hundred times till they were perfect. At last the film was released in February 1924. In splendid pictures the audience saw their hero Siegfried, court his beloved Kriemhild, they saw him slay the dragon and they watched him dying at the hands of Hagen von Tronje. They also saw the march of the proud Nibelungen to the East, and finally their extermination by the Huns, who were called gangsters or people of a lower race. Naturally, the impact of this film was great on the youth and it was remembered for many years.

The press was lavish in its praise of Lang's technique and photography. Enthusiastic praise also came from the members of the forbidden Nazi Party after their failed revolt in November 1923. Sigmund writes, "Adolf Hitler was interested in the topic, he admired Fritz Lang's ideas of directing and also appreciated the script written by Thea von Harbou. Nobody could have suspected at that time that the film, made by Thea von Harbou and Fritz Lang whose topic was the fall of the Nibelungen in the core of the Hun Empire, anticipated Hitler's visionary march of the Germans to the East, which was defeated in the battle of Stalingrad."

Thea did not elaborate further. She had learnt by now that it was prudent to not say too much to anyone. There were stories of people being rounded up and arrested for saying anything at all against the Third Reich. There was always a risk that Yeshwant

Thea von Harbou

might repeat too much of what he heard. Although she realized that the risk was small since he was a shy and quiet boy, Yeshwant gradually felt his world expand. In India, he had been familiar with the arrogant manner in which the British treated Indians. In Germany, he saw the same kind of discrimination towards the Jews.

Thea participated in a limited way in political activities and only when she felt she was acting in the country's best interest. Recently, to counteract inflation and save money, the Third Reich had instituted the custom of the 'one pot meal' or a sort of stew on Sundays. For several months now, the Sunday meal eaten at noon, which had been soup, roast meat, vegetables, salad and dessert, was reduced to a one pot meal where each household had a variety of thick lentil, green pea or cabbage stew. Party officials went door to door collecting the money that had thus been saved. Every door had a sticker to show that they had complied with this requirement. Sometimes officials made surprise checks. Overall, Thea's cooking standards had not been compromised. But she went along with the weekly one pot stew, a meal that she insisted everyone eat.

On a warm September afternoon in 1934, Tendulkar, Thea and Yeshwant were sitting on the porch, catching the last moments of the setting autumn sun while drinking their evening tea. Tendulkar was restless. He started pacing up and down, telling Thea about what he had heard – that the position which had been offered by the Propaganda Ministry to Fritz Lang, of making a film on the Nazis, had been given to actress and film maker Leni Riefenstahl. Apparently she had already been given the assignment of making a documentary based on the Nazi party convention that had been held a week earlier in Nurnberg. He was surprised that Thea had not mentioned anything to him about this. Thea had become increasingly reserved about the film industry, which otherwise had absorbed so much of her time. Now she was preoccupied with a new cause, that of looking after Indian students. If she knew about the film offer, she had not mentioned it.

"I've also heard the same thing," she said. "I remember, she had created quite a stir a few years ago, in 1928, actually. She was quite an actress, and dancer, and now she's interested in directing documentaries. Apparently, Hitler saw her on stage and 'liked' what he saw. So yes, she was asked to film the annual Nazi rally at Nurnberg. Just yesterday, at the UFA studios, I met several of the cameramen that I've worked with in the past. They told me that 30 cameras and a crew of 120 people were kept at her disposal. Herr Goebbels wants her to use the footage to make a two-hour documentary movie which she has decided to call *The Triumph of the Will*, for the Nazi Propaganda Ministry."

The 1934 rally was also reported in the newspapers. Every detail was described with great flourish and enthusiasm. Especially the scale and the dimensions of the Nurnberg rally. Hitler had made a dramatic entry down the central aisle of the assembly, followed by his close colleagues Hermann Göring, Josef Goebbels, Rudolph Hess and Heinrich Himmler, while 30,000 Nazi officers stood in uniforms with their hands raised in salute. The magnificent strains of a full symphony orchestra were heard in the background. News reporters were calling it a "gigantic assembly". The especially built stadium was filled with a sea of fluttering flags as thousands of SS men marched in perfect columns, reminiscent of the Roman legions. Nazi symbols such as the swastikas and eagles on flags and banners were shot in sequences from different angles, creating a rhythm and a sense of continuity in the visual presentation. All public appearances of the Führer were stage managed with a tremendous sense of drama and timing.

When Hitler made pronouncements like, "The German form of life is definitely determined for the next 1000 years. Germany has done everything possible to assure world peace," Germans cheered loudly, believing every word he said. Half a million people would go back to their homes talking about the Führer, the saviour of the Germans. The general population followed him blindly. It was also reported that at night, thousands of people stood shoulder to shoulder outside Hitler's hotel, shouting in unison, "Acht, neun, zehn…wir wollen unsern Führer sehn!" which meant, "Eight, nine, ten…We want to see our Führer."

Despite the political situation in the country, the three of them, Tendulkar, Thea and Yeshwant, managed to create a small, enchanted circle in their flat in Gelfertstrasse. Tendulkar had finally managed to enrol himself in Berlin University to do his Postgraduate degree in Mechanical Engineering. Yeshwant was still struggling with his German while continuing with high school. He missed India but didn't have the courage to tell either Thea or his brother. Tendulkar made it a point that both he and his brother remained in the background socially. He did not accompany Thea to award functions and receptions. According to the racial laws of the Third Reich, Indians were sometimes considered Indo-Aryans. He sensed that their relationship was under scrutiny. They lived a secluded life, and were seldom out in public together. One day Thea returned from the studio feeling very agitated.

"Fritz Lang has finally left for the USA, after his stay in Paris," she told Tendulkar. "But he has made some nasty remarks about me to the press. He told them I am a Nazi sympathiser and that I'm anti-Jewish. He has made it a point to announce this publicly, to hide the fact that he is actually half Jewish. He will say and do anything to promote himself. He knows that Hollywood is filled with prominent Jewish people, and therefore he is, in fact, strengthening his reputation by spreading rumours about me."

It had become known publicaly that Fritz Lang had a Jewish mother. Whether Thea had disclosed this to the press is not certain though in the press article which had agitated Thea so much, Fritz had blamed Thea for disclosing this. Thea maintained her silence about Fritz Lang and had gone on with her life, but she had not expected that he would blame her.

The Berlin Olympics

In August of 1936, Berlin became the venue for the Olympics. Whenever Thea and the Tendulkar brothers had some time to spare, they would get into their Mercedes and drive to the 325 acre complex that was just five kilometers away from Berlin city to watch the gigantic stadium being built. It was to hold 110,000 spectators. The size and the dimensions were absolutely overwhelming. And also, there was a bit of history about the place – the grounds had earlier been chosen for the 1916 Olympic games that were to have been held in Germany but that had to be cancelled because of World War I.

Thea would smile at the brothers' excitement as they walked around and discussed how "One day the Olympics will be held in India too!" Originally, when the decision to hold the Olympics in Berlin had been taken, the German government had decided that they would restore the earlier Olympiastadion of 1916, but once the Nazis came into power in 1933, this changed and the Nazis decided to erect on the same site a gigantic sports complex which they could then use for their nightly torch-lit processions and for other occasions.

Yeshwant listened for hours in fascination to the radio broadcasts of the Olympic games. The Nazi administration had developed special programmes to create a good impression on Berliners and make international tourists feel welcome during the Olympics. Tendulkar was amused by how the normally curt Nazi officers and

SS men tried hard to sound friendly, especially in dealings with the international press. Several of the public signboards saying "No Jews allowed" were taken down during the games.

The Treaty of Versailles signed after WWI had dictated that Germany's army be severely limited in size. However, it was now whispered that under the guise of athletic training, Germany was secretly training its people to become soldiers. Through the local newspapers, the Nazis encouraged Germans to use the forthcoming Summer Olympics as a showcase for the "New Germany", in other words, to exhibit the progress that Germany had made under the present regime. The Nazis also hoped to profit from the tens of thousands of souvenir-hungry tourists bringing much-needed foreign currency into the country.

Every day, the papers spoke of the new rules and regulations being created to shut out Jews from all aspects of German society. The official Aryan-only policy in selecting Olympic athletes to compete for Germany meant that many world-class athletes such as tennis star Daniel Prenn and boxer Erich Seelig were barred from participating. This was condemned internationally, since such a ban was a straight violation of the Olympic code that stressed equality and fair play. In fact, several countries boycotted the Olympics because of this discrimination. Meanwhile, many of the "acceptable" foreign athletes who arrived were given the red-carpet treatment by the Germans and lavish receptions were held in their honour. When Thea saw Yeshwant's excitement about meeting the Indian field hockey team she decided to hold a welcome reception for them in her house. My father spoke of how surprised the athletes were to see the 'Asian' influence in the house. Thea was a charming hostess. She made them all feel comfortable by telling them little stories about the movies she had made about India.

She insisted that they all call her Tai, but they insisted on calling her Mrs Tendulkar which she liked very much since the restrictive laws of marriage in Germany meant that to her colleagues she was still Frau Thea von Harbou. Tendulkar watched as his darling Thea played hostess to the Indians and was really amazed at how she didn't seem to feel out of place.

Thea was very happy to meet the captain of the Indian hockey team, Dhyan Chand. He was already an international legend in field hockey. Thea had seen him play in Amsterdam in the 1928 Olympics, when India had won a gold medal. My father described a conversation between them. I recreate it here from my memories of his accounts.

"How do you feel about participating in the Olympics here in Berlin?" she asked him.

"Mrs Tendulkar, I am very excited to play in Berlin and I do hope we can make our country proud," he replied. He went on to describe the victories of the Indian hockey team during their recent tour in Australia. Thea was very impressed by his unassuming manner and his experiences in the Indian Army in the Punjab Regiment.

"I was lucky!" said another player, Joseph Phillips. "I was chosen for the team at the last moment. There are so many players who were ready to play hockey in the Olympics that if any of us left, there would be at least two to three players ready to take our place. Half of Poona came to Khadki station to give us a send off." He said the long bumpy sea journey had taken almost 15 days on the ocean liner Aitheneaver during which the enthusiastic team constantly practised on the deck, losing hundreds of hockey balls in the sea!

Joseph informed everyone that Britain had not been keen that India, its colony, should participate in the Olympics. It was only after the British Indian hockey team had declined that they allowed the Indian one to participate. Tendulkar was keen to hear the latest news about what was happening on the political front in India. News was not too good either for the Indian leaders. Gandhi's ongoing Civil Disobedience Movement against the British was not yielding the desired results. India was fighting a war against the

British but there was a much larger problem brewing among its own people – the Hindu-Muslim divide. The colonial rulers and local politicians were instigating both sides and people who had lived peacefully for decades now began fighting with each other. Tendulkar found this development very disturbing, though he was happy to see that the Hindu-Muslim divide had not entered the realm of competitive sports, and winning the hockey match was the only thing on the minds of the Indian team! In fact the Indian Hockey team had an interesting mix of Anglo-Indians, Muslims and Hindus. The brothers were secretly curious to see who Thea would cheer for when Germany played against India. They knew she wanted to encourage the Indian hockey team, but deep down, Thea loved her country fiercely. Yet, she was open to India and had grown fond of a new culture, one that was very different from what she was accustomed to.

A few days later, the Indian team played a warm-up game against the Germans. They were not well prepared and their performance was quite dismal. They didn't score a single goal! During these trial matches with Germany, the Indian team lost every game and they became quite demoralised. Yeshwant, who was inseparable from them, was afraid that they had absolutely no chance of winning. He shared this concern with Thea and Tendulkar. Ultimately the Indian team sent an urgent cable message to India asking for an additional hockey player. Ahmed Sher Dara was air-dashed to Berlin just before India's semi-final match.

The opening ceremony of the Eleventh Olympic Games was held on 1 August 1936, inside the Olympic Stadium which was filled to capacity. Berlin's main boulevard Unter den Linden was decorated with large red, black and white swastika flags. The loud cheering of a hundred thousand spectators was punctuated with the boom of cannons. The German spectators, along with international participants and visitors cheered, wept, screamed and stamped their feet. The Olympic flag was towed by the Hindenberg, the largest Zeppelin airship in the world. It was

900-feet long and 160-feet wide, with huge swastika markings on its tail fins.

Thea had got special passes for herself and Tendulkar while Yeshwant tagged along with the Indian hockey team, assisting them in any way he could. He had never seen anything of this kind before and the scale of things completely overwhelmed him. The cloudy day with occasional rain showers did not dampen the mood of the spectators. Hitler and his entourage, along with the Olympic officials, walked into the stadium amid a chorus of three thousand Germans singing *Deutschland über Alles*, the German national anthem followed by *Horst Wessel Lied*, the Nazi anthem. A runner who had begun 13 days before in Olympia, Greece, ran into the stadium to light the Olympic flame. It was the first time in Olympic history that this had been done. Adolph Hitler, in full uniform, stood in the box of honour and officially opened the Berlin Olympics as twenty-thousand carrier pigeons were released into the sky. August 1, 1936 marked the beginning of an extravaganza the likes of which the world had never seen. Over 5,000 athletes from 51 nations marched by, with Greece leading the parade and the host country, Germany, following up at the end.

In field hockey, India beat Hungary 4-0, United States 7-0 and Japan 9-0. It was only after the last entrant had been called from India, Ahmed Sher Dara, that the Indian team had a stunning victory against France, scoring 10-0 in the semi-finals. No team had scored a single goal against India in their relentless march to the finals. Now it was their turn to play against Germany. Though the presence of A S Dara had revived the morale of the Indian hockey team and his presence was strongly felt after their warm-up games with Germany, the team was not confident of a victory.

As a British colony, the Indian players had been forced to march behind the Union Jack in the Opening Ceremony. Now, too, the Union Jack was all that was shown on the field. The manager of the Indian hockey team was aware of the feelings of his team from

The Indian Hockey Team, Berlin 1936

India and he knew that they would play their best if he could somehow rekindle their national pride. He thought that saluting the Indian flag would probably help. Just before the match Pankaj Gupta, the manager of the Indian hockey team, assembled the team around him in the changing room and quietly produced the Indian tricolour flag. There was a moment of pin-drop silence and then all the players saluted their national flag saying Jai Hind (victory to India). They sang *Vande Mataram* (One India), the song which is sung at all Indian national gatherings and stood in silence for a few moments, each one with a prayer on his lips. In the end, the players embraced to show their solidarity with each other and their country before marching onto the field.

Yeshwant told Tendulkar and Thea about this when he joined them in the stands. When the team appeared on the field Tendulkar explained to Thea the significance of what had transpired in the locker room. "I am sure this small gesture will charge the entire team with nationalistic fervour,"

Tendulkar concurred, "They will put their best foot forward for their motherland India."

India was facing Germany at 11 a.m. in the final fifth Field Hockey tournament on the Reichssportfeld near the Olympic Stadium. The air was vibrant as the spectators poured into the stands, a record crowd of 40,000 which included Indian royalty – the Maharaja of Baroda, the Princess of Bhopal, and a large number of Indians who had travelled from all over Europe to witness the final match. The vast crowd cheered as both teams entered the field.

The German team was convinced they would defeat the Indians, especially after their victory in the trial matches. In addition, Dhyan Chand, India's best player was incapacitated by a fever. He watched his team play from the sidelines, but at half-time when India had only scored one goal, he couldn't sit idle any more. The pitch was wet so Dhyan Chand removed his spiked shoes and took to the field. The crowd cheered as they watched the barefooted Dhyan Chand tear the German defence apart. India went on to score seven more goals in the second half. Dhyan Chand broke one of his teeth in an incident with the German keeper, but was soon back in action. He alone scored six goals, and India won the match 8-1. It was such an amazing victory that many Germans, including Thea, were loudly cheering the Indian team. It did not matter which side they had supported, true hockey fans of all nations were celebrating that India had played magnificently. They cheered the amazing Dhyan Chand, his brother Roop Singh, and the other members of the Indian team who had excelled. Thea, personally, was cheering for the determination that the Indian players had demonstrated. On the field the Indian team was ecstatic, as was the crowd, when the final score was announced. The Indian hockey team had won a gold medal. To celebrate the victory, the Maharaja and Maharani of Baroda invited the hockey team for a reception at the Hotel Adlon.

It was rumoured that even the Führer was very impressed by Dhyan Chand's performance in the finals. Gossip had it that after the finals, at a dinner party full of dignitaries Hitler had suggested that if Dhyan Chand decided to stay in Germany, he would be given the rank of a Colonel!

A New Life

Thea, my father and my uncle Yeshwant soon settled into a routine. Yeshwant had joined the Technical College in Berlin and was doing a course in Electrical Engineering. He was no longer the shy young man from India and had, as my father said, "found his voice". I was told that Thea, who loved him like a son, was always fearful that he might antagonize the Nazi authorities. I remember my uncle Yeshwant from when I was a child. Tall and lanky and always a little aloof from everyone he met, very different from my father. He would sometimes talk about his time in Berlin and describe how Thea expressed her concern and affection for him. He loved Berlin and told me many stories about how, on weekends, or whenever the weather was good, he would take canal boat trips through the Spreewald or swim in the Hundekehlsee, the Lake of the Dog's Gullet, in the Grunewald. He also spoke about the darker side of Berlin and the constant aggravation from the din of Nazi propaganda. He would talk about the Nazi newspaper *Der Sturmer* which was displayed in a glass case on street corners so that everyone could read the publication without even having to buy it. He spoke of how, after the excitement of the Olympics had died down, the rule of law in Germany had deteriorated to the point that the courts were unable to interfere with the activities of the Gestapo in any way. Hitler's rule was a dictatorship and his police occasionally put into prison those who were unpatriotic enough to ridicule him.

I found an interesting letter in my mother's collection from an Indian Congress party worker, J B Kriplani. It described how my father had gone to India in September 1936, shortly after the Berlin Olympics. He wanted to write about the All India Congress Committee session (AICC) in Faizpur near Lucknow which was to be held in December of that year. Pandit Jawaharlal Nehru was the President of the Congress session and the secretary was J B Kirplani. The letter is addressed to my father at the Taj Mahal Hotel, Mumbai and is a reply to his request for a press pass.

Swaraj Bhavan,
Allahabad.
17.12.1938.

My dear Tendulkar,

Thanks for your letter of the 6th instant. I was not here and the letter was wandering after me. Hence the delay.

I am very thankful to you for the kind sentiments expressed in your letter.

I am sure you will be able to secure press pass for the Congress and I am also sure that you will get some advantageous seat there. For the Press ticket you will have to write to the Reception Committee at Faizpur. The tickets are issued by them and not by us.

I hope you are enjoying your life here.

Yours sincerely,

J B Kirplani

Mr. A. Tendulkar,
c/o The Taj Mahal Hotel,
Bombay.

26/3525

Swaraj Bhawan, Allahabad.
17.12.1936.

My dear Tendulkar,

Thanks for your letter of the
6th instant. I was not here and the
letter was wandering after me. Hence
the delay.

I am very thankful to you for the
kind sentiments expressed in your letter.

I am sure you will be able to
secure press pass for the Congress and I
am also sure that you will get some advantageous seat there. For the Press
ticket you will have to write to the
Reception Committee at Faizpur. The
tickets are issued by them and not by us.

I hope you are enjoying your life,
here.

Yours sincerely,

Mr. A. Tendulkar,
C/o The Taj Mahal Hotel,
Bombay.

During the AICC, my father also had a chance to meet Nehru.
He described to Nehru how the AICC had given him a loan of
Rs 500 to go abroad when he was a young boy and expressed

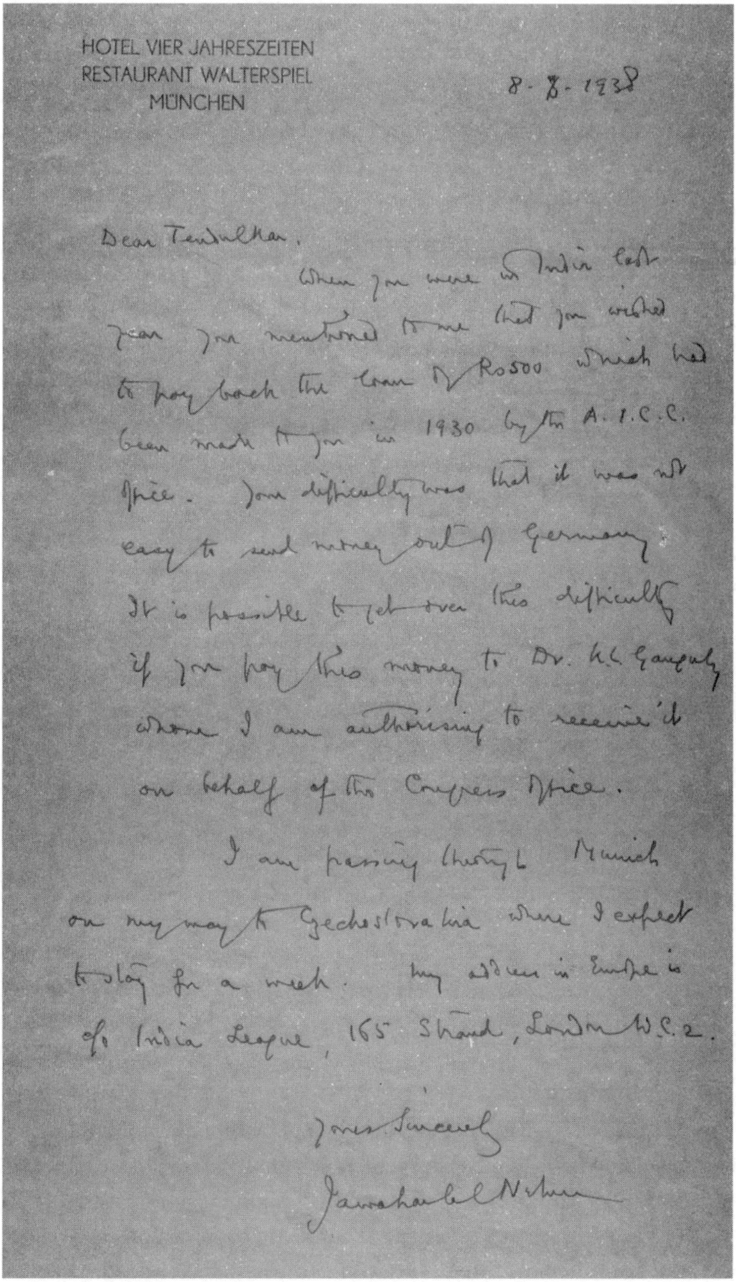

HOTEL VIER JAHRESZEITEN
RESTAURANT WALTERSPIEL
MÜNCHEN

8-8-1938

Dear Tendulkar,

When you were in India last year you mentioned to me that you wished to pay back the loan of Rs 500 which had been made to you in 1930 by the A.I.C.C. office. Your difficulty was that it was not easy to send money out of Germany. It is possible to get over this difficulty if you pay this money to Dr. K.C. Ganguly whom I am authorising to receive it on behalf of the Congress office.

I am passing through Munich on my way to Czechoslovakia where I expect to stay for a week. My address in Europe is c/o India League, 165 Strand, London W.C.2.

Yours sincerely,
Jawaharlal Nehru

a desire to return the loan, and Nehru replied to my father's letter, advising him how to do so. I give the text of this letter in Jawaharlal Nehru's handwriting to my father below. As I read it, I thought how much our political culture had changed – would this kind of thing even be possible today? Nehru mentions the loan given in 1930, but he must have meant in 1922 when my father left India for the first time, as in 1930 he was already a journalist and scholar!

8.8.1938

Dear Tendulkar,

When you were in India last year you mentioned to me that you wished to pay back the loan of Rs 500 which had been made to you in 1930 by the A.I.C.C. office. Your difficulty was that it was not easy to send money out of Germany. It is possible to get over this difficulty if you pay this money to Dr KK Ganguly whom I am authorising to receive it on behalf of the Congress office.

I am passing through Munich on my way to Czechoslovakia where I expect to stay for a week. My address in Europe is c/o of India League, 165 Strand, London W.C.2.

Yours sincerely

Jawaharlal Nehru

My mother's papers also held another letter, it was quite crumpled and when I managed to unfold it and spread it out a bit, I saw that it was a letter Yeshwant had written to Jawaharlal Nehru dated 11.4.1937. It read:

"Podbeilskiallee 59, Berlin-Dahlen, Germany

Dear Pandit Nehru,

Events in India have been occupying my thoughts for last few days and your statement to Reuters in Bombay which I read this morning in the German paper set me thinking seriously. Though not known to you personally, I take the liberty of addressing you for I consider you alone can give me the audience I need.

I am a young Indian of 24 and hail from Belgaum side. I am a student of Electrical Engineering at the Technical College in Berlin and I am already four years here. During my life in India I did not think much about my country and it is my close contact with German students that turned my thoughts to India. Every young German is a political soldier in the service of his country and is actively associated with the work of Germany's uplift. And I, a young Indian, am doing so little for India though India's needs are a thousand times more pressing. My work is in my studies in the college and my heart is with India and the Congress and you. Must I [deny] myself the great privilege of doing for my country what my German student friends do for their own?

I shall once be perhaps a good Engineer and work for the technical and industrial advancement of India. A week ago, I read about the spirited stand of the Congress in refusing office and I wrote to Bombay Congress enrolling myself as a member and enclosed four annas. Is this all I can do?

I have a brother (Dr Ayi Tendulkar) who is known to you. He non-cooperated in 1921, was at Gandhi's place for two years and for all I know is working intensely on a big industrial project for India. I know, he feels more keenly and more sincerely about India, than many Germans I know. He says that India has to develop technically in order to become a powerful nation. After his recent visit to India he became a member of the Congress. Can I do nothing more, else?

Mr Nehru, I ask what you expect from us, young Indian students? You know life and its struggles, [the] importance of financial independence. I remember having heard from my brother what you told him in India. India cannot wait till every man achieves financial independence and his place in life. I agree with you. But I am young and have little experience of this complex world. Would I be doing you and my country any good by returning to India on the impulse of the moment and joining [the] agitation for freedom? Hitler told my German fellow students what he expects from them, and you, Mr Nehru what do you expect from me? I should be thankful to hear from you, I am proud you are my countryman. Believe me please I have no better wish then to serve our common and unfortunate country in the most immediate and effective manner.

Yours truly

Y Tendulkar

My surmise is that Yeshwant must have written this letter on an impulse. Normally a reticent person, he was not given to great bursts of patriotic fervour. Whether Nehru replied to Yeshwant or not, I do not know but it seems that after he sent this letter, the British police made several enquiries about Yeshwant. The family learnt of this through my father's older brother, Purshottam Tendulkar, who lived in Bombay at the time. It seems he received a visit from the Bombay CID and was asked questions about what Yeshwant and Ganpat were doing in Germany. It was mandatory for the British police in India to open a file on everyone who travelled abroad. In fact Purshottam was the first to travel to Germany in 1925, and had returned to India in 1930 after obtaining a degree in Chemical Engineering from Konigsburg University. I was told that he had appealed to the British High Commissioner in Berlin to repatriate him to India as he had financial difficulties. Eventually he managed to pay for his passage, but only upto Ceylon by ship, and then had to appeal for assistance to travel from Colombo to Mumbai. It was not a large amount of money but the police knew his details and whereabouts from his records because the money had been returned by him to the British Home Department and the police had kept track of him since. So when Jawaharlal Nehru received Yeshwant's letter the police tracked down Purshottam in Mumbai. Purshottam had no idea about the letter that his brother had written to Nehru. During the questioning, he was quite shocked that his youngest brother, who had been quite shy and awkward when he left India, had mustered enough courage to write to Jawaharlal Nehru directly. I heard this story many times as a child, but it was only much later, when I was researching this book, that I actually came across the letter!

Before his return to Berlin, and after the AICC session in Lucknow, my father visited his family home in Mayem village in Goa. His brother Shripad was at the time the principal of a private school at Panjim. My father felt that Shripad too should be given a chance to better his situation in life and educate himself in Germany. Thea had often told my father that his brothers were always welcome in Berlin and she was emphatic that they all should have the same kind of academic opportunities that my father had had in Germany. Tendulkar therefore insisted that Shripad return with him to Berlin and both brothers left Bombay on 18 January 1937. They travelled onboard SS Conte Verde and disembarked at Venice on 29 January 1937 where Thea von Harbou was waiting to receive them, and from there the three flew to Berlin, arriving there on 31 January.

A few years older than Yeshwant, but much more worldly than him, Shripad was able to settle in more quickly than Yeshwant. Yeshwant still kept to himself whereas Shripad was gregarious, large-hearted and jovial. He had an amazing way with people. Thea loved being with the three of them and would listen to their banter as they teased each other, often using her as a referee for their arguments. Thea would describe the differences in their nature to close friends by saying that "When Ayi has to get some work done, he impresses people with his learning, his degrees and his contacts. He talks about the state of the world and the political situation in various parts of the world till the person finally agrees to what he wants. With Shripad, the technique is utterly different! Not so learned, but as clever, Shripad befriends the person, spends money on plying him with wine and whisky and gets his work done."

Being the youngest, Yeshwant never worked very hard at anything. This did not make any difference to Thea who was very partial to him and showered him with affection. He had stirred her maternal instincts in an inexplicable way. There was an instance when a letter they were sending to someone was accidentally put into the postbox and Thea had to retrieve it. Tendulkar appealed to the postmaster, but he was not impressed. Then Shripad went and spent many hours at the bar with him, treating him like his best buddy. The next morning the postmaster brought the letter to their flat!

Shripad, like Yeshwant, was tall and lanky and very thin. He soon made many friends in Berlin, being an extrovert and a great charmer. He took German lessons from a private tutor for two months. They all lived together in Thea von Harbou's villa at Podbeisktaller 59, Dahlem in Berlin. In April of that year, Shripad went to Oranienberg near Berlin, where he worked as an apprentice in a Civil Engineering firm called Dykerhoff & Widmann. On his return to Berlin he joined the Technical College to do a course in civil engineering. Within three weeks of arriving in Berlin, the family began to notice that Shripad was away from home for long periods of time. Thea was a little worried as she wondered what kind of friends he was mixing with. She tried explaining to him that the Nazis not only hated the Jews but also the communists and trade unionists and he had to be very careful about who he made friends with and especially about what he said to them. When finally they confronted him for being away from home for so long, he announced that he had fallen in love. He had met and become involved with Elizabeth Berghof. The romance soon became serious and in spite of being told how difficult the situation was for Germans who wanted to marry foreigners, Shripad moved into her apartment.

Since he had met Thea, my father had managed to do many things – he'd completed his dissertation and got a doctorate. He had then completed courses in Civil Engineering with distinction, impressing all the professors. They would often be invited home to discuss and formulate various projects that could be set up in India. He worked for a year in Siemens and then joined AEG, the engineering giant.

Thea knew that she would always be under observation and a

target for suspicion by the Nazi SS officers. Factors which would put her high on the list would be her celebrity status as a prominent member of the cinema community, Fritz Lang's sudden departure out of Germany and her relationship with Tendulkar, a foreigner. Everyone was alert that anything they said could be construed as anti-Nazi. Thea had heard of hidden microphones tapped by the Security Service. Rumour had it that a lot of displaced young intellectuals – unemployed university graduates – had joined the Secret service and had almost a hysterical interest in the Nazi philosophy of purity, the eugenics of a master race.

The Third Reich made life unbearable for Jews. In many towns, Jews could not find a place to live. Some found it difficult or impossible to buy food, including milk for their children, or medicine. Signs that read, "Jews Not Admitted," that had been removed during the Olympics, were put up once again. By 1937, Jews were excluded from public or private employment and at least half of them were left without a means of livelihood.

Surrounded by Jewish friends and colleagues Thea was, in fact, against the racial laws which were becoming more and more strict, and stood up for her Jewish friends with the political authorities. However, in 1941 she joined the Nazi party, something that has led to her being labelled a sympathizer and anti-jew. But it seems that in an official document called a Denazification certificate (which I speak of later) she gave a statement that she had enrolled in the Nazi party only to help the Indians that she had befriended. She also mentions that she never attended the meetings but reluctantly paid the membership fees.

A regular visitor to their home was her former husband Rudolph Kleine Rogge. It was an unusual friendship, their affection for each other was clearly evident, and the Tendulkar brothers developed a fondness for Rudolph who always wanted to hear about life in India under the British Raj. From various pieces of information, I gathered that Rudolph, despite his intense eyes and chiselled features, was quite a comedian at heart. One evening some friends were gathered together for a social occasion when Rudolph suddenly got on to his knees in front of Thea.

"When I met Thea for the first time, it was way back in 1914, she was a beautiful actress. She had bright blue eyes and golden hair. We were on stage together and I proposed to her the moment I saw her, like this!" Rudolph bent his head and bowed his hands with a flourish.

"Nonsense Rudolph, you had no courage, you forgot your lines and I had to prompt you. It took you three months to even describe your feelings," Thea said with a grin.

"Oh ho, Thea why must you always be so severe? Why do you only show your imagination in your writing? why can't you put your imagination to use in real life?"

Everyone had a good laugh. Thea and Rudolph often shared anecdotes like this from the time when they were a popular couple of the era in the arts, he a gifted and prominent stage actor in Nuremberg, she a beautiful and best-selling author. They moved a few years later, in 1919, to Berlin, and Thea began working as a screenwriter, adapting several of her novels into film scripts. Rudolph found it difficult to find good acting assignments in theatre and after some frustrating attempts, eventually attempted acting for the cinema. The following year, he began working for Fritz Lang. It was during this time that Thea became enamoured of Fritz Lang and they began a romantic affair, despite their respective marriages. Rudolph and Thea were divorced in 1920.

"Thea, what news do you have of Fritz?" Rudolph asked her as they were seated over a brandy after dinner. With Rudolph's mention of Fritz Lang the air in the room suddenly became charged. After all, Fritz's parting shot as he left Berlin had been to accuse Thea of anti-Semitism.

"Do you have news of how Hollywood is treating him, or Entshuldigung, let me rephrase it a little bit... how he is treating Hollywood?"

"Yes, I believe that he has settled down well," Thea replied, deciding to let bygones be bygones and not carry a grudge against her ex-husband.

"I have heard that *Fury*, which was released about two years ago with Spencer Tracy, has done well. He has just recently released *You Only Live Once* with Henry Ford as the main lead."

"But I am told that the actors in Hollywood complain that he is a fanatic and that they do not like working with him. I am told several actors have even refused to work with him," Thea added. There were moments when she remembered how they had all struggled together to finish their productions on time, but that era was long gone. "They say he takes a ridiculous number of retakes," she smiled.

"Fritz is also not very polite and sometimes forgets that he is no longer in Berlin. Do not forget, Thea that it must be hard for him in the USA. But he is moody, and I am sure he misses his Berlin days." Rudolph said.

Thea smiled. Life had changed so rapidly in the last five years since she had met Tendulkar. Now with his brothers also in Germany, she felt that she was part of a family, something she had craved for, something she had never had in her earlier marriages. She continued doing what she was best at, scripting movies and writing novels as she had a very large audience that appreciated her work. However, political uncertainities in the country loomed large and Thea was not confident that the three brothers would be able to live in Germany for much longer since all Indians were British subjects at that time.

Foreigners

It was at the Nurenberg annual rally in 1935 that the Nazis first announced new laws which enforced several racial theories prevalent in Nazi ideology. The laws excluded German Jews from Reich citizenship and prohibited them from marrying or having sexual relations with persons of "German or related blood". The Nazi obsession with the "Master race" did not permit Germans to marry foreigners. It became virtually impossible not only for Jews to live and work in Germany but also for people from other countries and other races. The Nazis kept tabs on all those who befriended foreigners.

Thea was called to the main Reich building for an interview. She arrived punctually, but was made to wait for over an hour. She was eventually called into a large room and was told to stand to one side of a wooden table. The room, like others in the Reich Ministry building, was unfriendly and bare. There was a painting of Adolf Hitler on the wall. An officer entered, giving her the Heil Hitler salute and asked her to sit down. Several other officers joined the interrogating officer and they seated themselves opposite her.

"Frau Harbou, we are sorry for calling you here, but we would like to question you about a topic that we think is very grave," the officer said.

"Yes officer, I have noticed that your men have been following me for the last few weeks," she said, wanting to show that she was not intimidated by them. "Is there something wrong?" She was not quite sure what offence she had committed, but she understood well that her guilt was implicit in the brusque way in which the officers treated her. They informed her that they had gone through her papers and had found that in 1922 she had married Fritz Lang. Further, it was on record that he had left for Hollywood in 1933, the reason being that he was half-Jewish from his mother's side. They now wished to interrogate Thea in relation to an investigation in a case of suicide. Liza Rosenthal, Fritz Lang's first wife had apparently committed suicide a few months before Lang married Thea. The case had been pending since then, and because Fritz Lang was no longer in Germany, they had called Thea to conduct a final interrogation which would close the case. The officers wanted to know whether Liza Rosenthal was also Jewish. Their records showed that she was of Russian descent, but her religion was not mentioned.

Thea was exasperated by the situation. "Officer, with all due respect, I do not know this woman's religion. It was not important to me what religion my friends and colleagues were and I never asked."

"Frau Harbou, it is reported that Frau Rosenthal shot herself with a pistol. It is understood that the pistol was in the possession of Herr Fritz Lang since his World War I military service in the Austrian army. Are you aware of any of these details?"

Thea fought to hold back tears of frustration. Why would the Nazis be interested in a Jewish woman who killed herself almost 15 years ago? Nasty rumours had been spread when Lisa had shot herself. The press had tried to point fingers at Fritz Lang. Still, she could not understand the Nazi party's real motivation behind this interrogation. More, she was surprised that they had wanted to question her. Maybe they were just trying to scare her.

"No, I am sorry, Officer, I cannot answer your questions, because I do not know the answers. What you are asking about happened many years ago."

Thea fought to control her anger and modulate the tone of her voice. She told them that she knew nothing about Liza Rosenthal. She suggested to them that since Fritz Lang was still alive and well, living in Hollywood in the United States, they should approach him as he would be the one who knew all the answers. Suddenly the interrogating officer changed tack.

"Frau Harbou, just a few more questions pertaining to the current moment. It has been reported that you are involved with Herr Tendulkar, an Indian. We understand that he is living in your house," the officer said, fixing Thea with a cold stare. She held his gaze and did not waver.

He went on. "We have come to believe that for several years Herr Tendulkar was working for *Berliner Tageblatt*, which was a Jewish newspaper."

"Yes that is correct," she replied quietly. "But the newspaper changed hands in 1933 and since then, Herr Tendulkar has been doing his Doctorate." She thought it better now to assume a more subdued manner.

"It is true, is it not, that the *Berliner Tageblatt* sent Herr Tendulkar to India on assignment?"

"Yes, they sent him to report on the Indian leaders fighting for their independence."

"Are you not aware, Frau Harbou, that India is ruled by the British?"

"Yes, and there is a strong movement against the British in India. *Berliner Tageblatt* has reported on it."

"Yes, Herr Tendulkar has reported on it. And we are now told that two of his brothers have also come to Germany?"

"Yes that is correct, Officer. They are all students."

Thea sat silently as the officers conferred with each other in undertones. The lead officer then told her that because of her association with "these foreigners", and because of "certain past incidents", it was imperative that her movements continue to be observed. They wished to inform her of this and apologized for any inconvenience caused to her. With that the officer stood up and gave the Heil Hitler salute. Thea, stunned by the officer's thinly veiled threat and insincere apology, gave a weak nod. She stood up shakily and left.

The last few years together with Tendulkar had given her a sense of belonging and stability. She had found solace in discovering a different culture through Tendulkar and his brothers. But now she had to finally accept the fact that Berlin was unsafe for foreigners. The time had come for them to return to India. That night Tendulkar found her very disturbed. The interrogation had upset her deeply and she was very quiet about it.

"I think that it is safer for you to return to India," she finally said to him.

Tendulkar had sensed that something like this would come out of the interrogation. He reassured her that they would return to India together. At least until the situation in the world had become more stable. Thea and Tendulkar pretended to sleep that night but they were both very restless and lost in their own thoughts. Thea was asking herself whether she could ever leave her Deutschland to live in a foreign country. She was scared of India's heat and the dust and the crowds. She was also apprehensive about how long Tendulkar's feelings for her would last. What would he do once he returned to his homeland? She knew that family was important for Indians and she had to acknowledge that one day he would want to have children. She had crossed the age barrier for bearing children and was soon to celebrate her 50th birthday. She saw that Tendulkar was also awake, tossing and turning. She put her hand out to touch him and quietly said, "No I cannot leave just now but you and the two boys must go ahead. I will follow later."

That night Tendulkar held Thea in his arms and they both wept. No one, least of all Thea and Tendulkar, was sure of what was going to happen in the unfolding tension and strife in the world, both in Europe and the Indian subcontinent. The next morning at breakfast, Tendulkar told his brothers that they must leave as soon as possible. Thea suggested they send a cargo container with all their furniture, books and clothes ahead by ship. Tendulkar protested, telling her that it was not necessary to carry everything back to India. But Thea insisted. She convinced them that it would be easier for them to set up a home and get everything ready for the time when she came to India. They decided that they would celebrate Thea's 50th birthday in December and then leave. Yeshwant was genuinely happy to be going home and he was happy that Thea had promised that she too would join them in India. Tendulkar, however, realized that Thea was being very careful about what she said. Her expressions gave her away. She was not really excited.

Tendulkar understood what she was thinking – despite her firm resolve of the night before, the question of whether or not she would go to India still troubled her. Were she to go, there would be just a thin thread holding her together before she broke down. He would have been happy to have her by his side, but life in India at the time was a great struggle. She would find it difficult to adjust. She would be a foreigner among the Indians as well as a foreigner among the British. The situation between Germany and Britain was volatile and if war was declared, she would be an enemy to the British in India.

Tendulkar, for his part, was keen to return to India and join in the movement against the British. He had dreams for India and wanted to use the skills and training that he had acquired over the last few years in Germany to do something at home. As the days passed, Thea cherished the moments all of them were able to spend together. A favourite topic for discussion amongst them was the British Raj. They often discussed how much longer the British would be able to withstand the agitations that were mounting in India on a day-to-day basis.

One evening at dinner, Thea tried to explain to Yeshwant and Shripad the concept of Lebensraum (living space). "Lebensraum was a popular political slogan coined during the establishment of a united Germany in the 19th century. At this time, Lebensraum meant finding additional living space by adding colonies, following the examples of the British and French empires." She explained that the Third Reich believed that adding Lebensraum would strengthen Germany and help solve its internal problems. It would make the military stronger, and would eventually allow Germany to become economically self-sufficient. They would gain greater access to food and raw materials. But, as was the case all over the world, this policy of adding living space to one's country could only be done by military invasion. Yeshwant replied emphatically that this was exactly what the British were doing in India. Tendulkar agreed, saying that the British had milked India dry by exporting her raw cotton at exceedingly low prices and importing it back as exorbitantly expensive spun cloth. The East India Company was trading in spices, coffee and other commodities and charging taxes to the Indians for everything. Thea knew this was a sensitive topic. She remarked quietly, "Hitler has changed the concept of Lebensraum. Rather than adding colonies to make Germany larger like the British have done, Hitler wants to enlarge Germany within Europe. He is looking East for Germany's expansion in Europe."

War in Europe was looming large but no one knew when it would begin. Germany had started manufacturing weapons at an enormous pace. There was a rise in organizations such as the Hitler Youth Paramilitary whose members believed that duty and loyalty to the Fuhrer and to the Fatherland was of paramount importance, even more important than their own lives. Tendulkar, with his journalist background, had been watching the events unravelling in Europe closely. He knew that any action Germany took would impact the entire world, including his beloved India.

Shortly afterwards, in March 1938, Hitler set his sights on Austria. "Look how Austria has been threatened by Germany's newfound military strength. And Nazi agitators are tearing the country apart from within," Tendulkar said to Thea as he was reading the newspaper at home one day. "Hitler has bullied and threatened various European leaders to concede to his demands of expanding the borders of his Reich by threatening them with warfare and bloodshed." Thea nodded her head in a resigned manner.

Tendulkar's opinions were those of everyone affected by the Third Reich, but no one could voice those opinions publicly. They stood on the sidelines watching how Hitler and Mussolini bullied the Austrian leaders with threats of war and bloodshed. On Saturday, 12 March 1938, they heard a radio broadcast: "German soldiers in tanks and armoured vehicles roared across the German-Austrian border on schedule. They met no resistance and in most places were welcomed like heroes. Hitler has drafted a law to provide for the immediate Anschluss (union) of Austria with Germany. Austria has ceased to exist, it is now a province of the German Reich. Hitler himself shed tears of joy when he was presented with the actual Anschluss document."

Subsequently, after the Anschluss, the world witnessed an outbreak of anti-Jewish violence in Austria. Vienna was home to about 180,000 Jews. Throughout the city, Jewish men and women were humiliated or jailed while their homes and businesses were ransacked.

"My dears now I am convinced it is time for all of you to return to India," Thea told the brothers. War was imminent. Hitler had taken Austria without firing a single shot. "Hitler will waste no time in pressing home his advantage. He will now make plans for the occupation of the Sudetenland, the western portion of Czechoslovakia which is home to about three million Germans. Other than Mussolini, Hitler has no friends and therefore he will start another war in Europe. When and how soon I cannot say. I hope that doesn't happen, but I believe it will."

"Thea I do not want to go to India without you," Tendulkar said to her.

She turned away, she could not stop the tears from falling. Yeshwant went up and embraced her and the atmosphere opened up a little. Everyone knew how eager Yeshwant was to return to his homeland. Thea was sure that another World War was imminent and she knew that even if it took a few years before that developed, it was no longer safe for foreigners to stay in Germany. She was aware that after the takeover of Czechoslovakia, Hitler had become more and more greedy. He had spoken about this theory of Lebensraum and that was what he was after.

The result was that Tendulkar reluctantly booked their tickets for India. Thea had already dispatched several cargo containers full of furniture, books and clothes. Tendulkar was surprised at the amount of stuff she had dispatched. She seemed so determined, and everything seemed so final.

"Do you really believe that the situation in Germany will worsen?" he asked.

She nodded and said, "I am not sure when, but one day I hope to also join all of you and live with you in India."

She was silent a moment and then added, "I hope you don't mind but I have also asked the movers to come tomorrow and pack the red Mercedes." Tendulkar was puzzled. He could not imagine driving such a magnificent car in India! He didn't resist but it troubled him that she was so adamant about wanting him to leave. A few days before their departure, Shripad requested his brother to accompany him for a walk. As they strolled the familiar streets of Berlin, Shripad suddenly said to Tendulkar, "I cannot return to India with you and Yeshwant." Tendulkar was stunned.

"My girlfriend Elizabeth is pregnant. I cannot and will not leave her alone at this delicate stage," Shripad said.

Tendulkar stopped walking and faced his brother. His heart went out to him and he said "Shripad, what will you do? You will not get permission from the German authorities to marry Elizabeth – after all, she's German."

"I know," said Shripad, who obviously had already thought at length about the situation. "Brother, I am in a dilemma. I cannot take her to India. You know that as a German national she may face problems when she enters the country."

The two brothers discussed the situation. The Nazi regime had changed the climate in the universities; scholarships and grants were impossible and it was getting more and more difficult to get employment. Shripad had to earn money to support his family. He was not confident that his options in India were better as Elizabeth would take time to get used to a tropical country and climate, and more so since she would have a baby with her. When he left India he was principal of a school in Goa, he was not confident of what he would do when and if he returned.

"You are right, Shripad," said Tendulkar, putting his hand on his brother's shoulder. "I think the only solution is that you stay back in Berlin and look after Elizabeth. In this way you can also be here for Thea, until she is ready to come to India." Tendulkar tried to lighten the atmosphere a bit and added with more eagerness than he had felt for days. "Maybe you can bring both Thea and Elizabeth with you to India once the baby is born. Nothing is predictable any more. God only knows what will happen tomorrow!"

So my uncle Shripad stayed back in Germany through the war and returned to India with his son in 1947. His wife Elizabeth followed later. Shripad was a wonderful raconteur, full of stories particularly of this period in his life and the time the three brothers had spent in Berlin. Many of the anecdotes and stories I've told here, the conversations I've recounted, come from him.

Departure

At the end of 1938, the Third Reich made a massive, coordinated attack against Jews across Germany. The incident came to be recorded in history as Kristallnacht, or The Night of the Broken Glass. Things escalated when a 17-year-old Jew named Herschel Grynszpan shot and killed a member of the German Embassy staff in Paris in retaliation for the poor treatment his family had been given by the Nazis in Germany. Just a few days before, Grynszpan's family and over 15,000 other Jews, originally from Poland, had been expelled from Germany without any warning. They were forcibly transported by freight trains in boxcars, and then dumped at the Polish border. The young boy's action was considered sufficient provocation for the Third Reich to take revenge on all Jews. Jewish synagogues were vandalized, their windows were smashed and the contents destroyed. Even the shops belonging to Jews weren't spared, and were sometimes set on fire. This happened across Germany, Austria and other Nazi-dominated areas. Thousands of Jews were rounded up and sent off to concentration camps, while those who remained behind made desperate attempts to get out of Germany.

Thea, Tendulkar, Yeshwant and Shripad stood at the end of the platform in the crowded Berlin Hauptbahnhof Railway Station. There were clusters of Jews waiting to escape by train. Amid the chilly breezes was a wind of uncertainty and fear. Yeshwant and

Tendulkar were preparing themselves for the long journey ahead, the train ride from Berlin to Genoa followed by a voyage by sea to India. Shripad would stay back in Germany.

My father told me how Thea looked at them anxiously, again and again, trying hard not to be overwhelmed by their departure. She held my father by the arm and her eyes scanned his face, as if she were trying to commit it to memory. She was half afraid she would never see him again and her eyes welled up with tears at the thought of losing this family that she had nurtured and loved for the last five years. It was a strange sight, a German woman with bright blue eyes and golden hair, circled by three Indian men. Still, no one who passed by even gave them a second glance. The despair and tears on the silent faces of the Jews who were trying to escape from Germany, or send their children and loved ones to safer homes, was too overwhelming. No one even glanced at other passengers. Each sigh, each cry of anguish had a thousand stories to tell of the abrupt end of a lifetime of happy, warm memories and the fear of future uncertainty. On everyone's face was the same question: would they ever see each other again? Would they make it to the border in time?

Tendulkar tried to control his feelings. He put his arm around Thea to protect her from the cold. He knew Thea was not the kind of person to express her emotions in public and he was not surprised that she had contained herself so well. Thea had loved and supported Tendulkar like no one else ever had. She had been everything to him; friend, lover, guide. He would not have been able to achieve so much had it not been for her support and encouragement. She shared his dream of building an India that was free from oppressive, colonial rule, and an India that was self-sufficient and where industry thrived.

"Even if I am not in India with you for some time, it doesn't mean that my soul and heart are not with you," she said to him.

Shripad sheepishly took out his silver hip flask that he had filled with brandy. He passed it around as a toast and everyone took a swig, almost as though this was a quaint but familiar farewell ritual. The brandy glided down their throats and warmed their bodies. They smiled at each other.

"You are taking Yeshwant with you, and you know I love him as though he were my own son. Promise me you'll look after him and treat him with patience. And don't scold him too much!" Thea said to Tendulkar.

As the moment of departure drew closer, Tendulkar took Thea aside.

"Thea, you won't be alone," he said. "Shripad is here, and you will have support from all the young Indian men and women that you've befriended and helped. They all love you and look up to you. I want you to promise me that you will look after them as though you were looking after me. Thea, you are like a real Indian goddess, in every sense of the word, towering above any other human being!"

Thea smiled at that last compliment. "Yes, they are my family now. I promise I will have them over at least once a week for dinner, and help them in whatever way I can. But I'll miss you," she said as she looked into his eyes. They both knew that she wouldn't have let him go had it not been for the warnings she had received from the various ministries. Things had changed drastically, and she was now constantly under surveillance.

"I will miss you too, Thea," he said and kissed her goodbye.

He then held his brother Shripad in a brief embrace and entered the carriage along with Yeshwant. Thea and Shripad followed. German immigration officers, Nazi officers and police were lined up there checking all the passengers' passports. Shripad guided them to their reserved seats and arranged their luggage. The warmth in the heated compartment was welcome. Thea sat down facing her husband so she could have a few more moments with him. Yeshwant was restless, and tried hard to suppress his emotions. Now that they were out of earshot of the passport officials he said, hoarsely,

"It's probably crowded on this train because of those inhuman Kristallnacht attacks. They even burnt the synagogues. Nobody could do anything. The fire department prevented the fire from spreading to nearby houses, but made no attempt to stop the synagogues from burning." He tried to stifle the slight tremor in his voice. He empathised with the Jewish people and felt their pain at having to leave their homes to migrate to countries they had never seen or, in some instances, never even heard of. Tendulkar commented on the mob violence that had broken out while the German police merely stood by and watched, along with the crowds of other spectators. Nazi storm troopers, along with members of the SS and Hitler Youth, beat up and murdered innocent Jews. They broke into and wrecked Jewish homes and brutalised the women and children.

"I am glad to be going home to India," Yeshwant said. "This has scared me enough. I believe that the US has recalled their ambassador permanently from Berlin and there is a very negative reaction outside Germany."

Thea reassuringly put her arm through his and looked at him with an effort at a smile. "I don't know what is in store for Germany," she said. "We have been reduced to a voiceless nation. Anyone who says anything in protest is immediately arrested."

The shrill sound of the train's whistle warned all the passengers to take their seats. Thea and Shripad got off the train and stood on the platform. Yeshwant and Tendulkar stood in the doorway to say their final farewells.

"Your ship leaves tomorrow in the afternoon at 2.30 from Genoa," Thea said as she waved goodbye. "Write to me when you can. Be safe, my dears, and have a comfortable journey!"

"Yes, leibling, I will do so," Tendulkar called to her. "Don't worry about me. I know that you will be following me shortly and I will set up house so that you can come and live like a Maharani."

Thea smiled. He often called her his Maharani, his queen. It always made Thea smile when he did that.

The train started moving and Thea didn't take her eyes off them as they waved. The smoke and the wind stung Tendulkar's eyes but he could see her standing tall in the crowd, waving to them. As the train gained momentum, he reluctantly took his seat next to Yeshwant. Their fellow passengers in the compartment looked tired and exhausted. Tendulkar suspected that most of them were Jewish businessmen leaving Germany while it was still possible, along with their families. He closed his eyes in exhaustion but the image of Thea standing on the platform waving to him was vivid in his mind. He knew that it could be several years before they met again. Suddenly, he realised it was entirely possible that he would never see her again.

He had come to Germany almost 16 years ago. He had loved Berlin, the city had welcomed him and had given him an opportunity to study and work. He loved the German language, which he spoke well. He looked out the window at the passing buildings and the hoardings of the city and remembered the many incidents he had lived through the Weimar Republic, the Bridge parties that extended into the early morning, the champagne breakfasts, the loitering in cafes. How he had enjoyed it all!

As the train pulled out of the station, the exhaustion of the last few days suddenly overwhelmed him. The train's rhythmic tempo calmed him a little. And yet, he could sense the tension in the streets. There were very few people to be seen and the streets were full of patrol cars and SS men. Swastika flags of the Nazi party were visible everywhere. Dark billows of smoke rose skyward from a few places, probably the remnants of the attacks on Jewish shops. He closed his eyes. "Goodbye Berlin," he said. His mind went back to 1933, when everyone in Germany had felt that Hitler's rise to power would transform their great country and he thought how tragically things had turned out.

2

Goa

My father returned from Germany and went straight to Goa. Although the rest of India was under British colonial rule, Goa continued to be under the control of the Portuguese, the first of the European powers to have entered India. For nearly four hundred years the Portuguese ruled Goa with a high degree of repression, converting Hindus to Roman Catholics and forcing many to flee to neighbouring areas. As a child, my father had spent several years with his maternal grandmother in a small village in Goa called Mayem.

I often marvelled at what a multi-faceted man my father was – at once a suave, sophisticated, western man, fluent in many European languages, a connoisseur of fine wines and elegant whiskies and yet, at heart, a simple Indian. He believed that Belgundi was home because he had been born there, but his early childhood had been spent in Goa and that too was home. But after he came back from Germany his thoughts often turned to that country.

The political situation in India was quite volatile and there was a lot of uncertainty in the air. At the same time, Europe too was in an uncertain state with the war having begun following Hitler's attack on Poland on 1 September 1939. England and France had defence treaties with Poland, so they got together and declared war on Germany two days later. Although he was happy to be back home, my father would often say that his attention at the time remained focused on what was happening in Germany where he had lived for over 15 years.

Once back, Father went to Mayem to visit his grandparents' home and found the house uninhabited, save for a few wild cats and pigeons. He walked about the empty old redstone house that had no running water or electricity, reliving memories. He walked about in the dense plantation of betel nut and coconut trees in front of the house. The hot sun and breeze and the peace of the place captivated him. Wild hens and roosters pecked at the ground for grain while stray dogs sat near the house. The smell of wet dung and freshly cut grass wafted from the cowshed where the black buffaloes were tied.

I remember my father telling me, "I was quite aghast when I met the neighbouring family in Mayem whom I had not seen for several years. I was surprised to see that their life had not progressed at all and I marvelled at how the entire family had lived on so little." He described how he had met and shaken hands with Kudaskar who had played with him and his brothers when they were children. He remembered how hard Kudaskar worked morning, noon and night in order to feed his wife and seven children rice and sour mango pickle – their meagre sustenance.

Kudaskar had rushed from his house the moment he heard someone from the Tendulkar family had come. He brought in his hand a small offering of especially selected and peeled raw cashewnuts. He held the nuts in his gnarled hands, a happy smile on his face but he could not conceal the sorrow in his eyes. He told my father "Tendulkar, see how smart you have become by going to Germany, who would have thought that you would have achieved so much? I still remember the days that we played together as children. But look at you now, you have become quite a *bada sahib*... how smart you look!" The old friends had slapped each other on the back and laughed and talked. My father started eating the freshly selected cashewnuts which had been plucked and peeled before the fruit ripened, They had a slightly sweet, nutty flavour. He savoured each cashew nut and was amazed at how the taste of something so simple could kindle a flood of childhood memories! He felt he had really come home.

"I am glad you have come home Tendulkar, you must help me – I want to send my sons to Europe to study. Maybe they'll become smart like you. With an education they can get a profitable job with the British administration, or become Congress leaders and bring some importance and some money to the family."

My father told him quietly that the world outside was going through a great transition and it was likely that a second World War was around the corner. This was not a good time to go abroad. He advised him to send his sons to a good school in Goa, especially a missionary school where the medium of instruction was English.

My father remembered how he had put his arm around Kudaskar's thin shoulders and Kudaskar had grinned, showing his teeth stained red by betelenut. Kudaskar led him inside his house. He had to bend low to enter and once inside, he stood to one side while Kudaskar lit a small oil lamp. The smell of food, rice and fish being cooked on a slow wood fire pervaded the house. They sat on woven grass mats on the ground and Kudaskar shuffled to the cupboard from where he brought out his prize possession – a bottle of freshly brewed Feni, the Goan's favourite drink, brewed from cashew fruit from his own garden. He had kept it carefully to share with a friend. They then sat on the floor and Kudaskar poured the alcohol neat into two small glasses.

"Here Tendulkar, drink up. I know you must have forgotten the taste of Feni. I have smelt that brown liquid – whisky – that the white sahibs drink. But it is no good! It has no fragrance," Kudaskar said with great pride. My father had recounted how he had gulped the Feni and felt the strong spirit hit his stomach. He had missed the drink for so long. He remembered Kudaskar's words "Feni is the only drink I know that is good for everything

– you drink it to celebrate, you drink it when you have a stomach upset, when you are constipated, when you have a cold and even when you are hung over!"

That encounter, he said, had taken him back to his roots, to the India he loved. He wanted to build India into a great country, a free country, a country he could be proud of, one where he could live, get married and bring up his children. My father had to spend several days waiting for his luggage to arrive by cargo ship from Germany. Thea sent it all in a container – furniture for a flat, and most of his wardrobe, complete with tuxedos and warm overcoats. Tendulkar's entire library had also been sent to India. The books were mainly technical books – on mathematics and engineering, and reference books such as encyclopedias. There were also several literary books, some of them printed in the old gothic script used in Germany at that time. When eventually the ship did arrive, he made arrangements to transport most of the things by truck to Belgaum where he had hired a spacious bungalow. Some of the smaller stuff was transported by bullock cart and the 140 km distance took several days to cover.

Germany and the Third Reich seemed very far away to my father at the time. He would tell me that he often thought of Thea and wondered how she was coping, and was grateful that at least she had his brother Shripad with her. He would often say, "It was only when I realized that my staying on in Germany would have jeopardized her life that I agreed to come back. I wanted her to come with me but India was still ruled by the British and they would have imprisoned her immediately! "

I was curious about what happened to my uncle Shripad who had remained behind with Thea in Berlin. My father told me that after he'd left Berlin, Shripad had moved out of Thea von Harbou's house – she was moving into an apartment in Frankenallee 14. He continued with his studies and Elizabeth gave birth to their son in January 1939. They hadn't married because the German government had not granted them permission to do so. Shripad then worked with Deutsche BAU AG as a civil engineer but had to give up his job when the war broke out in August of 1939. Life was very difficult for him and he was supported financially by Thea von Harbou. He had sent my father a letter describing how he'd been arrested on the 20 September 1939 by the German police and then released the same day after spending 8 hours in a cell in Alexander Platz. Before he was released, he was ordered to report to the police twice a week and was not allowed to leave Berlin without police permission.

My father said that he had promised Thea that once back in India, he would try to start an industry in the country but now he realised that the time was not right, that there would be various obstacles for setting up industry and it was better to wait till India became independent. Instead, he thought he would continue doing what he knew best, journalism. His years of working in several German newspapers in Berlin had given him a pretty good idea of how to run a newspaper. Within a few months he started a weekly newspaper in Marathi called *Warta*. He was able to buy an existing printing press and hire an editor. The newspaper had only eight pages, but it soon became quite important and Tendulkar would write fairly strongly worded anti-British editorials. The sales picked up quickly as the editorials touched a raw nerve and resonated with many readers.

Tendulkar used to recount how excited he had been to meet my mother when she came to his newspaper office. "Your mother Indumati wanted to submit an article for publication. I had fallen in love with her at first sight! But I had also become used to life in Europe and I could not understand why she constantly needed to seek approval of everything from her father. I sometimes felt it was easier for me to relate to the Indian villager than to the city person, I took some time to adjust to Indian society."

The red Mercedes made ripples in the small town of Belgaum and it was often troublesome when he had to drive it in the city – the lanes were too narrow. But, as he said, "the red Mercedes almost became a legend, and was probably the biggest car in Belgaum at that time."

The beginning of World War II marked a turning point for millions of people all over the world. It was also the beginning of a new life for my father. He had returned to India, as he knew he would one day, but in circumstances which he had not anticipated. Once back, he began to set up his life again.

Belgaum was a small town, but because of its strategic proximity to Goa it had a large army cantonment, and had a Divisional Commissioner's office. This is mainly because Goa was run by the Portugese while the rest of the Indian subcontinent was under the British. My father remained busy with the newspaper, often publishing anti-British articles and expressing his views in strong words.

While this was going on, the friendship between my parents had become very strong and their mutual fascination for each other had become a hot subject of gossip. But their work commitments often kept them apart. My mother had promised to volunteer at the 53rd session of the Indian National Congress to be held in March of 1940 in Ramgarh (now in the state of Jharkhand).

It was a long train journey and my father was not very keen that she travel almost 1500 kilometres alone by train, and he was unhappy that she would be away for almost 20 days. However she was stubborn and nothing would stop her from keeping her promise to her colleagues in the Congress party. She had once described this particular train journey and the events thereafter to me. This is what she told me.

Indumati recognized several freedom fighters who were on the train with her, but she sat a little apart from them. She simply was not in the mood to be party to their discussions about the latest political developments in the country. She had committed to go as a volunteer, and the party work was important to her, but she was leaving her home at a crucial time. She thought she would also use the time away to think about the events of the last few days and get some clarity in her thoughts.

Tendulkar was constantly on her mind and her head was full of all the things he had told her. She was also concerned about her current mission – the Ramgarh Congress – which was to be an important moment in India's history. World War II had started and Indian leaders had condemned the actions of fascist Italy and Nazi Germany but they were weary of the Imperialism of Britain. At the meeting, leaders would have to decide on the issue of their support to the British in World War II. Would India's demand for independence be conceded, and would Indians be able to form a national government if they cooperated with the British?

Once Indumati reached Ramgarh she got very involved in the work – she'd been given charge of various arrangements for the political leaders so there wasn't a moment to rest. The days were long and hot, the nights somewhat cooler, but overall the heat was quite intense and uncomfortable. The day after she arrived, she received a letter from her father.

Dear Indumati

I have come to know that in spite of promising that you would break all contact with Tendulkar, you have not done so. I am told that you were seen leaving his house the day you departed for Bihar. The family name is being tarnished because of your actions. I have repeatedly asked you to stop meeting him but you have not listened to me.

Dr Tendulkar is not a suitable man for you to marry. He has lived abroad for over twenty years and his experience of life is vastly different from what you have seen in your sheltered life. Indu, I implore you, please behave in a more responsible manner. And realize that what I'm saying is for your welfare. I am against your meeting such a man. If you repeatedly go against my wishes, I will have to resort to more drastic measures. I forbid you to enter this house until you promise to end all association with

Dr Tendulkar. I'm afraid you will have to choose between your
family and Dr Tendulkar.

Your Father

Nagesh Gunaji

Indumati was shocked. She had also received a letter from
Tendulkar that very morning. It was the first letter he had ever
written her. Her first love letter. She held both the letters in her
hand, her mind racing. What had she gotten into? Would Tendulkar
really marry her? She thought about this carefully.

She loved her parents, her family, but she knew she could no
longer go back to the life that she had left behind. She trusted
Tendulkar and took him at his word. She had to trust that eventually
her parents would see the situation from her point of view. One
day, she hoped, they too, would come to love and respect Tendulkar
as she did.

A week before she was due home she sent Tendulkar her father's
letter and informed him when she was due back in Belgaum and
gave him details of her train journey. All the way home she was
anxious about her return. What if Tendulkar was not sincere? But
as the train pulled into Belgaum, Indumati caught a glimpse of
him waiting for her on the platform. She was ecstatic and almost
ran to embrace him. There was something different about him.
Before she could identify what it was, he said, with a twinkle in
his eye. "Do you notice anything different about me?" He stood
back and opened his arms. "Look at my clothes, Indu, real khadi.
I had shirts and trousers stitched out of khadi. I've decided to
follow Gandhi's diktat of not using foreign goods, especially
foreign textiles."

"Finally the foreigner has become a native," Indumati teased
him. "Or at least somewhat native," she smiled, pointing to his
calf-leather shoes and his silver cigarette case.

"So where do we go, Indu?" Tendulkar asked, aware that she
had been ordered not to return home.

"Please take me straight to Belgundi. To your village. Didn't you read my father's letter? I have been thrown out of my father's house," she replied bluntly.

"Indu, I can make some arrangements in Belgaum for you," he said. "Staying in Belgundi may not be very comfortable for you. You are not used to living in a village with no help – please think again about this."

Indumati had made up her mind. She was going to work in the villages and this was the best opportunity to begin. "My new life begins here, and now," she told him.

Tendulkar didn't say a word as he drove. He was thinking of some of the problems she would have to face. It would take time before the villagers would get to know her. And he wasn't sure how she would react to the lack of amenities in the village. The 16 km

Mahatma Gandhi during the 53rd Indian National Congress in Jendha Chowk at Ramgarh, 14 March 1940.
© GandhiServe

distance between Belgaum and Belgundi mainly involved driving over a mud-track that posed as a road. There wasn't any other mode of transport available, and the bullock-cart ride would take at least five to six hours. It was a Tuesday, which was the market day for the nearby villages. People were returning to the village after having sold their goods in the market. Tendulkar was jolted out of his thoughts by the serpentine line of some 30 bullock carts along the uneven road. The driver of the first one, whose responsibility it was to navigate the others, was fast asleep, but his bullocks were trundling along and now the entire entourage had been led off the road and in a direction away from the village. Tendulkar startled the sleeping driver awake with the blare of his car horn and got him to rein in the wandering bullocks back onto the road. The startled look on the driver's face made Indumati and Tendulkar laugh heartily as they waved to his salaam.

When they arrived, Tendulkar told Indumati with much pride that he had been rebuilding portions of the house in which she would live. Indumati smiled at his excitement and looked around at the state of affairs. The roof was far from complete and the coarse red-roof tiles were piled in one room. The carpentry work hadn't begun as yet and there weren't any windows or doors. Later, Indumati would fashion curtains out of her hand-woven Khaddar saris. The only furniture in the room was a sturdy wooden bed. Indumati embraced her new home with all its charm and shortcomings. She had already decided to live by Gandhi's principle of "simple living and high thinking". Simple living in the village was no easy task, though. There was no running water, and no form of sanitation. She had to draw water from the well each morning and carry it home. She lived alone, though Tendulkar would often drive into Belgundi to help her and to spend time with her. This bold move by Indumati became the talk of the town. Rumours about her started to spread, both in Belgaum and Belgundi. Her living in Tendulkar's house, unmarried, along with her banishment from her father's home, was enough to set local tongues wagging.

But Indumati wasn't bothered about what people said or thought of her. She had so much to do in the village that she didn't have time to think. It was as if she could feel the heartbeat of the nation and the freedom movement embedded in her pulse. Tendulkar brought news of the political situation and current events when he visited, so she was aware of the latest events in the world. She felt as though she was caught in the vortex of worldwide change. She couldn't conceive of going back to her father's home and returning to her mundane life. She trusted Tendulkar implicitly and knew that he would never let her down. Despite his past and unorthodox ways, she knew she was meant to be by his side.

While the older villagers were filled with speculation about her, the children of the village were brimming with curiosity about this beautiful woman living alone in the partly finished dwelling. As soon as Indumati stepped out of her little home, she would be surrounded by a flock of village children. They stared at her intently and followed her around wherever she went. They turned out to be her first friends. They responded with smiles when she called them into her house and they loved it when she washed their faces for them, or combed and de-loused their hair, scrubbed them clean, and they didn't seem to mind that she scolded them for wiping their noses on their sleeves. She taught them to use handkerchiefs and clean their faces. She devised a small game with a little handheld mirror she had picked up from one of her trips to Belgaum. She started showing the young girls how unkempt and dirty their faces were, and then she would show them their reflection in the mirror after they were washed and clean. The girls would giggle and try to outdo each other in looking clean. She also taught them songs, and after a while she gave them slates and pieces of chalk so she could teach them to read and write. As the group got bigger, and they ran out of slates,

A young Indumati

she improvised by having the younger children draw their letters in the sand instead.

In due course, the children started to love Indumati, and gradually they managed to drag their reluctant mothers to her house to meet her. The women, skeptical at first, soon saw that Indumati was not only generous, but talented and sincere in her desire to contribute to the quality of life of everyone around her. Perhaps it was true that she had not been banished to the village, but chose of her own accord to live there among them. Over time, the group of women that assembled on a regular basis in her house got bigger. Indumati encouraged them by leading them in singing simple patriotic songs and getting them to recite prayers with her. These were the same prayers that were recited daily in Gandhi's ashram.

The caste system was very much in evidence, and in the village there were separate clusters of houses for Brahmins, for the farmers and for members of lower castes. Of all the unusual and curious behaviour of this new woman, the villagers were most surprised that Indumati never discriminated among them. She seemed to love them as equals, and never turned away when they touched or embraced her. The women started to bring her food; coarse, unleavened bread made of millet which they would eat with raw onions or chilly pickle. On festive occasions, they would bring sweetmeats made out of cane sugar. Often, the women would bring the food unwrapped, just covered with the edge of their saris, because they couldn't afford something to wrap it in. Indumati would graciously accept whatever was given to her, and would compliment them on its preparation. She started to teach the village women to read and write too. Despite living alone, there wasn't a moment when Indumati felt alone, since there was so much to do.

Soon, in appreciation for what she was doing in the village, the women started to help her with her chores of cooking and keeping her house clean. They would light her fire with dried cowdung cakes and would cook rice in stone pots and lentils in vessels made of mud. No matter what task they were in the middle of, the village women would flee from Indumati's house the moment Tendulkar arrived on one of his visits. But the children remained as curious about Tendulkar as they had been about Indumati. They would surround the car and draw shapes and signs in the layer of bright red laterite dust that covered the bonnet. Tendulkar was fascinated to see the progress each time he visited Belgundi. He always brought provisions and gifts for Indumati and was genuinely impressed with the amount of work he saw her do.

"Indu, watching you, I understand what it means to work for the nation. It's my dream to do something for my country, too. I want to build industry in free India. Cement, paper, steel. You have truly inspired me. You're a real leader in your own little way." As he exchanged the latest news and talked to her about his newspaper, he sat on her cot, drinking the tea she brewed with milk and jaggery. Sometimes, they poured the tea in the saucer to cool it before drinking, like the villagers did.

It was customary in the village for the women of the house to wake up at four-thirty in the morning to light the fire and cook the morning meal so that the men could go to work in the fields by daybreak. The first task each morning was to grind the grain for the day. This was done manually. It was strenous work, the more so because the flour had to be ready well before daybreak. Many of the wives in the village households were girls who had been married at the age of twelve, and once they reached puberty they were sent to live in their husbands' homes. The mothers-in-law of these young girls would beat them up if they didn't get up at four-thirty sharp to start work. Indumati was sometimes woken up early in the morning by crowing roosters, but sometimes by the screams of young girls. She couldn't bear this. She would rush to their houses and plead with the families not to beat the young girls, as they were still children. Usually the older women would stop at Indumati's request, but this didn't always happen.

One day, to Indumati's surprise, a familiar figure appeared at her door. It was Manorama Mody, her friend from her Pune University days with whom she had shared a room. Manorama did not have a family and had been sponsored in her studies by a charitable institution to complete a course in nursing. Indumati had befriended her and looked after her at University. Manorama had heard, from common friends who had recently visited Belgaum, about Indumati and her life in the village. The vicious rumours that had been rife in the early days hurt her deeply. Indumati had been her friend and supporter for over four years, and Manorama knew that Indumati probably needed her greatly right now. She immediately resigned from her nursing job at the military hospital in Pune and took the train to Belgaum to come and be with her friend. She felt it was time to finally repay Indumati for her kindness and her warmth.

"You can't imagine how happy I am to see you," Indumati cried, hugging Manorama.

Manorama had tears in her eyes when she saw how thin Indu had become, with her hair tied in a bun and coarse sandals on her feet. Was this the girl who had been considered the most beautiful girl on campus?

"Why didn't you call me earlier, Indu? How could you have taken such a drastic decision without even consulting me?" Manorama chided Indumati.

Manorama's training as a nurse and a midwife was a boon as she helped the village women to deliver their babies and taught them basic hygiene. The villagers soon grew to love both these women, as they realized how much they did for them. However, one bone of contention did exist between Indumati and Manorama, which was Manorama's frequent and insistent inquiry about Tendulkar's intentions as far as marriage to Indumati was concerned.

"Tell me, Indu, how do you know for sure that Tendulkar will marry you?"

It made Indumati frown whenever this question was put to her, which was usually about twice a day. Initially, it infuriated her, but gradually she realised that Manorama did not mean to be malicious. She only spoke out of genuine concern. Still, Indumati did not like it. Finally one day Manorama got Indumati to sit down and talk to her.

"Indu, how do you know that Tendulkar will keep his promise to marry you?" she asked. "You know that he is already married. Your marriage to him will be his fourth! He may just be waiting for the war to get over and then he will go back to Germany, to his old lifestyle, and he may never come back to India. He is used to sophisticated women who smoke and drink wine and whisky and put rouge on their cheeks and apply lipstick. Look at you. You look like a villager. Look at your hands, they are rough and calloused with all the cooking and cleaning. I don't know, Indu. Your Tendulkar is a very smart man, but you must not be a fool"

Indumati's face fell. She put her head down under the weight of Manorama's words. She felt the tears well up in her eyes. How many times had she not asked herself these very questions? She knew that Manorama's view was the commonly held one by everyone who knew her. Still, she did not believe them. Her tears were replaced by a look of resolve on her face when she raised her head to regard her friend.

"No, Manorama, he loves India and wants to build it into a great nation," she said, knowing as she spoke that she believed this with all her heart. "And he loves me, because we have a common goal and a common dream. I must support him. Who does he have in India? He knows I have already sacrificed my family for him and I am willing to sacrifice my life – what greater test of love do you want? I cannot go back to my family. This village is my home now."

The look on Manorama's face told Indumati that she was not quite convinced.

"Believe me, I of all people know, Indu, that when you love someone you do it with all your heart. But now you are acting like such a simpleton, even though I know you are so much smarter than me. I don't want you to suffer. You haven't seen the world in the real sense. You are so naïve!"

"I know exactly what I am doing, Manorama," Indumati replied. "I have not met anyone as brilliant as Tendulkar. Just look at his books, Manorama, they are so many and so technical. He will do great things and one day you will realise that I have put my trust in the right person."

Manorama was a little intimidated by Tendulkar and kept very quiet during his visits to Belgundi, but she was impressed by the manner in which he spoke. He was friendly and several of the village men would spend hours with him, discussing farming while he advised them about how to improve things in the village. He was getting more and more dependent on Indumati. Germany was receding from his mind.

One day, about a week after one of Tendulkar's visits, Indu heard the familiar voice of Digambar, Tendulkar's cousin, who lived in Belgaum. She rushed outside, wiping her forehead with the corner of her sari. Why would Digambar be here?

"Indu, I have come to share some terrible news with you," he said.

Indumati's heart stopped. She had been feeling a little insecure of late. Tendulkar had not come to see her for a few days and she had been more than a little unnerved by the bits of world news that filtered through to the village. She had been beset by fears, ranging from hyenas and wild jackals entering her house to the imminent outbreak of World War II. She hadn't slept or eaten for the last three nights. "Indu, I have rushed here to tell you that Tendulkar has been detained by the British. Major Rogers has arrested him this morning, and with great difficulty Tendulkar sent a messenger to me and asked me to inform you and to tell you not to worry." Indumati turned ashen and fainted. Manorama splashed water on her face and revived her. After drinking a cup of sweet tea she said, "What will I do now? When can I go and meet him?" She was trembling. She had turned her back on her family and had no one to support her. She had left her old life without thinking of the consequences. Now, the person for whom she had made this sacrifice had been put behind bars.

"Not for a while, Indu. Let the situation settle down a bit. The British have taken all those with links outside India into protective custody. When you are feeling better Indu, I have to speak to you about the logistics of Tendulkar's possessions."

"You can speak now, Digambar. I am fine. Tell me my dear friend, tell me how can I help you?"

"Tendulkar has left a fully furnished house and his Mercedes in my charge. He has asked me to look after you and to give you whatever money he had with him in the house. I don't know if you have heard the news recently. Although the British are ruling our country, they are anxious to obtain the support of our Indian leaders. The Indian nationalists have not forgotten their experience of World War I, and have refused to provide any support, unless their demands are met. The British are not willing to budge and have refused. Meanwhile, the Axis powers have conquered large portions of Europe, and the British are now anxious to enlist Indian support in the war effort. The Indian nationalists however reiterated their earlier stand of wanting a transfer of power to Indians in exchange for India's active co-operation in the war effort."

"But what does this have to do with Tendulkar? she asked weakly. "What has he done wrong?"

"You have to remember that Tendulkar was close to Thea von Harbou who they say had once enrolled in the German NASDP. Tendulkar, therefore, is also a suspect."

Indumati felt again like she might faint and asked Manorama for more tea before Digambar continued.

"Although Tendulkar is in prison," he explained, "he has been given the status of a political detainee. I am told that he has been kept in an 'A' class cell which has better facilities. I think that the A-class prisoners are allowed to receive visitors more often and also, in a few rare instances, home cooked food can be sent to them. I also know that the political detainees have common facilities like halls and areas where they assemble to chat and so forth."

Manorama clutched Indumati's hand and stroked her hair. Still, she felt quite alone and not a little scared. Indumati's shoulders shook as she started to weep. Digambar did not say any more, but waited while Manorama comforted her as best she could. She recovered and gave a weak smile to Digambar and thanked him for coming. A little colour had returned to her pale cheeks, but there were dark rings under her eyes and he could make out that she had been anxious and worried.

When the landlord of Tendulkar's spacious bungalow in Belgaum heard that Tendulkar had been imprisoned, he wanted his premises returned to him. He notified Digambar that he had a month in which to remove all of Tendulkar's belongings. This was not a small task.

Indumati had initially been startled by the number of items Tendulkar had brought back with him from Germany. It was an entire household, replete with crockery and cutlery. There were beautiful teak wood wardrobes, each containing Tendulkar's ties and jackets and tuxedos, the likes of which she had never seen before. Digambar stored the major portion of Tendulkar's furniture in his own house in Belgaum city. The remaining furniture was transported by bullock cart to Belgundi. Suddenly, the little hut in Belgundi was filled with huge wardrobes, fine art déco furniture and hundreds of books. The entire atmosphere of the house changed and she could feel Tendulkar's presence permeate everything. However, she soon realized that maintaining all this had increased her responsibilities several times over. Mildew and fungus started collecting on the beautiful German books due to the rain and damp. Indumati and Manorama toiled,

drying each book over warm sand but it was not easy to keep
the damp at bay.

Slowly, word spread to Belgaum about how Indumati had made
her mark on the village. Her family felt terrible on hearing news
of her kindness, how she set about teaching the local women and
children about hygiene, cleanliness and diet. They were humbled to
hear how hard she worked in very difficult conditions. Gradually
the ugly rumours that had been spread about her in Belgaum
were silenced. Old friends and acquaintances would often make
the 15 mile trip either on cycle or horse cart to visit her, She was
totally absorbed in what she was doing, and waited patiently for
the War to be over and for Tendulkar to be released.

Wardha

Six months had passed since Indumati had left her family home, and her father missed his favourite child immensely. He missed their evenings together, which had assumed the form of a ritual. First the oil lamp in the temple was lit, this was followed by the evening Sandhya, a short daily prayer, and then the lighting of joss sticks. Indumati's mother would place freshly plucked jasmine and hibiscus around the idols. After this, the kerosene lamps were lit and one was placed in every room. Indumati would carry a lamp to her father's study, and would then spend hours there chatting with her parents.

Evenings at home were no longer the same. Her parents, especially her father Nagesh Gunaji, could not stop worrying about her. He had too much pride to visit her in the village, even though it was barely sixteen kilometres away. He was still hurt that his daughter had rebelled against him and the family. However, when he heard that Tendulkar had been detained by the British for his long stay and association with Germany, he became genuinely distressed. Indumati would not come back home even now, and Gunaji struggled with a strategy, a tactful way in which he could approach her. He knew for certain that this was not the right time to go to her and say, 'I told you so' He spent several sleepless nights worrying about what to do, before finally deciding on sending his youngest son, Narender, by bicycle to Belgundi to meet with Indumati.

It was a long cycle ride, but Narender had sensed the panic in his father's request and had agreed immediately. He carried with him a letter from his father asking how his daughter was faring and urging her to come back and live with them, at least until Tendulkar's release from prison. Gunaji believed that the British would detain Tendulkar until the war ended, and no one knew for how long the war would go on. It could be years. It was unthinkable that Indumati wait out her time for him in those village conditions. Along with the letter, Narender carried a package put together by Indumati's mother containing a new sari and some home-made delicacies.

"Narender, how nice to see you," said Indumati, thrilled to see him, but a little puzzled at his unexpected appearance. "I hope all is well at home."

Before hearing his news, she insisted that she cook him lunch. Narender was amused to watch his elder sister light the wood stove, the black soot staining her pretty face. Her hair was tied in a knot and she was wearing an old sari. He silently ate everything that she served him, trying hard not to make faces at the acrid taste of the slightly burnt chapattis and vegetable curry.

"Indu Akka," he began when they were done eating. "Everyone is saying that you are wasting your life in this village. They all say that Tendulkar will go back to Germany after the war is over, that he will leave you." Narender's innocent tone made the familiar words less offensive to Indumati's ears.

"Whoever told you that is a liar, and is trying to spread stories about me," she replied with a smile. "Don't worry Narender, Tendulkar will marry me, and we will live in Belgaum. Everyone is just spreading nasty rumours about me."

"Well, Indu Akka, please learn to cook a little better before you marry," Narender said. "Otherwise whoever you marry will run away from you if he is forced to eat this kind of food!"

Indumati burst out laughing and gave him a playful pat on his back. "I promise, Narender. I will take your suggestion most seriously!"

Then he handed his sister the letter from their father and the package from their mother. She opened the package first, and exclaimed in joy at the lovely sari. It had been a long time since she'd had anything new, and she looked at it with the deep appreciation any of the village women might have felt. She made her brother taste the sweets with her, and then she opened her father's letter. She felt a surge of mixed emotions rise in her as she read it once briefly and then once again more slowly, listening as she did to her father's voice speaking the words in her mind. She had not allowed herself to slow down in her daily routine and had kept at bay the thought of her parents, but now she realised how much she missed them. She sat down and penned a reply for her brother to take back. Before he left, she handed him a parcel of chopped sugarcane stems she had brought from the nearby fields.

"Now you take care of yourself, and give my love to mother and father," she said as she waved goodbye.

Oblivious to the beautiful sky colours of the setting sun, Indumati's mother and father were anxiously watching the horizon for signs of their youngest son returning home on his bicycle with Indumati. Finally, they saw him. He cycled past the entrance, and they saw he was alone.

"Where is Indu?" his father asked him as he entered.

"Here, father, she has sent a letter for you," Narender said as he handed him the letter, chewing on the sugarcane stick that he had taken off his cycle. He was tired and was sweating profusely, but clearly happy to have met his favourite sibling.

Dear Father,

Thank you for your letter, and for sending Narender to bring me home. But I have commitments in the village and cannot leave

just now. Please do not worry about me. I am well and happy. I
am waiting for Dr Tendulkar's release from prison and will stay
in the village until he is released.

My love to mother and to all at home.

Your loving daughter,

Indu

This was the first direct word from Indumati since he had
delivered his ultimatum. Gunaji felt hurt. He had hoped against
hope that reaching out to her with an offer to come home
without blame or shame would be all it would take, but he had
to admit to himself that there was no one to blame but himself.
It was his impulsive action that had led to her separation from
the family. It wasn't common for young girls of their community
to choose their own husbands, or to even talk to strangers, but
he had encouraged his daughters to be independent thinkers. He
had just never foreseen what shape that independent thinking
could take.

His wife had been upset with him for months. She wasn't
accustomed to speaking to him openly in front of other people,
but when they were alone, she often expressed her thoughts.

"It's all your fault," she would say. "You brought up your
daughters all wrong. Educating them has only made it difficult
for them to get husbands. She is not happy with simple middle
class men from our community. That is why she is running after
Tendulkar. See how many proposals she had turned down."

Gunaji would scowl and leave the room quietly. He realised that
he would have to make his peace with Dr Tendulkar, and that if
he continued to oppose the relationship, he would probably lose
his daughter. One evening, he was sitting with his wife on the
terrace of their house. His wife was unusually outspoken.

"Why don't you write to Gandhiji and tell him about Indu.
You have already mentioned to him that your daughter worked
as Rector of the Ladies Ashram in Wardha for several months.
Now, tell the great man the truth, that she has disobeyed you

and has left her home to work in the villages. Ask Gandhiji to write to her, and summon her to his Ashram and put some sense in her head. She will only listen to Gandhiji. It's no use our speaking to her."

Gunaji mulled over his wife's suggestion for a couple of days. Though uneducated, her instincts were sharp and often right. Gandhiji had attended the annual All India Congress Committee meeting held in Belgaum some years ago. When he had fallen ill, it was Gunaji who had been summoned to treat him. They had taken to each other instantly and Gunaji would often correspond with Gandhi about health remedies, and would send him advice about various exercises. He decided to appeal to Mahatma Gandhi to intervene on his behalf and ask Indumati to return to her family home. He wrote him a letter in which he mentioned Indumati's work in Belgundi and the appalling conditions in which she lived. He also wrote about her decision to stay there until Dr Tendulkar's release from prison.

"I know my daughter will not listen to anyone else, and I know she has great regard for you, and the principles you stand for. I humbly request you to kindly intercede on my behalf, and please ask Indu to return home. May I suggest that you call her to Sewagram and talk to her in person? Your decision in the matter will be final, and my wife and I will adhere to whatever you suggest as a solution."

At the Sewagram ashram, the letter was received by Mahadev Desai, Gandhi's right-hand man. Gandhi told Desai to reply to Gunaji and to enclose a letter for Indu, inviting her to Sewagram, so they could talk. So Narender had to make another trip to Belgundi, this time with two letters, one from her father and another from Gandhi. Narender also handed her some money so she could travel comfortably from Belgaum to Wardha. She was touched by her father's concern and overwhelmed that he was willing to go to such lengths. She re-read his letter:

My dearest daughter,

I know that you have taken the decision to leave the family home.

I also know that you have great faith and trust in what Bapuji thinks and says. Please talk to him and let him advise you on what you should do, given the present situation. He is the leader of our nation and a great human being. I will honour whatever his decision is, as I would expect you to also do, in the same spirit.

With love
Your loving father
Nagesh Gunaji

"Please tell father that I will travel next week to Nagpur by train. Request him to book my ticket for me," she told Narender.

He said he would, and then handed her a small container which was filled with home-cooked food. Narender didn't want to sample Indumati's culinary skills again, and still scarred from the last time, he had come prepared. They both laughed as Indumati laid out the simple meal.

Indumati travelled to Wardha alone. She had made this trip several times before. She was hoping to meet her old friends in the Mahila Ashram in Wardha, but when she visited the ashram she learned that they had moved away. She spent the night there and left for Sewagram early the next morning. It was an eight kilometre walk to the village where Gandhi had built his ashram in 1936. Wardha was really the only link Sewagram had to the rest of the world as there was no post office or telegraph office there. Sewagram was surrounded by forests on all sides. Snakes and scorpions were common there. As Indumati entered the ashram, the first person she met was Kakasaheb Kalelkar, her father's friend from Belgaum. He had been told by her father about the situation. He made her comfortable and reassured her that Gandhi would help her as much as he could and that she should open her heart to him. It was a new experience for her, discussing intimate details of her personal life with so many people and such important people at that!

The walls of the huts in the ashram were neatly plastered with white clay and were decorated with folk art depicting palm trees, peacocks, the charkha and the letter *Om*, a strange mix. The windows and doors of the huts were made out of bamboo stalks fastened together with rope. They were decorated with local designs. Mats made out of palms were strewn on the floor. There was a single telephone which had been installed in Gandhi's office at the behest of Lord Wavell, the Governor General of India. Each hut had a spinning wheel so that raw cotton could be spun daily.

This was the first time that Indumati would have a one-to-one audience with Gandhi. She was quite nervous and was unsure what she would say to him. She missed having Tendulkar by her side. He was her strength. She began to think that she had perhaps been too rash in leaving her parents' home, that the statement her actions had made was just too far-reaching and that she would probably have to bear the consequences. Yet, she was aware that had her father not asked her to choose between the family and Tendulkar, she would probably not have taken such a drastic step and in the manner in which she had. She had understood her father's plight though, the fact that both her brothers couldn't join the army because of her political activities, and that the whole town was abuzz with rumours of her affair. Although she was touched by her father's concern, Indumati was also somewhat upset that he had decided to involve Gandhi in what was essentially a family matter.

When Indumati was shown into Gandhi's quarters, his eyes lit up through his steel-framed glasses as he smiled and signalled to her to sit down. His wife was sitting beside him while Madhavbhai took a seat in front of Gandhi. Indumati immediately felt at ease in his presence. She could see that his body had taken the toll of all the fasting and the political uncertainty. He seemed terribly frail, all skin and bone. Indumati had heard that he walked four or five miles each morning at a pace so brisk it was difficult to keep up with him. He wore a loosely wrapped dhoti and a coarsely spun white shawl which he hung over his bony shoulders. Indumati was awestruck by the humility of this man who almost single-handedly had managed to shake the very foundations of the British Empire. She addressed him as though she were speaking to her father and quickly decided to bare her heart to this thin, small man who ruled India's heart. Despite knowing his views about sex, she didn't hide the details about her relationship with Tendulkar. Gandhi sat spinning as he listened patiently to her words, without commenting on them. When she had finished, he stopped spinning and looked into her eyes.

"Does Dr Tendulkar want to marry you, beti?" he said. Without waiting for her to respond he continued. "Are you sure that your service and your sacrifice for the country will be realized by marrying him? Beti, he has an exciting background. But what do you know of Europe? Why do you want to take such a big risk? Why don't you devote your life to the country instead? You could live here in Sewagram. The country needs more people like you."

Indumati knew that Gandhi had placed service to the country above everything else. She, too, had worked selflessly for many years. But things had changed since she had met Tendulkar. She now felt that it was doubly important that she marry Tendulkar in order that her family could save face. She held up her chin almost defiantly, and quietly but resolutely said, "Bapuji, I will work for the country and do whatever is required of me. But Bapu, Tendulkar has agreed to marry me and I cannot refuse him. I want to have a family and bring up children. I will wait for him."

Bapu and the others were amazed to see the spirit of this young woman who had made up her mind and who resolutely defied everyone around her.

"Indumati, you tell me that Tendulkar is unofficially married to a German lady. What is her name, Thea…"

"Thea von Harbou," said Indumati. "Yes, the German authorities would not allow their marriage to take place officially."

"Well, then I would also request you that before we make any decision regarding your marriage with Tendulkar, you must show me a letter from this woman saying she had no objection to Tendulkar marrying you."

"Yes, Bapuji. I will ask Tendulkar to get a letter from her, although correspondence between Germany and India is quite difficult at the moment."

"Beti, I think you must meditate on what you want. I would also like you to give us a little time until we can resolve this issue," said Gandhi. Indumati joined both her hands in a namaste and left Gandhi's hut.

The next morning, Kakasahib Kalelkar met Indumati near the community temple. "Come, Indumati. We can sit under the tree and talk for a while. I have a message for you from Bapu," he said. Once they were seated, he continued, "You know that Gandhiji holds service and sacrifice to the country as being above all else. You are also aware that in the ashram, there are several followers who are married and who are yet required to follow the vow of celibacy, right?"

Indumati looked at him. She had known Kakasaheb for many years. He was from Belgundi and he knew the Tendulkar family personally. He was also a writer and a close friend of her father's. She was aware that her father had written to him separately, explaining the situation. She had read about Gandhi's views on celibacy and abstinence and was aware of his stance. She wondered with a growing sense of dread what was to come next.

"Bapu appreciated your honesty and your boldness," Kakasaheb continued. "He saw immediately that you are the kind of person who will stick to your word and do only what you believe in. I have also told him about the wonderful work you have been doing in Belgundi, single-handedly, almost, with no one to help or support you, especially since Tendulkar is in prison."

"But what is Bapu's verdict," she asked, a little impatient now.

"Bapu feels that before anything else can follow, you must first atone for your sins. He feels you have sinned against society by living with Tendulkar out of marriage. He says the only solution is that you do not meet each other for some time. It is only through separation that you can test your love for each other, and also decide for yourselves how you must lead your lives."

"But, Kakasaheb, Tendulkar is in prison and I don't know when he will be released. I don't know how long this war will last," she said, now weeping loudly. She leaned her back against the tree, completely devastated, she had taken everything in her stride till then and now the tears would not stop.

"Don't worry beta. Whatever happens will be for your own good. I am sure the time will pass quickly. It will be a wise idea to wait and not do anything rash. Bapu will let you know through a letter what the period of separation ought to be. He also said that if both of you fulfil these conditions, then he will personally preside over the wedding ceremony, in front of all the freedom fighters. Finally, Bapu has requested that you return to your father's home and to stay with him as long as possible."

"But Kakasaheb, what about my work in the village? I cannot abandon my friends and my students!" Indumati exclaimed.

"No, No, Indu, you must not do anything drastic. All you must do is visit your parents once in a while, and let them know where you are and how you are faring. After all, they are your parents. They love you very much."

"Thank you, Kakasaheb, for all your help and support," Indumati said, quite relieved. She joined her hands in a namaste and returned to her hut.

Indumati had the opportunity to meet Bapu once more before she left. He was busy with various people and acknowledged her with a smile and a small wave. "Beta, I will write to your father soon," was all he said. She had bowed down doing a namaste and quietly left to return to Belgaum. She did not want to think of what was going to happen next, realising that life was only going to get more complicated.

My Mother Speaks

Belgundi, August 1984: It was a wet monsoon evening and I was sitting at home with my mother in Belgundi. It was part of her routine to light the lamp in the puja room as the sun set every evening and to sing a few Sanskrit shlokas. Then, if I was with her, we would sit down and talk. I had been married some four years and was expecting my second child, and my husband and I had moved to Belgundi to start a small cement factory. Away from the busy life of Mumbai, I had time on my hands and so would demand that my mother tell me about her life. The drumming of the monsoon rain coming down in torrents outside and the erratic voltage making lights flicker inside, set a very charged atmosphere to our conversations. My mother was 70 and she cut a very handsome figure. Her face was virtually wrinkle-free and a shock of white hair framed her regal features.

One evening, as we sat together, I could sense that she was in a nostalgic mood and wanted to talk and share her memories. Suddenly the lights failed and soon after, fireflies began to glow in the dark and small night flies started circling the flame of the few candles we had lit. I persuaded my mother to talk about her meeting with Gandhi in Wardha way back in 1941, and asked her to tell me what happened in detail.

"It's strange that you ask me to talk about my wedding in Gandhi's Sewagram Ashram today Laxmi. We got married on the

19th of August 1945, and in fact, it's precisely that date today, the 19th of August. It was on this day that I married your father 39 years ago!" I was curious and it took me some coaxing to make her resume her story from the point when she had gone to meet Gandhiji at Sewagram to resolve the issue of her marriage.

"I was returning from Wardha where I had gone to meet Bapuji in 1939. Bapuji and Mahadevbhai had called me to explain why I had not returned to my parents' home since your father was now in prison. My mind was reeling and Gandhiji's words kept going round and round in my head. I was lost in my thoughts till I realised it was noon, and the train had stopped for an hour at Victoria Terminus in Bombay. I had enough time to get off the train and pick up food for the remaining journey. I marvelled at the Gothic architecture of the station and was amused to see the porters in their red shirts and white dhotis jostle noisily, competing with each other to find customers. I had forgotten what life in a busy metropolis was like. Living alone in Belgundi had made me insensitive to the sidelong glances of my fellow passengers. Khadi had become the symbol of the freedom movement, so I was instantly recognised as a freedom fighter because that's what I wore.

The train pulled into Belgaum late at night. I was happy to find my younger brother Narender waiting for me in a hired horse carriage. He smiled and said, "Where to this time? Belgundi?"

"No, home to our parents first," I said, giving him a quick hug. The next day, the entire family gathered to listen to me narrate my encounter with Gandhi in detail, and my subsequent meeting with Kakasaheb Kalelkar. My father was a little disturbed when he heard about the condition that Gandhiji had laid down for us. He was surprised to hear that Gandhiji had said we would have to be apart for a stipulated amount of time to test our love for the country and for each other. The duration of the separation hadn't yet been specified. I explained to him that Gandhiji would be writing to tell us his decision about what I should do while Tendulkar was still in prison.

"Father remained silent and allowed mother to fuss over me over the next few days. He knew that Gandhi could be very harsh. The duration he would prescribe would in all likelihood be at least a year. He knew that nothing would make me go back on my decision. My mother tried to coax me to eat and talk to the rest of the family. I was uncharacteristically listless and quiet. My brothers tried to tease me, hoping I would react to their banter. I missed Tendulkar terribly and was anxious about how he would react to Gandhi's intervention. I knew how western he was in his outlook and was worried he may not honour Gandhi's diktat. I grew increasingly tense and kept worrying about how I could possibly explain this complex and difficult situation to Tendulkar. In a few days, we received the much-awaited letter from Gandhiji, it was sent to Gangadhar Rao, a freedom fighter well known to the family in Belgaum."

At this point of the narrative my mother stopped. "Here Laxmi," she said," why don't I show you the letters?"

Luckily the lights had come on and my mother got up and went to the cupboard and took out an old cigar box from a drawer right at the bottom. She opened the box and I could see her face light up, it was just a fleeting second, a flash, these were her memories, her treasures. We sat on the bed looking at them. The letters clearly dated forty to fifty years back, they had become brown with age and some had moisture stains, they were of all shapes and sizes and were neatly folded and kept in the box at the bottom of her cupboard. I was fascinated. I touched them gingerly, not wanting to cause damage, and then began to read them little by little. There were many letters from Gandhi, addressed to my parents in his own hand writing. Some were in English, others in Hindi. There were also notes that were written in pencil on bits of brown paper. "On certain days Gandhiji maintained silence and if anyone went to see him he would scribble a comment or message," my mother said, explaining these bits of paper to me.

We spent the next few hours in silence and carefully sorted

through the letters. "Here, see, this is only a typed copy of the original but I have kept it carefully, it was addressed to Gangadhar Rao Deshpande who was a Gandhian and a political leader of Belgaum and also a family friend," said my mother as I began to read.

(original letter)

27-3-41

My dear Gangadhar Rao,

Bapu and I had long talks with Indu.

Her frankness and truthfulness are admirable and make it possible for one to be of some help to her. I have an impression that she has seen her error and is prepared to make amends for it. She realizes that she was fed on a false philosophy and she must shake herself free from it. Bapu says that if she really wants to do so, and love and service of the country is her sole end and aim her other inclinations must take a subordinate place, and in as much as she has defied her and you and society so far she must now bid good-bye to the old life and dedicate herself, not to an individual who had led her astray, no doubt with her full cooperation, but to the service of the country. Her friendship with Dr. Tendulkar she says, should be transformed and purified and elevated into a holy passion for the country, because she says that it was the common ideal of service of the country that bought them together and still binds them.

She says and I agree with her that that is an impossible ideal for her. She knows her limitations and she cannot fly in the face of them. She says she cannot possibly give up the thought of marriage with the Doctor, and she cannot dare to think that she would not be able to live an unsullied life maintaining friendly but unwedded contact with the Doctor. I have therefore suggested a way out which apparently has applied [sic] to her. I think she owes it to you and to her parents to make genuine amends for her error. If a pure bond of friendship and love unites them both she and her friend must be prepared to impose self restraint upon themselves. All contact between them excepting perhaps through correspondence must cease for the period of restraint, and she may spend that period either under the parental roof or with you or even at Sevagram, according to your direction. I propose that the period of restraint and penance if I may so put it should be five years or two years after the Doctor's release, whichever is shorter.

Shri. Gunaji should receive her back in the family with all the affection that I know he still has for her even in the justly lacerated heart. I would suggest that he should make a sympathetic attempt to understand her, forget and forgive her error and shower more affection on her than he has hitherto done. After this period of self restraint is over and if everyone is satisfied that both have observed the rules of restraint faithfully and cheerfully you and her parents should give them blessings and unite them as husband and wife.

This seems to me to be the only solution in the circumstances. Indu says that she is going to have a talk with doctor regarding this. It is likely that he will resent this letter and the proposal contained in it. Indu has to exercise all her influence with him to make him see his error and the value and implication of this proposal. If he does not Indu should either forget him and if she cannot do so she must forget every one of us, and go her own way. She has our prayers that God may guide her aright.

Yours sincerely
S/D Mahadev Desai

Gandhiji himself has added the following to the letter

"At paragraph 2 Mahadevbhai has not brought out my position clearly. It is this. Indu has grievously erred against her father, friend, society, herself and her beloved and therefore against the country. She can purify all by purifying her friendship for Dr. Tendulkar. This she can do by forgetting the physical relationship altogether.
    Bapu."

They were to be separated for five years! Gandhi specified that they could communicate with each other only through letters, and could occasionally even visit each other, but they were not to live together or marry each other before that time was up. I was also somewhat taken aback by Gandhiji's postscript: "She can purify all by purifying her friendship for Tendulkar. This she can do by forgetting the physical relationship altogether."

"What did you do then?" I asked my mother. "I would never have accepted such a harsh condition. Papa must have been hopping mad!"

"Gandhiji must have thought that a five-year period would be long enough for both of us to prove to ourselves that we truly loved and cared for each other," she said to me.

"How did the rest of your family react? How did your mother react?" I asked her.

"She was really upset and worried for me. My mother blamed everything on my father. She had disapproved of all the steps he had taken, right from the beginning – even when we had been sent to study in college. For years she had prided herself on being the mother of the most beautiful girls in the neighbourhood. Now everyone gossiped about my love affair. She kept repeating that it was a shame, for her, and for the rest of the family. She must have felt that your father would only be released when the war was over. But no one knew when that would be! What an absurd situation we were in. Gandhiji had also stipulated that even if Tendulkar were released before the five-year period of 'restraint and penance' was over, we could only maintain contact through letters.

"My mother had thought that Gandhiji would just write to me telling me to go home. Instead he called me to Sewagram and then he himself got involved in the situation. Once the national political leaders had got involved in our lives, we could not act independently. We could not go back, we were trapped. I was so scared of how I would break the news to your father who was in prison."

"I remember how anxious I was to meet your father and how scared I was about how he would react to my meeting with

Gandhiji in Sewagram. I had to wait for ten days as one could meet
political detenus only on certain days. He was quite shocked when
I told him about the five-year period of separation that Gandhiji
had stipulated. He was also surprised why a matter which was so
personal and close to our hearts had now become an issue that was
to be watched closely by leaders of Gandhiji's stature and other
politicians. He was aghast by the phrase Gandhi had added, "Indu
has grievously erred against her father, friend, society, herself and
her beloved and therefore against the country. She can purify all
by purifying her friendship for Dr Tendulkar. This she can do by
forgetting the physical relationship altogether."

"He told me that he loved me and could not understand what
all the fuss was about. He said he was committed to me. He asked
me why my father had involved Gandhiji in the issue of our
marriage. Was he still uncertain that he, Tendulkar, would marry
his daughter? He had great respect for Gandhiji, and felt he was
a great leader and should not deviate from the more important
national issues like the freedom struggle. He told me that if I was
still insecure about his commitment to me and thought that he may
go back on his promise, then he would seek special permission to
marry me immediately in prison. It must have been very frustrating
for him, being in prison and having no control over his life at
all. Especially after the interesting time he'd had in Germany for
almost two decades. He kept repeating to me, 'How can anyone
tell us that we have sinned against society? What have we done
that is wrong? Have we hurt anyone? Have we been untruthful?
What is this sin that has been committed?'"

"Both of us realized then that after my meeting with Gandhiji
we could never go back to taking any decisions without his
approval. Our relationship would thereafter be monitored by a
larger circle of people. I didn't know it then, but I was not going
to meet your father for a long time after that. He was transferred
to Nashik prison shortly thereafter, and after some time I too was
imprisoned for my anti-British activities."

My mother went on to describe the next few days at home with her family. She went about her day-to-day chores like a zombie. She seemed to have lost track of time, days flowed into nights. Sometimes her father found her sitting around, extremely depressed and morose, and at other times she would feign cheerfulness which he knew she wouldn't be able to sustain for too long. Her father was afraid she would suffer from a nervous breakdown.

The next letter I picked up from the box was written by Gandhiji himself. It read:

Letter to Indumati N Gunaji

SEVAGRAM, WARDHA,
April 17, 1941

CHI INDU,
I have your letter. The truth is that restraint, to be natural, must have the co-operation of the mind, which again cannot be

had without knowledge. If I have the clear knowledge that consumption of alcoholic drinks will harm me I will never touch alcohol, whatever its attraction. In your case the fact is that you do not accept abstinence a hundred per cent. You think you have two different duties, in fact you have only one. But that is what I think. God alone can guide you in your dilemma. Make an effort. It will certainly do you good.

Blessings from
BAPU
(From a photostat of the Hindi: C.W. 10944. Courtesy: Indumati Tendulkar)

"Here Laxmi" said my mother, "this is the letter that your father received while he was in Nashik prison. This was in reply to the conditions laid down for the next five years. I am sure your father must have written to Gandhiji expressing his concern on what would happen to me until he was released. This is what Gandhiji wrote:

Bardoli
21.12.41

My dear Tendulkar,
    I was glad to hear from you. Nasik weather must suit you well.
    I would like to see Indumati again and have her in the Ashram as long as she wishes to be there.

Love
Bapu (M.K.Gandhi)

"A few days later I returned to Belgundi to continue my work there. My friend Manorama was quite alone, and she had sent me several messages that the villagers had been asking for me. My father was initially surprised that I was going back, but he said to me, 'Indumati, you are a brave girl. I respect the fact that you have been able to stand up to your decision to be with

Tendulkar, despite the consequences. I wish you had decided otherwise, but henceforth, I will respect all the choices that you make. Please remember, we will support you always, in whatever way we can.'"

"My brother Narender offered to take me to the village on his cycle. I was grateful to him. My mother was more articulate than anyone else, that day. 'How will my daughter stay for five years without Tendulkar? What has this Gandhiji done to their lives? Does he realize the consequences of his decision? What will happen to my daughter?' She cried as she embraced me.

"That evening, the villagers were excited to see me cycle into the village. Everyone gathered around to welcome me back and Manorama, hearing the commotion, rushed out of our little hut. She hugged me, anxious to hear about everything that had transpired. Manorama led me inside the house, where she had been cooking on a wood stove. She had a pile of freshly picked vegetables that had been peeled and diced. She was about to sauté them with spices.

'Five years, aah-ya-oh!' said Manorama, slapping her hand to her forehead. 'This is sheer madness. What does the Doctor have to say? I don't believe that your doctor will listen to anything so absurd, not even if it comes from Gandhiji.'

"I was amused by her irreverent comments about Gandhi. 'Manorama, you can't understand how wonderful it was to meet Gandhiji,' I said. 'He spoke to me just like a father talking to his daughter. He's so interested in all our lives.'

'No, no, Indumati. I am very frank, and I will tell you that all this is humbug. You can call your Gandhiji a saint, fine, but you cannot allow him to control your life like this. You are a silly girl.'

"I was quite amazed at the simplicity of my friend's reasoning. Manorama had always been a very practical person, she'd had to fend for herself for many years."

'Manorama, while Tendulkar is in prison, there is nothing much that either of us can do. Who knows how long this war will last. I don't think the British will release any of the political detainees until the war is over. So what is the point of resisting this?'

'No, Indumati. I still feel you are making a big mistake. I think you should do what your Tendulkar suggests and get married to him in prison. I don't trust him. What if he changes his mind and decides not to marry you after all?'

"I was exasperated by Manorama's distrust of Tendulkar. She had always disliked him and been doubtful about our compatibility and the stability of our future, but this was not what I wanted to hear."

'Manorama, please let me decide what I to do with my life,' I retorted.

"Manorama smiled at me, flashing her white teeth."

'Yes, Indumati. Just know that I care for you. You are the only friend I have in the world. I am willing to give my life for you. You should know that I will stand by you no matter what you decide.'

'Let us start our work in the village. We can leave the future to our destiny,' I said.

'Oh, Manorama, another thing I learned from some of the leaders I met in the ashram is that women like you and me can play a crucial role in the freedom struggle. We will soon be called upon to travel outside of Belgundi and encourage the boycott campaigns and participate in the non-cooperation movement. I have heard that in most of the rallies organised by the Congress, women attend in large numbers, often with little children in tow.'

'Indumati, you do the political work. I will stay in Belgundi and help the women with their babies!' said Manorama.

"Over the next few days, we threw ourselves into our daily chores and into looking after the villagers, educating them, helping them with their day-to-day lives. I wrote to Gandhiji often and he replied to me. Here are some more letters I received from him."

Letter to Indumati N Gunaji

SEVAGRAM,
via WARDHA,
May 3, 1942

Daughter Indu,

I have your letter. Bharatanandji's plan is only an idea. Nothing has yet materialised. It will be all right if you take something from what I have written in Harijan.

Blessings from BAPU

Just under Gandhi's handwriting, there were a few words written by Madhav Desai. They read:

Indu, I have not received any news from you or Doctor. I have had to ask others. What are you up to these days?

Mahadev Desai

Indumati brought out another letter which was handwritten by Gandhiji's close aide Amrita Kaur but dictated by Gandhiji. Gandhiji often asked his aides to write letters on his behalf. In fact the letter shows that though it was written by Amrita Kaur, the address has been written in Gandhiji's own handwriting.

May 1942

Dear Indu

You must be well. Bapu is busy with a lot of work and therefore cannot reply to your letter. You will find what you are looking for in Shri Rajendra Babu's compilation.

It is very hot here. All is well except for a few children who have whooping cough here.

Blessings
Amrita Kaur

In August 1942, the Indian National Congress met in Bombay and launched the Quit India movement, calling for a mass struggle against British rule. "Do or Die" was the mantra that Gandhi gave to the people of India. However, even before the movement could get into gear, the British came down heavily on the protesters. All major leaders were arrested and the Indian National Congress was declared an illegal institution. Indians from different strata of society reacted spontaneously to this act of repression. Revolts broke out across the length and breadth of the country.

After my mother's visit to Gandhiji in Sewagram ashram, many freedom fighters came to visit her. On Kakasahib Kalelkar's guidance, she joined hands with another freedom fighter named Murlidhar Ghate. They were to go to every village and encourage the villagers to fight the British, not be intimidated by them and to not cooperate with the British administration. It was a difficult assignment. The villages were poorly connected and travel between them was often done on foot, sometimes in bullock carts and sometimes on bicycles.

Indumati's reputation as a social worker went with her and all the villagers welcomed her. Their target was to visit at least seventy villages and to spread the message of the Quit India movement. They often spent days away from home and would lodge for the night in a village, usually in the house of the village head.

My mother recounts:

I would be offered a place to sleep with the women and the children of the family. I found it difficult to adjust because of the lack of light and fresh air in the overcrowded dwellings. There was very poor sanitation in most of the villages. The houses were long and narrow and often had cattle and goats as well as people. It took me some time to get used to the rich smells from the kitchen, which combined the aroma of food cooking with the earthy smell of livestock and fresh fodder. I would fall asleep at the end of the day out of sheer exhaustion. In the morning I would rise early, bring all the villagers together and explain to them Gandhi's mission.

After two months of such extensive travel, a group of policemen were waiting to arrest me when I arrived at a village near Belgundi. The arrest warrant had been made on the charges of instigating the public against the Raj. Both Ghate and I were to be imprisoned. We were taken to Hindalga prison, near Belgaum. The lawyers who were supporting the freedom struggle were themselves in prison and the others too frightened to openly fight the British Raj. It was only later that I learned the name of the person who had informed the British about our activities. He was a villager with contacts in the army, a supplier of freshly-brewed alcohol to the officers. He had been well-rewarded for this information.

I was placed in the Hindalga prison near Belgaum, the same prison where Tendulkar had been detained for two years. The jail complex was spread over five acres of land, with two distinct divisions for men and women. Different single-storeyed buildings housed private cells and general barracks. The tall, imposing gates and the visiting area were all familiar to me, but I was shocked when I found out that I was being sent to the general barracks with the other convicts. Initially, I was made to sleep in a large bare room, the same cell as those who were under trial for criminal acts. Each prisoner was given a coarse mat to sleep on and a thick woven sheet to cover themselves with. The bedding was ridden with bedbugs, between them and the mosquitoes, I'd be up all night. More than once, some of the other prisoners spent the night wailing at the unjust treatment meted out to them. Some of the prisoners were completely innocent, while others were guilty of terrible crimes. The complex also housed mentally ill women, as there was no more space in the mental asylums in the district.

I could hear their shrieks early in the morning. The first few days were the most difficult for me. I was constantly in tears, miserable at the thought of what fate held in store for me. But I would focus my mind on Tendulkar and try to remember his vitality and energy. This would give me strength. 'He is definitely worth the wait,' I would say to myself. I had grown to believe that even if Gandhi had not imposed the five-year separation on us, the political situation of the country would have separated us anyway. I was soon moved to an eight foot by eight foot cell, which I shared with three other women. We were given thick cotton saris, white, with horizontal black stripes to wear. The sanitation and bathing facilities were deplorable. What we were given to eat was pathetic – ice-cold food that had been prepared by other convicts at least six hours before it was served.

The only relief in the miserable conditions was that every afternoon the prisoners were allowed to sit outside in the vast compound, under the shade of the large tamarind trees. Here, we sang songs or chatted with each other. There were several small children among us who ran around in the open air. These children were either born while their mothers were held captive or they had been brought to the prison along with their mothers. They afforded a welcome distraction, their innocent smiles touched our hearts. I quickly fell into my previous role of a village worker and showed the mothers how to fashion toys from pieces of wood or string that they found lying in the compound. I also taught them rhymes and chants.

My fellow prisoners were curious about what crime I had committed. They often regarded me with curiosity. Once in a while the bravest ones would inquire: 'Bai, what are you doing here? Women from high-class families like yours don't come to places like this. What crime have you done? Did you kill someone?

Your mother-in-law? Or your husband?' I would shake my head, horrified at their assumptions, and explain that I had been arrested for instigating the villagers against the British. The prisoners were not always impressed with my reply.

However as the Quit India movement spread, and more and more freedom fighters were jailed in the prison, we all formed a small group and bonded with each other.

I eagerly awaited the fortnightly visits by my family. They took turns to visit me, all except my mother who was too frightened of the prison to come. She devoted her time to worrying about me and praying for me. Tendulkar's cousin visited me often as well, but it was the letters from Tendulkar that were the highlight of my meagre existence. I looked forward to them like nothing I had ever done before. His letters expressed his worry for me and in them he would try to cheer me up with stories about what had been happening with him. He also related whatever news he had of what was transpiring in the outside world. As a political prisoner, he was given access to radio broadcasts and current affairs. Although the Quit India movement was only moderately successful in arousing anti-British activity among the citizens of India, it was ruthlessly suppressed by the British. I was sentenced to at least two years in prison.

Meanwhile, Gandhi and almost all the members of the Congress Working Committee were also arrested in Bombay. Gandhi was held under house arrest for two years in the palatial bungalow known as the Aga Khan Palace in Pune. I was saddened when I heard, while I was still there, that Mahadev Desai, Gandhiji's friend and secretary, had died of a heart attack at the age of 50. By the end of 1943, the British finally gave indications that power would be transferred to Indian hands at the end of World War II. At this point, Gandhi called off the struggle, and around 100,000 political prisoners were released.

The warden of the prison where I was housed had become very concerned about my failing health. He had realised early on that I was no ordinary convict, so in the wake of the waning freedom movement, he shortened my sentence on grounds of poor health. I was released in early 1944, after a little over eighteen months in prison. Too weak to think, all I could do was thank God for my release. My father arrived to take me home, I had difficulty walking as I was weak and too malnourished to walk. My mother was shocked to see the dark, black circles around my eyes and how thin I had become. The tension and uncertainty of my life, coupled with the deplorable physical conditions in which I had lived served to weaken my heart and I suffered from a nervous breakdown. Gradually, day by day, my parents nursed me back to health, massaging me with their own hands and using naturopathy. My father took me to a heart specialist in Pune, and then to Bombay where I stayed with my elder brother, Dattaram. It took a year, but over time, I grew stronger.

One day my father came to me and said, "Indu, I was wrong to have closed my doors to you. Please forgive your father."

I hugged him, sobbing with remorse and relief.

"I never meant to hurt you – or any of my family," I said. "I love you all deeply. All I did was to follow my heart and serve my country – how terrible can that be?"

Once home, I was able to update myself on Tendulkar's activities and read his letters over and over again. It was a difficult time for the country and for my family, but everything in Tendulkar's letters was positive. He was confident that the World War would be over soon and that India would get independence and that we would be married soon.

My mother had a faraway look on her face and I could still feel the emotion in her voice when she recounted these incidents. She didn't talk about them often and I still remember the moment vividly, being in Belgundi in the heart of the monsoon with letters from her little box in front of her. She picked up another yellow paper lying at the bottom of the box – it was her certificate of imprisonment at Hindalga prison way back in 1942. I read the judgement...

IN THE COURT OF THE MAGISTRATE FC BELGAUM
CITY JUDGMENT

The prosecution case is as follows. Government have issued orders to the effect that no public meeting or assembly or procession should be held at any place in the province of Bombay except with permission in writing of the District Magistrate of the Place concerned. These orders were published in Bombay Government Gazette Part1 at page 2881 dated the 9th August 1942. These orders were also published in the Village by beat of drum by the Police Patil of Tudiya, Belgundi and other places. Both the accused are Congress workers and stay at Belgundi. On the 19th August both these accused went to Tudiya and collecting people at several places made speeches before them saying that Mr Gandhi was sent to Jail and the British Government was at an end. The Police Patil of Tudiya sent report to the Police about these meetings. The Police registered the offence and an investigation [was made and they] have sent up a charge sheet against the accused who now stand charged with having committed an offence punishable under Rule 56(4) of the Defense of India rules.

Both the accused plead guilty to the charge. I convict them on their plea. I sentence accused No. 1 to two years rigorous imprisonment and accused No 2 to two years simple imprisonment Rule 56(4) of the Defense of India Rules.

s/d V.V. Velling
Magistrate F.C.
Belgaum city

"How strange" I said, "the date that you were arrested was 9 August 1942, just three years before you were married in 1945 on 19 August. What a coincidence!" My mother gave me her beautiful smile and look which said. "You haven't seen anything in life yet". We put the little box away but there were still many more papers that I wanted to see.

Release from Prison

A fierce monsoon rain lashed the dark, brooding walls of Hindalga prison on the outskirts of Belgaum. The wind howled through the trees and the leaves swayed and rustled loudly. The potholes around the prison compound were filling up as the red laterite soil sucked up the water. It was almost as if the fury of the monsoon rain was a response to the events that had led up to this day.

Gandhi had lost his wife Kasturba on the 22 February 1944. Gandhi did not keep good health himself and a few weeks later he suffered a severe malaria attack. He was released from prison on the 6 May, because of his failing health. A year later, in May 1945 World War II would come to an end and the Allies would celebrate their victory. India, however, still remained under the yoke of colonial rule.

It was a June day in 1945. Large numbers of political prisoners who had been detained during the war were scheduled to be released on that day. Across the road from the massive prison gates, under a cluster of trees, a small crowd of people awaited the release of their loved ones. Among them, huddled against the fury of the rain, was Indumati with her brother Bal. Indumati made a slight wispy figure in the grey deluge. Just a few days earlier she had received word from Tendulkar that he would be among the prisoners released on that day. In the letter he avowed his abiding love for her.

She peered through the lashing rain at the figures coming out of the prison. She had waited four and a half long years for this. Dressed in a white khaddar sari that was now soggy with rain water, she scanned the prisoners as they walked out the gates. Her long hair was styled in a simple plait. Her face was radiant, and her eyes glowed with the hope of meeting Tendulkar again. Her tears mingled with the rain water when she saw Tendulkar emerge.

Her younger brother Bal nudged her. "You better go quickly Induakka" he said, smiling slyly. "In case the jailer changes his mind and locks him up again." Indumati was too happy to be annoyed by her younger brother's teasing. She tapped him playfully on the arm and he smiled at her apologetically. Tendulkar waved as he approached. As Indumati strained her eyes to see in the rain, she could make out his tall figure, clad in a khaddar kurta, carrying a small parcel with his possessions.

When he reached them, Tendulkar wrapped his arms around Indumati. Immediately, the emptiness and loneliness of their separation seemed to evaporate.

"Are you two just going to stand together like that or do you want to get out of this raging torrent and go home?" Bal's voice brought their attention back to their immediate surroundings.

"Thank you, Bal," Tendulkar whispered as he looked into Indumati's eyes, "for bringing her to me." He then offered his hand to Bal in a warm grasp. He liked this bright and spirited young man.

Though Tendulkar looked tired and thin, Indian prison life had not diminished his impeccable demeanour, or his European manners. He wore a coarse Kurta pyjama and his shock of black hair was combed back on his face. His time in prison had not broken his resolve or his dignity.

Indumati quietly held his hand as Bal guided them to a horse carriage parked a short distance away from them. As they climbed in, Tendulkar lit his cigarette and continued smoking all the way to Indumati's father's house. Because of the heavy downpour, the journey took almost an hour, although it felt as though it was over in a few minutes. Tendulkar looked at Indumati and listened to her attentively while she poured her heart to him about the events that had transpired since they had last met. Their longing and their uncertainty about the future was palpable through the bumpy ride.

They knew how closely their future was tied into that of India, struggling to free herself from British rule. This was the beginning of what the whole world had waited for – the end of World War II and the start of a new era.

"When you meet my father, you will see how much he has changed in his attitude towards us. He respects us for having honoured Gandhiji's injunction that we stay apart for five years. He has seen how much we have both suffered," Indumati said, smiling encouragingly at Tendulkar.

Bal nodded and then added, "Induakka's state of health after her release from prison truly touched father. She was very weak and could hardly walk. But we all nursed her back to become strong enough to bully us."

Smiling into Tendulkar's eyes she said, "That's true. Father nursed me back to health. He will no longer stand in our way and is prepared to let us go to Gandhiji's ashram in Sewagram." Tendulkar held her small hand tightly and said, "I will do whatever you want Indu, will go wherever you want to take me. You have stood by me and I am committed to you."

Happy to be together at last, they huddled together in the back of the horse carriage. Bal sat in front whistling. He was happy for his sister, who, it seemed to him, constantly needed to be bailed out of trouble. But what else are brothers for? he thought as they made their way through the rain, the slushy muddy road and the glistening green trees.

"Whatever happened to your joining the army, Bal? You would have been a commissioned officer in the British army by now!" Tendulkar shouted to Bal, in an effort to be heard against the rain and the sounds of the horse carriage. "I have only Induakka, my dear sister, to blame. The British army did not want the 'freedom fighter' Indumati Gunaji's brother in their ranks – we were shown the door. As simple as that! The British consider all Gandhiji's followers as rebels and will do anything to make their lives difficult. Even punish innocent people like me!"

Though they laughed together at his assessment, Indumati knew how bad Bal had felt. Of her three brothers, he was the most keen to join the army. She was only too well aware of how her family had been affected by her nationalistic fervour and her determination that the British quit India. Tendulkar put his arms around her and drew her close, whispering in her ear, "You have made us all freedom fighters and diehard swatantra sainiks. You are quite amazing and I am proud of you!" Beneath Indumati's fragility was a fierce commitment to causes she believed in. Had she not had the heart and mind of a freedom fighter, a woman like her would have easily found refuge in the safety and comfort of a marriage arranged by her parents and would even have had children by now.

Finally, the back-breaking ride was over – they had arrived at her family home. Indumati's father greeted them as they got down from the horse carriage.

"Namaste," he said in a friendly voice. He led them into the house. The archway to the kitchen was low and Tendulkar had to bend his tall frame to enter. Indumati's mother was in the kitchen waiting to serve him hot tea and several homemade savouries. They saw him in a new light now. He was a respected freedom fighter, worthy of their daughter. Tendulkar tried to converse with Indumati's mother but she shook her elegant head in embarrassment and continued to serve him food. He saw a different woman now – so vastly different from the angry mother who had stormed into his home at Belgundi and had unceremoniously, without deigning to say a word to him, taken her daughter out of the house. A man with a very keen eye and discerning taste, he could not help but notice how beautiful Indumati's mother really was. That first day, all he had noticed was her indignation. Now he took note of her ivory skin and quiet manners. She was indeed startlingly good looking. She wore the traditional nine yard sari which was draped in the old-fashioned way. She wore a large bindi on her forehead and her eyes would constantly rest on Indumati's face with concern, anxiety and a kind of tenderness peculiar to mothers. She knew how much her daughter had been waiting for this day.

Tendulkar understood that this welcome and friendly attitude was a tremendous reversal of what the family had shown towards him earlier. They had been more than a little unsure about whether he would follow through and marry Indumati. When the rumours had started spreading that Indu and Tendulkar were in love, the entire town had been amused. However, when news broke out that even Indumati's father had asked her to leave the house and that Tendulkar had been arrested by the British, the town had been aghast. Indumati was delighted to see Tendulkar so completely at ease, teasing her brother and making everyone laugh. He recounted amusing anecdotes about how he used to wait for Indumati's tiffin to arrive. But turning to Indumati's mother, he said in all earnestness, "Madam, I have never eaten such exquisite food, such delicacies. The tiffin box Indu would send me while I was in prison was delightful. But what I have eaten today in your home is ambrosia."

Indumati's mother smiled and bowed her head, accepting the lavish praise. What a way he had with women, she thought. Tendulkar regaled them with stories of how more than the treats in the tiffin, what he looked forward to was the letter from Indu that she would tape under the lid. Once a week, the tiffin box would reach the prison and as Tendulkar's friends pounced on the food, Tendulkar would look inside the lid for the letters. Those letters were the highlight of his stay.

"My constant friends in prison were my friend Joachim

Alva and an Iranian called Agha. We would spend a lot of time playing Bridge, exchanging books and having long discussions," Tendulkar continued.

Indumati sat blushing demurely as she listened to the jovial stories. Her father stood in the shadows watching the whole scene. He saw Tendulkar as a brilliant but ruthless man, who was also deeply ambitious. His daughter was the joy of his life and he had always been so proud of her independent manner and her boldness in the face of all adversity. These very qualities now frightened him. What kind of life would be in store for her now? The sound of Indumati's voice joining in the conversation interrupted his thoughts.

"What he hasn't told you is that gradually my cooking got better... but because it took so long for me to actually cook the food, my letters grew shorter and shorter." She laughed and her father couldn't help but laugh at that remark too. As he watched Indumati and Tendulkar sitting in the midst of his family, fearless in their love for each other, he knew it was the beginning of a new era in the world and in their lives.

After the mirth of Indumati's remark subsided, Anuradha, said, "One day a prison guard landed at our door. He had a tree sapling in his hands. It was a gift from Tendulkar to Indumati and the guard had been convinced to deliver it here." Everyone looked amused.

"What a lovely present to send someone – and under what tragic conditions!" Anuradha continued, holding aloft the potted plant.

"Induakka asked me to plant it in the garden. Every day I water it and just see how beautifully it has grown." A tender look was exchanged between Indumati and Tendulkar.

Bal also had a story to share. Apparently, once, he had gone to the outskirts of Belgaum city and had come across a slightly bent man wearing a dhoti and a long jacket and a Nehru cap. Bal recognised him as Murlidhar Ghate, the freedom fighter who had been arrested along with Indumati.

"Namaskar, I don't know if you recognise me. I am Indumati Gunaji's younger brother," Bal had said.

"Oh Namaskar!" Murlidhar Ghate had replied, "How is Indu? How is her health now? I have not seen her in Belgundi for quite some time, in fact I have had no news from her ever since I was released from prison."

"I told him that Tendulkar was to be released shortly and he wanted me to convey his namaskars to you. He was very keen to know when the marriage ceremony was to be held." Bal continued "He mentioned that one of the important leaders of Gandhiji's ashram, Kaka Saheb Kalelkar, was currently in Sewagram and would be very happy to receive both of you."

As the sky darkened, Tendulkar had a chance to take a short stroll with Indumati in the compound. She noticed some changes in him. He seemed somewhat quieter and more pensive. "I want very much to go to Belgundi, even if it is just for a few hours tomorrow and visit the house. We can leave early in the morning and be back by sunset," he said.

Indumati was happy at the suggestion. She had been back to the village just once since her arrest, when Narender had offered to take her on his bicycle. It had been a tiring journey and she had not yet built the stamina to go alone. She knew that visiting Belgundi was important for Tendulkar; it was like his pilgrimage and she agreed readily. In addition, she looked forward to some time alone with Tendulkar, because she wanted him to talk to her about his ex-wife Thea. She needed to tell him that Gandhiji had insisted on a letter from Thea von Harbou stating that she had no objection to Tendulkar marrying again. She also wanted Tendulkar to prove to her that he was as committed to marrying her today, after his release from prison, as when he was in prison.

After the War

Tendulkar and Indumati planned to make a day trip to Belgundi the next morning. Tendulkar's cousin, Digambar Tendulkar, also known as Nana, had come to meet him. Having kept in touch with Tendulkar whilst he was in prison he had also looked after Indumati. When she required money to sustain herself in the village, she would approach him, and on Tendulkar's request he would sell a radio, or a gramophone player or one of Tendulkar's fancy German trinkets.

The three of them were happy to be in each other's company. My father often recounted to us that on his release from prison he was curious to know how his beautiful Mercedes had been transported from Belgaum and kept in the village. He would chuckle when he quoted what his cousin told him. "Oh, quite simple," he said, "We used an age old tradition. We actually tied the car to two buffaloes who pulled it all the way to Belgundi! I sat in the car and was driven in great style, the longest drive ever in a Mercedes! Don't worry, there was no damage! Incidentally, the owner of the bullock cart who dragged the Mercedes is coming to take you and Indu back to Belgundi and I am sure he will be here in just a few minutes."

My father had been amused and had told him "That was very resourceful. I take it that you saved on petrol as well."

Tendulkar also told Indu that he had heard from Thea who had given her permission and blessings for the marriage. Tendulkar had explained to Indumati that his relationship with Thea had been unique, and Thea had been much more than a wife to him. She was like the mother he had never had, and his benefactor – the one person who urged him to study further and convinced him to build industry in India.

He told her that he had received a letter from her in 1941, while he was in prison. She had written that she had just released a novel on India called *Aufblühender Lotos* or Blossoming Lotus. Surprisingly, the book, which was pure fiction, was the story of a young Indian Brahmin who had studied medicine in the UK. He returned to India impressed with the colonial power, but within months of his return, he actively joined the freedom movement, having witnessed the heartless and cruel treatment meted out by the British to Indians. Tendulkar was sure that she had got a lot of the details from Shripad who was in Berlin and had spent time with her. Tendulkar realized that the story also involved age-old Indian malaises such as child widows, untouchability, etc., and that she was finally expressing her understanding of Indian culture as it was. Her novels on India which she had written as a young girl were fantastic fables of Maharajas and their obsession for white-skinned princesses.

I had come across two newspaper cuttings in my mother's box which pertained to my father's release from prison. Both were news items that had appeared in the *Bombay Press Chronicle*. The first, dated 28 April 1945, mentioned that Mr H R Mohrey, Editor of the *Samyukta Karnataka* had requested support from the editors of all newspapers to pass a resolution that along with other stalwarts of the press community, they would form a committee to present the matter to the Government to secure release for Tendulkar who was imprisoned in spite of the World War II being over.

TENDULKAR MUST BE RELEASED

Editors' Conference Move

HUBLI, Jan. 24 : Mr H. R. Mohray, Editor of the "Samyukta Karnataka", has given notice of a resolution to be moved at the forthcoming session of the All-India Newspaper Editors' Conference at Calcutta protesting against the continued detention of Dr. A. G. Tendulkar, editor of the "Varta" a Marathi weekly of Belgaum since 1940 for the publication of certain articles in the weekly and urging his immediate release or the institution of a judicial inquiry of his case.

The resolution adds that a committee consisting of Mr. S. A. Brelvi, Sir Francis Low, Mr. K. Srinivasan (Commerce), Mr. J. S. Karandikar and Mr. H. R. Mohray be appointed to represent the matter to the Bombay Government and secure justice for Dr. Tendulkar.—United Press.

TENDULKAR MUST BE RELEASED

Editors' Conference Move

Hubli, Jan 24: Mr H. R. Mohray, Editor of the "Samyukta Karnataka", has given notice of a resolution to be moved at the forthcoming session of the All-India Newspaper Editors' conference at Calcutta protesting against the continued detention of Dr. A. G. Tedulkar, editor of the "Varta", a Marathi weekly of Belgaum since 1940 for the publication of certain articles in the weekly and urging his immediate release or the institution of a judicial inquiry of his case.

The resolution adds that a committee consisting of Mr. S. A. Brelvi, Sir Francis Low, Mr. K. Srinivasa (Commerce), Mr. J. S. Karandikar and Mr. H. R. Mohray be appointed to represent the matter to the Bombay Government and secure justice for Dr. Tendulkar – United Press

Another cutting which appeared a few days later, on 1 June 1945, reported that a resolution had been passed to release my father from detention at the All India Newspapers Editors Conference at Calcutta.

RELEASE HIM FORTHWITH

The war against Germany ended for the British Governement on the day the Germans surrendered unconditionally or immediately after. But so far as the Government of India is concerned, it does not appear to have ended yet. Dr. A. G. Tendulkar, an Indian journalist with connections with Germany – he had lived and married there – was interned by the Government of Bombay on the outbreak of war, obviously as a security measure. So far as we are aware, there have been no charges against Dr. Tendulkar except a presumption of pro-German sympathy, To have proceeded against him on mere suspicion was bad enough but it is something worse than foolish to keep him in detention even now. Oswald Mosley's, pronounced and self-proclaimed Fascists have been released promptly in Britain. Dr Tendulkar, a mere suspect and that too in the illogical mind of the bureaucracy, detained because of war with Germany is not freed yet! The All-India Newspapers Editors' conference at Calcutta passed a resolution on the subject of Dr Tendulkar's detention. That has been ignored. And now the Government is ignoring even the end of war with Germany. Dr. Tendulkar must be released forthwith.

Release Him Forthwith

The war against Germany ended for the British Government on the day the Germans surrendered unconditionally or immediately after. But so far as the Government of India is concerned, it does not appear to have ended yet. Dr. A. G. Tendulkar, an Indian journalist with connections with Germany—he had lived and married there—was interned by the Government of Bombay on the outbreak of war, obviously as a security measure. So far as we are aware, there have been no charges against Dr. Tendulkar except a presumption of pro-German sympathy. To have proceeded against him on mere suspicion was bad enough but it is something worse than foolish to keep him in detention even now. Oswald Mosleys, pronounced and self-proclaimed Fascists have been released promptly in Britain. Dr. Tendulkar, a mere suspect and that too in the illogical mind of the bureaucracy, detained because of war with Germany is not freed yet! The All-India Newspapers Editors' Conference at Calcutta passed a resolution on the subject of Dr. Tendulkar's detention. That has been ignored. And now the Government is ignoring even the end of the war with Germany. Dr. Tendulkar must be released forthwith.

It must have been a very frustrating experience for my father who had long awaited the end of the war. He probably never thought that he would be held back in prison because of his long stay in Germany. He was very touched by all the people who had supported him.

Digambar went to see Tendulkar in jail and handed over two letters to him that had come overland via hand from his brother Shripad. The first one had been trailing him for a long time and was dated December 1944. It was enclosed in an envelope that was stained and dirty. Shripad's letter told him about Thea's involvement with Subhash Chandra Bose in Berlin. Bose, the eminent freedom fighter who had staged various demonstrations in Calcutta against the British, did not agree with Gandhi's principle of non-violence. Instead, he believed in the very simple premise that "an enemy's enemy is a friend". So, in order to remove the stranglehold that the British had over India, he had decided that he would try to convince Hitler to help India fight against the British. He'd travelled to Berlin to do so – a journey that had not been easy. For a start he had to stealthily escape house arrest in Calcutta by the British. And then, he had to travel incognito, going on foot, by truck, or by bus via Kabul until he finally reached Berlin, his spirit exhausted but not defeated.

With the help of a few Indian supporters, Bose was able to establish a base in Berlin. His attempts to convince Hitler's officers to give him support against their common enemy were successful. People were amazed by his ability to negotiate with the Third Reich. The manner in which he dealt with the Germans was remarkable and he was able to achieve diplomatic status for his free-India movement which came to be known as the "Azad Hind Movement". Thea had written to Tendulkar earlier, saying she had been in touch with Bose. At one point, Bose made a broadcast to Indians in English and several Indian languages, via radio from Berlin. This shocked the British Raj in India and motivated hundreds of Indians to continue their fight for freedom. Indeed, Indians from all over the world had tuned in to the radio programme. Tendulkar had heard rumours of the broadcast while he was still in prison and he had paid special attention knowing that Thea had supported Bose in this endeavour. Now, Shripad's letter gave him more information on this.

Shripad wrote:

....Once Bose was asked whether he was not scared of being caught by the Gestapo and being but into prison. Bose retorted saying 'Had I been scared of going to prison, I would have stayed back in India. The British officers are brutal and cruel to Indian freedom fighters, torturing them and giving them inhuman punishments.' The Azad Hind army is also known as the 'Indian Infantry Regiment 950'. About 3500 men from four battalions took an oath of loyalty to Hitler, Bose and "Free India" in September 1942. The Legion was paraded on 6th of November 1943 at a ceremony at the Hotel Kaiserhof in Berlin to announce the creation of the Indian National Government. I have been very friendly with a group of them – Nambiar and others. They were very actively involved with Subhash Chandra Bose and were part of the Azad Hind programme to liberate India, especially during 1941 and 1942. Thea told me that she had taken special care of those Indians who gathered around Subhas Chandra Bose and who worked in Radio Azad Hind and in the Indian Legion. Apparently, together with Subhas Chandra Bose, she said goodbye to the eight Indian students at the Anhalter Bahnhof railway station. They were leaving for Frankenberg for military training, and were to later form the core of the Indian Legion. It is such a refreshing change to hear Indians greet each other with the words "Jai Hind".

On 5.1.1942 I received a call from the Foreign Office inviting me to come to the Kaiserhof Hotel. I met Mr S C Bose there for the first time. A few days later a gentleman from Bose's inner circle called Mr Vyas rang me up and asked me to come to the Free India Centre at Leichstein Allee. I took my friend P B Sarma with me and we were both taken to S.C. Bose. He explained his plans and told us about his organization and requested us both

Thea von Harbou with Indian students in her house during Christmas, 1940

Thea von Harbou and Michaela Purchner with Indians in Berlin,
in front of the sports palace, 1941

to join him. Sarma agreed but I refused telling him that I had come to Germany to study and had no interest in politics. In January 1942, my friend Keni asked me to give him the details of my marriage and said that Bose was willing to help me get permission. I refused the offer once again as I did not want to apply through Bose.

A few months later I was able to get a job in MARQUARDT City planning Company in Berlin which would have counted as practical training for my Diploma exam. But I was asked to produce a work permit from either the Foreign Office or the Free India centre, which I could not do and permission was cancelled! In December 1942 once again Bose called me and asked me to join the Free India centre which I refused.

Life has been very difficult for me. My son Klaus was operated for appendicitis in September 1944. I finally joined the Siemens civil engineering branch in October 1944. The Gestapo called me in Berlin and asked me whether I had joined the Free India centre. I told them I had not and yet I was asked to report to the police station once a week. This was just shortly after an attempt had been made on the life of Hitler. I told them that I had never taken part in politics nor had I ever helped the Germans in any way during the War.

Thea loves us, as though we were her family. I do not know what I could have done without her help. I hope to come to India once I am out of this terrible place. I hope you will be released from prison soon and I can bring Elizabeth and Klaus back to India!

Your loving brother
Shripad

Tendulkar was apparently amused that despite having lived in Berlin for so long, Shripad had steadfastly refused to join the Free India movement. The second, moe recent letter was hand delivered to their elder brother, Purshottam in Bombay by a traveller from Berlin.

Berlin
June 1945

My dear Brother

I have not heard from you for a very long time. Elizabeth and I have had a very tough time during the war, but thank God that is now over! I have been in touch with Tai. Our son Klaus is doing very well. He is six years old, a good-looking boy, but speaks only German. He is very close to Thea. I was put into the Staumühl detention camp, close to the city of Paderborn. I am writing this letter to you from there.

The camp has about 3,500 inmates, mainly German. There are a few foreigners and altogether we are about 35 Indians. We have all been accommodated in barracks and there is an adjoining camp for women which has about 500 prisoners. One of the first persons I spotted was Thea von Harbou. From the messages we managed to exchange with each other, I feel that she was happy to be in the same camp as the Indians. She had accepted her fate stoically. The conditions after the war are indeed depressing and there is a scarcity of everything, especially food.

One day, quite by chance or fate, I came face to face with Thea and that was the time when she made a sign telling me that she would be at the dentist at 11 a.m. the next day. I pretended to have a sore tooth and made such a good pretence that the dentist actually extracted my molar tooth! I think he suspected that I was shamming and wanted to teach me a lesson. It's okay, after all what is it to lose a tooth? I had been worried about Thea and was happy to see her well and composed. She was very keen to know whether I had any news from you. She wanted to know whether you were still in prison and the present condition in India. She believes that once you are released, you will be marrying Indumati Gunaji. She is convinced that only an Indian woman can give you the family life that you deserve and that only an Indian woman can make you happy. She has always told me that water reaches its own level and keeping your age differences and differences in background in mind, she always felt that you would want to settle down and put your roots down in the land in which you were born.

Thea also told me that the army and police have started occupying houses that lie vacant and she has asked me to move my family into her flat in Frankanallee. I have already sent a message to Elizabeth to move into Frankanallee with baby Klaus.

How are you? And what is the situation in India like now? Please write to me as soon as you are released.

How I long to be back in India, especially in our grandfather's home in Mayem, Goa, where we grew up. How I long to swim in the river next to our house and fish in the Mayem lake. I never knew that our lives would take the turns that they have. I never expected that I would start my family in Germany.

Tendulkar put down the letter. He had not met his brothers for the last five years. He had to make up for all the time that had been lost in prison. He had no idea about Thea and Shripad being put in the same detention camp after the War was over. He was also sad that Thea, at her age, had to undergo so much trouble.

The bullock cart that had to come to take them to Belgundi had finally arrived and both Tendulkar and Indumati got into the old-fashioned vehicle. Tendulkar was silent for some time as he was thinking of what Shripad had written to him. There were several light showers on their way and Belgundi was a veritable paradise in the monsoon season. It was situated in the middle of undulating hillocks and valleys of the Western Ghats. The land was fertile, the farmers were progressive, though uneducated.

They were in high spirits, talking and generally enjoying each other's company. Indumati felt like a queen. Tendulkar was attentive to every nuance of her feelings. He seemed as though he was willing to place his life at her feet. But much as he was in love with Indumati, a part of his mind and heart was still occupied with his life before the war. He had promised Thea that he would dedicate his life to the service of his country and he never expected that he would have to face political detention for almost five years. The five long years had made him very impatient. He had returned from Germany determined to do so much, and rather than using his talents he had been made to languish in prison!

He showed Indumati the telegram that he had received that morning from Gandhiji in Simla, expressing his happiness that he had been released from prison. Indumati had read about the telegram in the newspaper, the clipping of which is produced below dated 17 July 1945.

Gandhiji Happy At Tendulkar's Release

BELGAUM, July 17.
Dr. A. G. Tendulkar, who was re
leased from the Belgaum Central
Prison on Saturday after five years
detention, has received a telegram
from Mahatma Gandhi from Simla
expressing his happiness on Dr.
Tendulkar's release.

"Yes, Father had mentioned that to me in the morning. We must go to Sewagram soon so that Bapu can get us officially married. We have fulfilled his condition of being separated for five years and now there is no one who can stand in our way!"

They both climbed the hillock near the village and stopped to rest under a Jamun tree. Tendulkar had a smile on his face and a faraway look in his eyes as he suddenly felt a wave of nostalgia sweep over him.

"Indu, do you see that Jamun tree?" he asked, pointing to another tree not too far away from them.

"Every day during recess at school, my friends and I would race each other to the top of the tree, touch its topmost branch, admire the view from the top of this hill, and race down again! What unbridled energy we had then!"

He watched Indumati as her eyes roamed over the scene of his childhood pranks. She looked so serene, so beautiful, so happy to be with him! He admired her chiselled profile with its broad forehead and well-defined contours. She had worn a thin, pink cotton sari with a maroon border and not the khaddar she normally wore. The shade of her sari brought out the colour in her cheeks and she looked radiant. Tendulkar, too, wore a half sleeve shirt over black trousers and a pair of sandals. He felt rested and energetic. He was relieved at being out of prison. He gently touched Indumati's face.

"One day Indu, I am going to build a palace on this hill – and I will offer it to you, my Queen," he said, almost as if he were making a vow.

"How dramatic!" said Indumati, delighted.

Indumati's smile widened. Her experience of living in the village in an unfinished house, constantly having to ward off animals and rodents, had not been a very comfortable one. But now, with Tendulkar by her side, she felt bold, even ecstatic. She could take on anything. She had stood her ground all these years despite the malicious rumours circulated about Tendulkar and her, despite opposition from her family and friends.

"Love makes the impossible easy, no obstacle seems too big," sighed Indu romantically as she lay, her head on Tendulkar's broad shoulders and felt the warmth of strong arms embracing her.

"Indu, my darling, we could have just had a simple ceremony here in Belgaum in front of your parents and family. I know your father meant well when he wrote to Gandhiji five years ago but how complicated the issue has become now, and we have to go to Sevagram."

Indu looked away "We have complied with Gandhiji's request of staying away from each other for five years and the worst is behind us now. Let us get his blessings – it's only a matter of a few more days."

Tendulkar lit his cigarette and had a faraway look in his eyes" I have lost so many years for no fault of mine, we are both older and more mature, if your wish to go to Sevagram to get married is so strong we will leave as soon as we can."

Marriage

Gandhi had recently announced through his newsletter – *The Harijan* – that he would only give his blessings or officiate at those marriages in which one of the parties was a Harijan. He had forgotten about the promise that he had made Indumati five years ago. Five years later, she and Tendulkar suddenly appeared in front of him, without any prior notice. Indumati stood before a thin and frail Gandhi. She was wearing a hand-spun sari and looked confident and determined.

"Tendulkar, I am happy to see you released from prison. It must have been a long ordeal. But you are looking the gainer and are looking healthy and fresh!" This from Gandhi.

They both did their Namastes to Bapu and sat down in front of him. Bapu wanted to hear about Tendulkar's experiences in prison and about the people he had met while there. "Now tell me – why have you both come here? What can I do for you?" said Gandhi.

This statement, in all its simplicity, shook the young couple. Indumati was the first to speak.

"Bapu, Dr. Tendulkar is now free. I have honoured my word to you and Madhavbhai Desai. I haven't met Dr Tendulkar in five years, as was asked of me. He himself has served a sentence for four and half years. We have come here because, after fulfilling all your conditions, we want to get married, and we want our wedding to be done in your presence, and with your blessings."

Mahatma Gandhi lowered his eyeglasses further down his nose and peered at Indumati and Tendulkar. "Have you not read my article in *Young India*? Last week, I published a statement that I would officiate only at those weddings where someone was marrying a Harijan. If I remember correctly, both of you are Brahmins."

Indumati was shocked at Gandhi's statement, but she stood her ground. "But, Bapu, we have stuck to your conditions. Tendulkar has just been released from prison and I, too, had to serve 18 months of imprisonment and we are here now together to work towards the independence of our country. Madhavbhai Desai had written to us, on your instructions, and this was conveyed to me through a senior Indian Congress worker. He even came to meet my father in Belgaum and gave him your letter. I have suffered very much during the last few years and it is only your promise that has kept me going. I have been ill with worry and unhappiness. I have fulfilled my promise to you and have also worked in a manner in which I have always put the needs of the nation above my personal ones."

Gandhi looked at her kindly and said in a small, silent voice, "Indumati, can you bring me the letter I had sent your father five years ago? It will be a testimony to my promise and no one can then criticise me for not honouring a word given prior to my statement published in *Young India*."

"Yes Bapu, I will try and find it," she replied. Tendulkar looked at Indumati questioningly. She reassured him with a nod. She knew that her father Mr Gunaji would have kept the letter safely. With that Gandhi got up from his seat on the floor. He stretched out his hands and placed them on the shoulders of the two girls on either side of him, walking slowly and made his way towards the kitchen of the ashram. Tendulkar and Indumati accompanied them. They then sat down on a stool with a small table in front of him, and started peeling vegetables along with the others. Light conversation, interspersed with jokes and laughter, followed. This made Indumati feel at home and at ease.

"How does he find time for such a trivial occupation as the peeling of vegetables in the midst of his multifarious activities and with the heavy responsibilities of handling issues of national importance?" muttered Tendulkar softly to Indu, sounding somewhat exasperated. "His actions and decisions are responsible for guiding big movements which shape the destiny of millions…"

"During my visits, both at Wardha and at Sevagram, I'd watch him engrossed in his daily chores. I realised that with him there was no 'high' or 'low' ranking, neither in work nor in men. He believes that all work is service, and all service is dedication, and so work has no rank. He calls the duties that are assigned to each member of the ashram "bread money" and he often carries them out himself, whether it means cleaning the cowsheds or the water closets!"

"I really do wish he had taken our request a little more seriously. How can Bapu go back on what he has promised five years ago?" Tendulkar asked.

"I am sure he will do what he has promised. It is, of course, important that it does not appear that he has gone back on his most recent promise. Every action of his is scrutinised by the whole world, and you know that in supporting the Harijans, he has single handedly opposed the entire caste system in India." Although Indumati was upset herself, she would not let anyone criticise Gandhi.

"I have seen him spending time serving food to the residents of the ashram with his own trembling hands, both morning and evening. I have seen him devotedly attending to the sick. I have seen him giving as much time and attention to settling trivial disputes amongst his disciples, as one would give to settling matters concerning the most intricate affairs of politics or the State," she continued.

But Tendulkar was still critical. "If Gandhiji spent his time a little more judiciously, saved it from these trivialities, and spent it on higher and greater objects that require his attention, things would be better managed," he said.

"Bapu believes that he must love all without any discrimination. It is the wisdom of these spontaneous actions which is the real secret of the hold he has over millions. I can tell you from personal experience what joy I've felt just reading a few uneven and illegible lines written in his own hand," said Indumati.

As they left the kitchen, Indumati was called to Mrs Madhav Desai's hut. She was very close to her and to her teenage son Narayan. Seated on the mat in Mrs Desai's hut, Indumati told her the whole story about how she had been asked to come to Sevagram to meet Gandhi and Madhav bhai Desai when Tendulkar was still in prison. Mrs Desai realized that she was emotionally exhausted and very nervous and encouraged her to speak.

"Kaka sahib Kalelkar was here just this afternoon and he mentioned that he knew your family well and that your father is a respected writer. He says that he also knows Tendulkar who comes from Belgundi," said a smiling Mrs Desai. "But Indu why hasn't your father come here today? What were his reservations?" she asked.

"I can never understand why so many people object to my marrying Tendulkar. It doesn't matter to me in the least that he has been married to other women before me. I believe him when he tells me that we will serve the nation together and that his reasons for returning to India will be fulfilled by marrying me. I believe him when he says that he loves his country and wants to settle down in India. I dream that we will work side by side in building the nation. Why then are my father and even the great and compassionate Bapu not supporting me?"

Mrs Desai put her arms around Indumati. She felt sad, she knew that Indumati would one day understand that though these words of promise and motivation were straight from Tendulkar's heart and were genuinely meant by him, there was a huge price to be paid. There was too much difference in their backgrounds and lifestyles and it was obvious to all that they were so ill matched – Tendulkar, experienced and very European, and Indu, a simple though stubborn and strong-headed young woman from a conventional middle-class family.

The following day Tendulkar went to meet Indumati – she was at the time in one of the huts reserved for women. During the free time in the ashram routine, they both went for a walk around the ashram and then settled down beside the river to talk. It was August, the heart of the monsoon season, the skies were full of thick, dark grey rain clouds which made the weather sultry and warm. Tendulkar took Indumati's hand and said very plainly.

"Indu, we cannot go on like this. We have to settle down. If Bapu cannot officiate at our wedding, we should look for alternatives."

He lifted the few stray curls that were covering Indumati's forehead and stroked her hair. Indumati had tears in her eyes. "Yes I know, our love story has been the subject of discussion of so many people for so long. When I met Bapu five years ago, I was absolutely frank and open with him and told him that we were already living as a couple. I remember the words that he used to me in his letter he said 'Indu you have erred against society and your family.' That is why he felt a need to punish us with the long separation. I think in view of the kind of attention we have received after Bapu got involved personally in our lives, we cannot go back and have another official perform our wedding. It's also important that people know that we have done no wrong. What Bapu said was acceptable to me because I love and revere him, but I will not allow any other soul to tell me that I have erred against society. I am not shy or embarrassed by what I have done. I have paid the price willingly!"

Tendulkar looked at Indumati's flushed face. She had a strong sense of pride and duty and honour. He saw and loved the spirit in her eyes. She was stubborn, yet righteous. "Indumati, you are right. Let's try and implore Gandhi to fulfil his promise, but remember, he is known as the father of the nation. We are not the only people with problems; there are others whose problems are more pressing. Not to mention the world of politics that he has to address constantly. Let me try and meet him tomorrow. He has told us that he cannot do anything unless we produce the letter."

"I am sure you will be able to convince him my darling, but please do not be impatient or say something that you will regret later," Indumati said with a smile. Tendulkar smiled back at her. She knew him well.

Telephone services to small towns like Belgaum were quite erratic. Tendulkar and Indumati would have to make another trip to Belgaum and return once again after having found the letter Gandhi had asked them to produce. Gandhi believed that abstaining from food by fasting was good for the body and to abstain from communication by not speaking was good for the spirit. He often spent days in silence. When there were pressing demands, he would make an exception and would scribble out his answers on paper. When Tendulkar called on Gandhi that evening there were many leaders assembled in the hut. There were also other people who had come to visit and discuss things with him on which they sought his intervention or advice. Tendulkar recognised Manilal, Gandhi's son, and Meera Behn, who was attending to him. As soon as Tendulkar entered, the light banter between these two ceased. Tendulkar brought in a certain amount of tension into the hut, as everyone had heard the rumours that were circulating in the ashram about him. Manilal and Meera Behn regarded Tendulkar with curiosity, wondering how Gandhi was going to handle the strange situation in which this man found himself.

"Namaste Bapu," said Tendulkar and Gandhi gestured, inviting him to sit by his side. Then he patted him gently on his back.

"Bapu," Tendulkar continued. "I know today is your maun vrat, your day of silence, but I had to speak to you."

Bapu nodded and made a sign encouraging him to continue speaking.

"Indumati and I have both come here with so much expectation. We did not meet each other during the last five years, as you requested. We have stood by your wishes in every sense of the word. We have been through hard times including detention in prison. Indumati has worked in the villages all alone and she has even developed a heart ailment because she is so exhausted."

Tendulkar paused. He was aware that several people were staring at him. Some of the senior members of the ashram had heard about Tendulkar's stay in Germnay and they knew that he had been married. They didn't feel that Gandhi should allow the wedding to be held in the ashram, and had already had a meeting with Gandhi to this effect. But Gandhi had not committed anything to them.

"Bapu," Tendulkar continued, "I cannot bear to see the tension that Indumati is in. Forgive me, Bapu but I have come to say that if you do not marry us, I am afraid I will have to go outside the ashram and get the first priest from the roadside to perform our wedding rites. I can no longer bear to see Indumati in this state," Tendulkar said, his voice rising to a higher pitch than usual.

There was pin drop silence. Tendulkar's habit of bringing up issues with the sheer power of his own audacity had worked well in other instances. But this was not the case in front of Gandhi for whom silence, non violence and passive resistance were the foundations on which he planned to build India. Gandhi smiled, then nodded to Manilal to pass the writing pad and pencil. He looked at Tendulkar and scribbled a small note which he then handed him. "Let's look into the whole issue clearly tomorrow," it said.

With that, Gandhi got up, gestured for his walking stick and made his way across the compound towards the large central hut where the evening communal prayer was conducted. The sounds of devotional songs sung each evening – one from every religion – had just started and the oil lamps were lit in strategic places to facilitate movement in the ashram. Gandhi held his walking stick in one hand while the other hand rested firmly on the shoulder of his niece whose duty it was to escort him.

Gandhi's steps were small but amazingly quick for someone his age and with his frail build.

Tendulkar also followed the duo for some distance before heading for the hut in which he was staying. As he described it, many thoughts were going through his mind at the time. He thought it strange that when he wanted to marry Thea von Harbou, he was not allowed to do so because of his nationality. Almost ten years later, he wasn't being allowed to marry an Indian woman of the same nationality because he was considered a foreigner, due to all the years he had spent in Germany. Indumati had become his life and he loved her dearly and he realized that once the political situation within the country settled down, he would need some kind of stability in his life. He realized that he had not behaved properly with Gandhi. Tendulkar always had mixed views about Gandhi; there were times when he appreciated his policies and political strategies and others when he criticised the passive manner in which Gandhi was conducting Indian politics. He had not planned to make that remark about picking up the first priest on the roadside, but something had irked him. He had agreed to the conditions that were laid down by Gandhi initially, because he knew that it made a lot of difference to Indumati.

The next morning, Indumati received a message from Gandhi asking her to come to him immediately. "Indumati, my daughter, Dr Tendulkar says that he will pick up the first priest from the road if I do not get both of you married. Does he speak only for himself or do you have the same wish?" he asked. He had grown very fond of this young girl and wanted to make sure that he would do what he could to make her happy.

Indumati was embarrassed and felt put in an awkward position. She had not met Tendulkar since his audience of the night before, and she was quite shocked by this account of him trying to bully Gandhi. Tendulkar should not have taken the liberty to speak thus to Gandhiji, but she knew how frustrated he was and how impatient he was to make up for the last five years that he had spent in prison. She also realized that Tendulkar's words had been said on impulse.

"No Bapu, I will only marry Tendulkar if you will perform the rites. Otherwise I will not get married," Indumati said quietly but with firm resolve. Bapu looked intently into her face. He saw that she had been crying and was very tense.

Calm and affectionate, he said to her, "Tell me what I had written to your father. Do you have the letter I sent with you?" Indumati looked up at him. He continued, "At least tell me what was inside it. It is a letter I had written over five years ago, and so much has happened since then."

Indumati suddenly realized that Gandhi was trying to give her a chance and she responded, "I know the letter by heart! You said that if we fulfilled the conditions that you and Madhavbhai Desai had laid down, of us not meeting each other for five years, and thereby proved to you our love for each other and for the country, then you would perform our wedding in Sevagram once the separation period of five years was over." She spoke breathlessly, and quickly added, "My father has also agreed to everything. He has told me that he will accept Tendulkar as my husband, because you had agreed to marry us once the separation was over. He now knows that after five years our love is true and will last forever!

"Let me think about it," was Gandhi's reply.

Indumati quickly went back to the hut of Mrs Desai to apprise her of this recent development. She found her sitting on the floor gently working her wooden spinning wheel, which was a compulsory ritual for everyone in the ashram. Her fifteen year old son Narayan was rolling the yarn she produced into bundles. The hut was austere like the other huts. In one corner was a pile of books that belonged to her late husband.

After Indumati narrated the story to them, Narayan said with an excited voice, "Indumati, I think I can help you. I remember this letter. I was with Bapu and my father in Panchgani when Bapu wrote this letter. I copied this letter while I was in Panchgani.

It was a task given to me and my companions to actually keep a record of all correspondence by copying the letters in dairies. I know which diary it is in and I know where these dairies are kept in the office. I will bring it to you and then you can show it to Bapu."

Indumati was astounded and overjoyed. She had no idea such a simple solution might be found. She rushed to Narayan and gave him a sisterly embrace.

"Go Narayan," Mrs Desai said. "Go quickly and see if you can find the draft of the letter recorded in the dairy. It will help my poor Indumati out of her difficulties."

Narayan went to the main administrative hut and after what seemed to Indumati like an eternity, he returned with the diary tucked into his cloth shoulder bag that hung from his shoulder. Indumati felt reassured the moment she saw the young boy's grin. Mrs Desai and Indumati both read the letter over and over again while Narayan watched them, happy that he had been the one to provide such important help to Indumati. It was already afternoon and they were anxious to show the copy of the letter to Gandhi. Mrs Desai accompanied Indumati to Gandhi's hut. They peered inside and saw that he was sleeping.

Mrs Desai signalled to her to leave it on the head table. Indumati placed the dairy carefully down and then they returned to Mrs Desai's hut to wait till Bapu awoke. When Narayan returned from his chores and heard how they had left the dairy behind, he became visibly concerned. "No, No," he cried. "If Bapu is sleeping, don't leave it behind. Somebody may take it. The people in the ashram are not at all keen on this wedding. You must not let that letter get out of your hands until Bapu sees it."

In a panic, Indumati immediately retraced her steps and entered Gandhi's hut. Luckily he was still sleeping and the diary was still on the head table. She quickly took hold of the frayed diary and hurried away to find Tendulkar and tell him the good news. He had been in a strange mood ever since his meeting with Gandhi.

"Look, I have the letter!" Indumati cried rushing into his hut.

Tendulkar got up slowly from the bench on which he had been sitting. He hadn't met Indumati since the incident with Gandhi and he wasn't quite sure how she had reacted to what he had said. But he took one look at the diary in her hand and understood the situation. They both smiled at each other, but he still felt awkward about what had transpired between him and Gandhi.

He tried to say something to ease his embarrassment, but Indumati silenced him by putting her hands on his lips. "That is all behind us now," she said firmly. "Look, we have finally found it. Here is Bapu's letter."

19.9.1944
Panchgani

Bhai Gunaji,

In case you cannot read this Indu will read it to you. Why should we write to one another in English? I am glad that you have had a change of heart about Indu and brother Tendulkar. If all of you agree I will perform the wedding in Sevagram, they know the conditions. With blessings from Bapu.

They sat down on the bench in Tendulkar's hut and read the letter over and over. It was strange to think that in this one piece of paper lay the key to so many years of their suffering and an entire future of their happiness. Another hurdle in their life was finally over. That afternoon they went and waited outside Gandhi's hut. At about 4 p.m., Indumati and Tendulkar were granted audience to read the extract from the dairy to Gandhi. Narayan had joined them there, and as the young man bent to salute Gandhi, he mischievously tweaked Narayan's ear. "So young man, you are also behind all this?" he teased. Narayan grinned sheepishly.

Reading the promise given to Indumati and actually seeing it in front of him seemed to give Gandhi tremendous pleasure. He truly respected Indumati and Tendulkar for keeping their word. He looked up from the diary, took off his glasses and said, "Now I have to perform your wedding in the ashram as I had promised you. I had made this promise to you almost five years ago. Today, with the letter in front of me, I can only say that I am your slave in this matter. Many people are against me in this, but now I can prove to them my promise, which I will certainly not go back on."

Tendulkar, Narayan and Indumati were filled with jubilation, and left to share the good news with Mrs Desai. Several of the prominent leaders in the ashram, like Susheela Nayyar, Pyarelal, and Mushroowalla, came to meet Gandhi that evening to reiterate that they were still against this wedding. They regarded Tendulkar as a foreigner and not a true Gandhian at heart. There was also some objection to the plan of the marriage ceremony being performed in the hut of Gandhiji's late wife Kasturba. Gandhi made a statement that evening to all those assembled.

"I have promised Indu that I will get her married," he said, "and I have to stick to that. Here is the written proof of the promise I had given her several years earlier. I had made this promise even before I made a statement in the *Harijan* magazine. I will not comment on who she marries. That is her concern."

The next morning a messenger brought a handwritten note in Hindi to Indumati. She took the letter to Tendulkar and they read it together.

Dear Indu,

This letter is for both of you.

I would like to perform your wedding on the 19th August. The rituals will be performed by Prabhakar. He is born of Harijan parents who converted to Christianity. Kaka Sahib Kalelkar is preparing the pledges that you both will take during the ceremony. I am presuming that this is acceptable to both of you.

You have to inform your parents and take their permission. I consider that this wedding is not being undertaken for pleasure. You both are embarking on this marriage for the sole purpose of service. You will have to promise to me that you will not have children till India gets independence from the British. I would also like you to promise to me that till then you will not take any measures for contraception. What is the use of getting married? You have no idea how much effort I am making and thinking about the marriage. But if you want to have children and we do not get independence then how will you feel? If you want to invite some guests I will not object. They will eat with us. Think and tell me

Stay involved with the ashram and keep your mind on God. I want you to also keep in mind that I have not considered the legal aspect of the marriage ceremony.

With the blessings of Bapu

The forthcoming wedding had now become the subject of conversation in the ashram and many of the distinguished residents were discussing it in detail. One of the issues that came up and was put in front of Gandhiji was the legal aspect of the ceremony. Gandhiji sent another note to my parents a few days later telling them that since he had not considered the legal aspects of the wedding they could get it registered.

After August 10, 1945

If both of you want to have protection of the law you may have [the marriage] registered. Devdas has done it. So has Kanu. I never wanted it, but the girls' fathers were keen on it. I have only expressed an opinion. I never pay any attention to the law in whatever I do. We may regard Prabhakar as more than a Brahmin, but what can we do if society and the law would not recognize him?

(Also C.W. 10951.)

Tendulkar decided that as that particular day was a day of silence for Bapu, he would frame out a written reply to Gandhi's letter and also the note he had sent "about registration" and send it to him. He and Indumati went to the office of the ashram where there was a typewriter. Tendulkar sat at the machine and started typing as though he was in a frenzy. Indumati sat nearby watching. She could hear the rain outside and the noisy clicking of the typewriter. There was a dreamy look in her eyes, she was happy that the uncertainty about their marriage would soon end!

There was a sentence in Gandhiji's letter that unnerved Indumati substantially. Bapu's words kept reverberating in her mind. He had said that they had promised him not to have children till independence. Then he had said that if "you want to have children and we do not get independence, how will you feel?" Indumati was disturbed that the Father of the nation had written that he was not confident India would get independence from the British! After everything that the freedom movement had been through he still doubted Swaraj? She was confused, but being practical she had decided that she would handle things in her life one at a time. The first hurdle was the wedding ceremony and an end to the delays and uncertainty and all the noise and fuss it had caused. It seemed a lifetime and finally she was to be married! She thought to herself that she would see what was to be done with the remaining issues when they arose.

"Here, Indu, read my letter and tell me if you think I have covered all the points adequately," Tendulkar said, handing over the three typewritten sheets he had produced.

Sewagram
11 August 1945

Dear and great Bapu,

We received your letter of the 10th insant this morning and we both have read it with the closest attention it deserves. We are happy in the thought that you will get us married on the 19th instant which is a Sunday. This represents the fulfilment of a long-cherished desire on our part and we have no adequate words to express to you our deep gratefulness for your kindness. We would greatly feel the absence of Madhavbhai on this occasion and it would be difficult to express Indu's sorrow that the person who stood steadily by her (Madhavbhai Desai) in all kindness and gentility in her moments of confusion, trouble and difficulties, and guided her to a conception of love, marriage and family, a true and noble conception but within her reach, should be no more there to bless her marriage. We have fulfilled all the conditions set by you five years ago and permit us to say that during this long stretch of time, we have been often reminded that you have tested our love of each other and our devotion to you all the more severely in order to bless it all the more truly.

You are perfectly welcome to enlist the services of Prabhakarji to aid you in the performance of rites; and we fully grasp your noble idea of associating at the supremely auspicious occasion of our marriage a member of the Harijan community. The implications of this revolutionary step are very clear to us and we rejoice that our marriage should be the one to illustrate a new departure in your outlook touching the very fundamentals of sanctity and auspiciousness of the inside of Hindu society. We are happy that Kaka Saheb's aid has been enlisted to decide upon the appropriate rites and rituals. Apart from the great esteem and admiration in which we both hold him, he is dear to us, his name being closely associated with the village of Belgundi which has been a field of our uplift activity and whose welfare and progress remain a matter of utmost concern to us.

We are informing Indu's family about the marriage date. It is certainly not necessary to wait for their permission regarding the form and pattern of marriage we are entering into. They are more than content to leave all these details entirely to us as they know that we are fully responsible persons who should decide for themselves. Indu's father wrote to you immediately after your release in May 1944 to say that his one wish was to see us soon married and he left it to you to bring this about in the way you think best. It is in response to this letter that you wrote to him expressing your own agreement to marry us. Indu's mother has already written to you on her own behalf and it is proposed that Indu's brother Chandrakant should be present at the ceremony representing the family. For the convenience of Chandrakant and a few other friends I would request you to fix our marriage ceremony not earlier than 9 a. m. on Sunday the 19th.

In fixing upon the marriage rites you say, you have not taken into consideration the aspect of legal validity of our marriage. Both of us considered this point very earnestly this morning as it affects not only us but our future children, their prospects and even their legitimacy. We feel, however, that you are perfectly entitled and within your own good rights to marry us in the manner you yourself consider fit, proper and adequate. And this, irrespective of everything else. We are much touched by your forethought and its mention of this aspect of our marriage which we shall fully bear in our mind.

I shall now come to the other part of your letter in which you have stated your own conception of marriage and certain assumptions which you would like to be safe in entertaining in regard to us and our approach to the same problem. You say that:

a) the aim of marriage is not pleasure or gratification but the service of the country.

b) In actual practice this would mean that continence would be observed by us until after India becomes really free.

c) You state your opposition to the use of contraceptives and warn us before it.

On these points, I would prefer to speak for myself as Indu says she has already and very fully discussed this aspect of the question with Mahadevbhai in December 1940 and settled it to their mutual satisfaction. She would rather have a talk with you about it if you wish it or permit it. My own ideas of marriage have considerably changed since 1940 and have moved in the same direction as yours. The kind way in which you lent me a helping hand and put faith in my word has proved a turning point in my life and in my world of thought. The enforced leisure of years gave me an opportunity to think and re-think over my own small little world within me and this with surprising results. It is no longer today a mere matter of loyalty on my part to your person or personality as it was in 1940, no mere theoretical agreement with your ideas or a more intellectual alignment either. I understood the full force of my inner re-approachment to you and to what you stand for and what you symbolize for the future of humanity, when on the third day of your fast in 1943 without the least premeditation I found myself fasting in sympathy with you and lived on bare water for eighteen days. This would not have been possible except for my inner solidarity with your stand.

Even in the matter of our proposed marriage, I accepted your advice and your award in 1940, not because my ideas then corresponded with yours but in my faith of your superior wisdom. I have the good conscience today that I kept my word with you. You wrote to me in 1941 that your advice would do good all round and help me to rebuild a shattered home. I have not been wrong and have never regretted having followed your advice.

But growing years bring me a keener realization of my own weakness and limitations and ceaselessly teach me humility. I cannot have too much of it. I would much rather take up a lower position however unsatisfactory it may seem to you and steadily improve upon it, rather than in enthusiasm of the moment or in order to look well in your eyes make a bid for something which would be beyond my capacity. I should state therefore my position as follows:

a) My conception of marriage is very similar to yours. Its aim is not pleasure, its basis is not gratification of senses. Its real fulfilment can only be in the service of the country. I shall look upon Indu as my friend and colleague in the service of the country. Indu has been always that so far and my marriage to her will offer a further opportunity for the above purpose. I shall never lose sight of the fact that it is you, with your conception of marriage that has got us married and you have blessed our marriage in the faith that it would help us both individually and together in India's service. Your conception and example of marriage would be an inspiration and ideal before me.

b) In actual practice it would mean for me that I would not permit domestic happiness either to absorb me or lend me away from country's service. The ideal of continence I would hold in great respect and strive after attaining it. But this without impairing in any way Indu's right to motherhood, to which, if and when she chooses, she remains fully entitled. I would wish that my life partakes of that ceaseless urge for the country's freedom, which I see is consuming you and that all my vital and other energy is dedicated to the self-same cause; that continence grows within as in strength and beauty (sic). I hope, however, to have understood your position correctly when I have read elsewhere in your literature that married life in its fullest sense is certainly preferable to a forced mechanical continence which lends to perversity or obsession.

c) I know all the reasons for your opposition to the use of contraceptives. I agree fully with these reasons.

Dear Bapu, this represents my mind in all sincerity and frankness. May you always help us and guide us.

Your obedient
A G Tendulkar

Indumati looked up at him. "How beautifully you have expressed your thoughts. I know now what a great writer you are, that you are a master with your words! I am glad that you have mentioned Madhavbhai Desai's demise. I do miss his presence."

They sent the letter to Bapu's hut, happy that most of the issues regarding their wedding had been sorted out. The next morning, Tendulkar accompanied Indumati to Gandhi's hut and said to him, "Please forgive me, Bapu, for what I said to you earlier. I was impatient and frustrated. We are happy with the thought that you will get us married."

Gandhi looked at Tendulkar and quietly said, "Tendulkar bhai, it is forgotten. However, I have read your letter and I am glad that we have agreed on most of the issues. In fact Kaka Saheb Kalelkar was here just now and we were discussing the appropriate rites and rituals for the nuptial ceremony, as per the fundamental principles that the ashram would like to uphold in a marriage ceremony."

Gandhi put his book down, removed his glasses, and drank a little water. Then, in a serious tone, he said, "Have you both taken into consideration the aspect of the legal validity of your marriage? I would urge both of you to also register the wedding in the Registrar's office in Wardha."

Tendulkar replied, "Both of us have considered this point very earnestly this morning. We feel, however, that as the 'Father of the Nation', your presence and blessings are sufficient to give our union sanctity and irrespective of everything else, we are much touched by your thoughts on this aspect of our marriage."

Bapu looked at both of them and nodded, "Tendulkar you are aware that I believe the aim of marriage is not pleasure or gratification but the service of the country. I would therefore like both of you to practise and take a vow of celibacy in your life. I would like you to enter into this wedded state as brother and sister. Other people in the ashram have been married and still maintain their vow of celibacy and I feel that both of you should also follow suit."

Tendulkar replied, "Bapu I have written in my letter that in my marriage to Indu I shall look upon her as my friend and colleague in the service of the country. But I believe that she cannot be deprived from her wish to have children, how can I deny her the right to motherhood?"

Gandhi looked at Tendulkar. He had been listening to him carefully, evaluating him all the time. He looked into Indumati's nervous face. She was biting her lips, unsure of what Tendulkar would say next.

"Yes, Tendulkar, you have a point there and I must say you have expressed yourself rather well. I cannot force anyone to do anything. I would then make a request that you promise me that you will not have children till India is independent."

Both Indumati and Tendulkar were relieved by Gandhi's suggestion.

"Bapu, I promise you that we will not have children till India is independent from the British," said Indumati on Tendulkar's behalf.

Gandhi looked at her, "My daughter, you are aware about my feelings against contraception and I expect you to respect my views!"

Both Indumati and Tendulkar bowed to Bapu and left his hut. The next few days were relatively normal and they were both involved in performing the ashram duties assigned to them. Indumati sent a small note to Bapu expressing her concern about the attention their forthcoming wedding was beginning to receive. She received a letter in Hindi from Bapu written in Pune a few days later. It read.

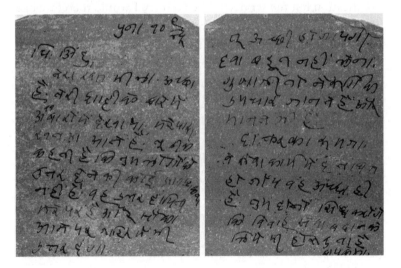

10.9.1945
Pune

Dear Indu,

I received your letter. It is good. I saw the mention of your marriage in the newspapers. Letters are coming to me also. You were correct when you say there is no reason to reply to each letter individually. I will answer the queries in a notice in the newspapers. Your health will be OK. Do not expose yourself to too much air. You know Gunaji's natural remedies and follow them.

Explain to Dr Tendulkar that it is only through involvement in seva actions (service) [unclear]. Both of you will show that there can be marriages whose main intention is for seva.

Bapu

Indumati appreciated the interest Bapu showed in the planning of their wedding. It was a very busy time at the ashram as the Working Committee meeting of the Congress party was being convened at the Sevagram ashram and a large number of political leaders had assembled for the meeting. Indumati was able to get an audience with Gandhiji for only a few minutes the next day. There were many people around him when he said to her, "Did you read my note and do you still want to go ahead as planned?" Indumati said, "Yes Bapu we will follow what we have promised." She did a namaste and silently left his hut.

A few days later, Tendulkar came striding up to Indumati outside her hut. "Come quickly," he said. "We can sit under the tree. I have to show you this note from Bapu, it was given to me just this morning." They walked briskly toward the tree at the far end of the ashram. Tendulkar handed Bapu's handwritten note to her. Indu read it out in an undertone.

(original letter)

18.8.1945
1.35 am

My dear Tendulkar,

Many are protesting to me that I am officiating at your marriage tomorrow. Among them are Manilal and his wife. She tells me that this will be your 3rd marriage, though I believe in one man one wife and vice versa for all time. I know about your German wife but nothing about your previous wife. My son says

18-8-45
1·35 AM

My dear Tendulkar,

Many are protesting to me that I am officiating at your marriage tomorrow. Among them are mainly ___ his wife. She tells me that this will be your 3rd marriage, though I believe in one man one wife & vice versa for all time. I know about your German wife but nothing about your previous wife. My son says none of my ideals will be realised in this

2

union & that neither you nor Indu will carry out my wish that you two may not procreate during the country's ___ -dependence. I have told them that I ___ not go back on my promise which is not in itself immoral or not for a manifestly immoral purpose. Therefore the promise shall be fulfilled by ___. But you will please give me such an answer as you can.

3

Now for your preparation for tomorrow. (1) Both should fast till the marriage ceremony is performed ___ between (2) You will both read 12th ch. of Gita & contemplate its meaning. (3) Each will clean up separate plots of ground with reason (4) Each will tend cows in the goshala (5) Each will clean up the well side (6) Each will clean a closet ___ daily & do all these with the intention so far

Bapu

none of my ideals will be realised in this union and that neither you nor Indu will carry out my wish that you may not procreate during the country's dependence. I have told them that I cannot go back on my promise which is not in itself immoral or not for a manifestly immoral purpose. Therefore the promise shall be fulfilled [unclear]. But you will please give me such answer as (soon as) you can.

Now for your preparations for tomorrow

1. Both should fast till the marriage is performed, fruits may be taken
2. You will both read 12th ch[apter] of Gita and contemplate its meaning
3. Each will clean up separate plots of ground with reason
4. Each will tend cows in the Goshala
5. Each will clean up the well side
6. Each will clean a closet
7. Each will pray daily and do all these with the intention so far to carry out these yagnas daily

Bapu

"You know, Bapu is really going out of his way to keep his promise to us," said Indumati.

"Yes Indu," said Tendulkar. "And we will honour his wishes to the utmost, but really I am getting a little impatient at the manner in which everyone is voicing their opinions to Bapu. How are they affected by our marriage?"

Indumati smiled at him. "We have come so far, please my dear have a little more patience. Once the wedding is over there is no one and nothing that can come between us!"

The monsoon skies suddenly burst into a torrential downpour and there was accompanying thunder and lightning. They were now seated in a covered area of the ashram where the prayer meetings were held. Indumati observed that Tendulkar was a lot more pensive than she had ever seen him before. She wondered whether he was disturbed and had reservations about the wedding. After all, Thea von Harbou was still alive and World War II was finally over. Travel to Germany would soon be permitted. She asked him why he was so pensive and disturbed.

He said, "Indu, I have been thinking about the marriage, this big step that we're going to take. Deep in the night, suddenly, the thought comes to my mind – am I worthy of you, your love and your purity of mind. I ask myself if I am fit enough to look after you? Will I be able to give you the same single-minded devotion that you have given me?"

Indu was a little shocked to hear this and was silent for a few minutes. Was this the end to her long romantic involvement? Suddenly the events of the last few years flashed in her mind, their meeting, their time in Belgundi, the prison visits, her imprisonment, release and reconcilement with the family and now this. Through it all she could only see the overriding emotion – her love for him. She looked at him and that's what she saw again. She put her fingers on his lips, as if to stop him from speaking.

"Please stop," she said. "I don't know why you're saying all this to me, that too, at the eleventh hour, just when Bapu is to marry us. We have crossed so many hurdles together. It has been my trust in you, my belief in our love that has made all these years apart bearable. Why are you telling me all this now?"

Tendulkar took her palm and kissed it, "No, Indu, I love you more than you will ever know. But I feel that I may not be able to live up to your expectations of me. I have lived so many years in the West and I have acquired certain European habits. I have been married before. You deserve someone better than me." He replied quietly but in a very clear and matter-of-fact way.

Indumati was devastated. Tendulkar took her arms and placed them around him. "Please Indu, hear me out. I do not mean to upset you in any manner. But I have to be honest with you. I know my nature. How do I tell you that I am scared about the prospect of settling down like this? It will take me a few years to establish myself. The last few years in prison have been a huge setback for me in every aspect – emotionally and financially. I do not want to make your life difficult after everything that you have been through already!"

"How can you say something like this to me now, especially after all that we've been through?" Indumati replied. "No, Indu, please don't cry. I don't mean to hurt you in any way. I just want you to consider carefully once again what we are about to do. Once married, especially in the presence of Gandhi and all the Indian National Leaders, we cannot go back…"

"If you had these doubts, why did you pursue me so relentlessly and make me fall in love with you?" Indumati said bitterly. "I always thought that you had chosen me because you really wanted to settle down in life and start a family. We cannot go back on our promises now."

"No Indu, I love you deeply. I just wanted to give you a chance to reconsider our decision. I cannot imagine life in India without you. Let us start life in the best way we can, in front of Gandhiji and the whole nation." He put his arms around her and she could feel his deep sobs as he held her. It was as though his whole inner being was purging. All the frustration and suffering of the last five years were finally released.

Indumati wrote in her journal that night:

A lot of people criticise me and ask me why it is so important for me to have the endorsement of Bapu for our wedding. I realize now that I am a little scared and insecure with him [Tendulkar]. The difference in our years and education make things very difficult. I believe that if we are to take a vow of marriage in front of Bapu and all the other leaders of India's freedom struggle, he will take it much more seriously. Tendulkar has promised me that we will stick to our promise of not having children till independence. I was amazed that Tendulkar should also be anxious and he told me that I should not marry him because he was not deserving of me. After so much has happened there is

absolutely no way of going back on our words! I always seem to
be caught in a turmoil. Now that Bapu has agreed to marry us
the leaders in the ashram are objecting. My family has accepted
the marriage but I feel that Tendulkar himself is getting cold
feet. What should I do? I will be bold and go through with it.
God help me!'

Indumati replayed the whole scene in her mind. She thought
about the manner in which Tendulkar had spoken to her and
how she had broken down. It had unnerved her greatly, but in
her heart she knew that she wanted to be only with him and
wanted to live as his wife. As far as she was concerned, there was
no turning back now!

The forthcoming wedding ceremony had created quite a stir
in the ashram as Gandhi had gone back on his public vow to not
officiate at the wedding of a non-Harijan. But Gandhi was firm
in his decision to go through with this. He had given his word to
Indumati five years ago.

Rameshwari Nehru, a prominent social worker of India,
married to Brij Lal Nehru, a cousin of Jawaharlal Nehru was
present at the wedding ceremony of my parents and she describes
it in her book *Reminiscences of Gandhi*. She writes:

> He (Gandhiji) values an ounce of practice more than a pound
> of precept. All rituals and conventions of society, therefore, have
> value for him only present in so far as they conform to the actual
> facts of life and are based on moral principles. Mere assertions
> of principles, however learned, are like empty shells if they are
> not followed by practice. He pushes this love of living the truth
> to dimensions beyond the conception of ordinary individuals.
> The latest instance of this love for the living truth regardless of
> consequences was the Indumati Tendulkar marriage celebrated
> last year at Sevagram under his instructions.
>
> The procedure he adopted in this marriage gave a practical
> shape to the whole ritual of Hindu marriage, disregarding the
> fact that this ritual of his making was not recognized by the law

of the land. He gave a new shape to the rite of Saptapadi which in its orthodox symbolic form represents seven steps taken by the couple jointly in the path of life. In this new ritual the bride and the bridegroom were made to accomplish in company with each other seven pieces of activities like the reading of the *Bhagavadgita*, spinning, tending of the cow, cleaning the well-side and the land for cultivation etc., on the eve of the marriage. The priest who officiated at the marriage was a Harijan by caste and belonged to the Christian religion by profession. The whole proceedings were held in Hindustani. Amongst the list of pledges given and taken, some old unnecessary ones were omitted and new ones were introduced. In evolving this form of marriage the only one principle he regarded was strict adherence in life to the moral principles held by him and professed by the couple. At one stroke and in one action so many reforms which he advocates were woven into the fabric of life.

The marriage was much discussed, although Gandhiji forbade the presence of photographers and the press. Rameshwari Nehru further quotes what Bapu himself had written on the occasion

The very word 'Hindu' is modern. The label was given to us. The name of our religion is 'Manava Dharma', i.e., man's religion. *Manusmriti* is the code of man's religion. The fountain of all is the Vedas. But no one possesses all the Vedas – Man's religion has been undergoing evolution. Before the advent of British rule, society was undergoing change from time to time. British rule changed all this. What was fit for change became petrified. If there was a change, it came from either the Privy Council or the British-made legislatures. Owing to this much harm has been done, and society has become inert like the superimposed laws. In this state of things, my advice is to perform marriage rites according to morals prescribed by man's religion. That should be binding. We need not heed those British rules which are inconsistent with [the] highest morals. We must run risks, if there be any in so doing.

Rameshwari's comment on this was "In the immensity of his work, he covers the whole of human life. No aspect is neglected. He has tried to solve all questions confronting individual and collective life. His solutions are made with a view to evolving a civilization in which there is peace on earth and goodwill among men." (New Delhi, 4-3-1946)

Before the wedding Gandhi wrote down the rituals of marriage that would be performed. The first was that the marriage couple were to fast up to the day of the marriage ceremony. If they so desired they could eat a little fruit. Gandhi made it compulsory that they read an excerpt from the *Bhagvadgita* each day. In particular, he told them they must read chapter 12 daily as this chapter explained the process of Bhakti yoga. "This is a devotional service," he said. "It must form the basis of your new life together as husband and wife."

Bapu's choice of Prabhakarji to conduct the wedding ceremony raised a few eyebrows in the ashram as he was a Harijan and had converted to Christianity.

On the morning of the 19th of August, 1945 the entire ashram was invited to attend the wedding ceremony of Indumati and Tendulkar. Gandhiji had personally hand spun and made two garlands out of yarn. It was customary in Hindu weddings for the bride and groom to exchange floral garlands, but Gandhiji wanted them to exchange khaddar garlands which had been made by him. They were both touched by the gesture. Indumati was happy to see her younger brother Chandrakant. He brought some presents from their parents, a sari for her and a gold chain with black beads known as a mangalsutra worn by married women, and he brought that most welcome item, a note from their father blessing them.

The evening had been hectic for both of them while they completed all the prenuptial instructions including fasting from the night before, and cleaning various places in the ashram in the form of service. Their duties left them quite exhausted. Indumati rushed to her hut to freshen up before the ceremony. To her surprise she saw a fresh hand spun khaddar sari waiting for her with fresh jasmine flowers tied in a string. These had been put there by Mrs Madhavbhai Desai, who followed Indumati into the hut.

"These are for you Indu," she said. "I know your mother is not here today and I have taken the liberty of giving you this sari. But you don't have to worry, because you will look beautiful in whatever you wear. These flowers are for you to put in your hair." The two women embraced each other. Indumati was feeling overwhelmed, she was excited, emotionally charged and exhausted. She had never in her wildest dreams thought that any bride would have to work so hard!

Mrs Desai led Indumati to Kasturba koti where everyone had assembled. Tendulkar was already there with Kaka Sahib Kalelkar by his side. He wore a dhoti and stood respectfully behind Bapu. Indumati saw him and suddenly a thought flashed in her mind – this is the place where his life had begun. Here, from Gandhiji's ashram he had been sent to England to study as a young boy. It was auspicious how their lives had led them here, and how now, finally, everything was coming together.

There were no wedding decorations and the wedding music consisted of members of the ashram singing devotional songs, including Bapu's favourite song "Raghupati Raghav Raja Ram…". There were no joss sticks and in place of the ceremonial fire there was a small lamp. Bapu welcomed the couple and handed each of them a copy of the Bhagavad Gita and asked them to read Chapter 12. When they were done reading, Prabhakarji stood in front of them and asked them to take the matrimonial pledge as had been instructed by Bapu. Indumati stood beside Tendulkar and their eyes met. After the tremendous strain of the last few days, she had developed a slight fever that morning. Tendulkar saw her flushed face and smiled at her. Reassured, she tried to concentrate on what Prabhakarji was reciting.

Ganpat Narayan Mahadev Tendulkar and Indumati Nagesh Vasudev Gunaji are to be married with the blessings of the Almighty today. I would request you to keep your minds pure and take the sacred vows of matrimony. Let us thank the Almighty by singing the bhajan "Aaj Mil Kar Geet Gao".

Please now answer my questions:

Are you both healthy?

Have you fulfilled the seven services that you were told to perform this morning and do you promise to continue to do these actions every day henceforth?

Are you both aware that this ceremony is being performed not with the aim of happiness?

Are you both aware that you are entering in the state of sacred matrimony for the purpose of serving your country?

Do you promise to work together and stay honest to each other?

Do you promise that you will not have children till India gets independence?

Indumati and Tendulkar answered in the affirmative to each of the questions. There was pin drop silence while the pledges were taken, with the chirping of the sparrows and screeching of parrots in the trees giving sanctity to the moment.

Prabhakarji continued. "Now I join you by asking you to exchange these garlands of hand spun yarn. Keep these yarn garlands with you always and maintain the sanctity of this union by upholding the promises you have made today. By ritual I pray that God bless and support you both and give your union strength. Now we will sing: 'Raghupati Raghav Raja Ram'."

They exchanged the garlands that Bapu had made, and both of them touched his feet as he gave them his blessings. Bapu then announced them officially married and everyone applauded. The women in the ashram had put together trays of crumbled jaggery and dried peanuts which they distributed to all present.

Although Gandhiji did not want the press present in the

ashram during the ceremony, several press reports appeared in various newspapers the next day. There was criticism from many quarters that Gandhi had insisted on continence in the marriage, that he had opposed the use of contraceptives and had insisted on the condition that my parents would not have children prior to independence. The nature of the ceremony was very unusual and the vows taken included the aspect of 'seva' or service. My parents had to wait for five years as per Gandhiji's conditions, and finally when my father was released from prison they found themselves in the midst of so much controversy! I found these newspaper cuttings about the wedding in my mother's special box guarded carefully for prosterity.

Mahatma Gandhi officiated at the m arriage of Dr. A. G. Tendulkar and Miss Indumati at Sewagram recently when he put into practice a rite of his own drafting which represents a r evolution in Hindu Marriage ritual. This new marriage concept is nothing s hort of a full-pledged political formula enjoining on the couple to look to the ir marriage as a pledge for life-long national service. Dr. Tendulkar was re leased last month after five years' detention. He was 15 years in Germa ny and worked for some time on the Editorial Staff of the "Berliner Tagebl att". Miss Indumati was also in prison in 1942.

BOMBAY CHRONICLE 2.9.1945

UNION OF MAN AND WOMAN FOR SOCIAL SERVICE
UNIQUE SEWAGRAM WEDDING
(From Our Correspondent)

Wardha. Aug. 19. Breaker of traditions and maker of revolutions, Mahatma Gandhi today introduced new MANTRAS and a ritual of marriage when he supported by Kaka Kalelkar and Vinoba Bhave, assisted at the wedding ceremony of Dr A. G. Tendulkar and Srimati Indumathi Gunaji at Sewagram.

"With God as witness", he said, "I am performing this marriage ceremony between Tendulkar and Indumathi. Those who are present and are witnessing the ceremony lend them help to keep their vows pure and fulfil them."

After this preliminary exhortation, a pledge in the form of ten questions was read out to the couple who answered the questions in the proper manner.

These questions are:

(1) Are you in full possession of your faculties when you mean to unite?

(2) Have you performed the seven 'Yegnas' (some of these are Gopuja and Jalapuja)?

(3) Do you believe that marriage is not meant for mere gratification of pleasure?

(4) Do you enter on married life with 'Dharamabhava', 'Thyagabhava' and 'Sevabhava'?

(5) Do you, therefore, undertake not to obstruct each other in the mission of your service but to help each other in mind, word and deed?

(6) As long as India is not free will you make an honest effort to see that you do not indulge in procreation?

(7) Do you believe or give sanction to interdining and inter marriage with so called untouchables?

(8) Do you believe in the equality of men and women?

(9) Do you believe in living as friends without the sense of master and servant in your relationships?

UNION OF MAN AND WOMAN FOR SOCIAL SERVICE

UNIQUE SEWAGRAM WEDDING
(FROM OUR CORRESPONDENT)

WARDHA, Aug. 19.

Breaker of traditions and maker of revolutions, Mahatma Gandhi today introduced new MANTRAS and a ritual of marriage when he supported by Kaka Kalelkar and Vinoba Bhave, assisted at the wedding ceremony of Doctor A. G. Tendulkar and Shrimati Indumathi Gunaji at Sewagram.

"With God as witness," he said, "I am performing this marriage ceremony between Tendulkar and Indumathi. Those who are present and are witnessing the ceremony lend them help to keep their vows pure and fulfil them."

After this preliminary exhortation, a pledge in the form of ten questions was read out to the couple who answered the questions in the proper manner.

These questions are:

(1) Are you in full possession of your faculties when you mean to unite?

(2) Have you performed the seven 'Yagnas' (some of these are Gopuja and Jalapuja).

(3) Do you believe that marriage is not meant for mere gratification of pleasure?

(4) Do you enter on married life with 'Dharamabhava', 'Thyagbhava' and 'Sevabhava'?

(5) Do you, therefore, undertake not to obstruct each other in the mission of your service but to help each other in mind, word and deed?

(6) As long as India is not free will you make an honest effort to see that you do not indulge in procreation?

(7) Do you believe or give sanction to interdining and inter-marriage with so called untouchables?

(8) Do you believe in the equality of men and women?

(9) Do you believe in living as friends without the sense of master and servant in your relationships?

(10) Do you agree that the seven 'Yagnas' replace the 'Sapthapathi'?

After obtaining satisfactory answers, Gandhiji said "I am uniting you in this bond with yarn spun by my hand. Both of you preserve this garland with utmost care. And you will remember that you never break this bond. You will pray to God to give you strength in observing the pledge and in remembering rites performed here."

The first point to note in connection with today's marriage is that the priest was a Harijan, Prabhakar by name, coming from Andhra. This means a frontal attack on Bhrahminical sacredotalism and holiness and auspiciousness associated with it. When young persons so long brought up in Hindu society are married by a Harijan, they are not likely to forget that the Harijan who had been kept so far away from the Hindu fold has been given a place of honour, the highest in any society.

The second point is the equality of sexes and the rights of sexes which spells emancipation of women.

Thirdly even a marriage to which Gandhiji makes himself a party, hereafter should be directed to and end in the service of Swaraj and not the creation of more slaves. He wants this conception to prevail universally.

Fourthly, the medium of today's ceremony was Hindustiani and not Sanskrit.

Fifthly a breach of the pledge of service of the country involves obvious risks to the married couple.

Sixthly, old Sapthapathi goes by board with all its archaic ideology and a new one comes in with the supreme ideology of social service as the first and paramount aim of marriage, especially when winning of Swaraj and consolidating its gains is the main task before every Indian, man and woman.

The shadow of politics lay thick on today's marriage. The engagement was as old as 1940 between Tendulkar and Indumathi. However they had to wait for five years as Tendulkar was jailed under the Defence of India Rules on the suspicion of being a Pro Nazi.

Gandhiji these days refuses to allow any marriage in Sewagram unless it is a definte departure from caste and convention but he made exception today as the engagement is of long standing. Both Tendulkar and Indumati belong to Prabhu community and come from Belgaum. Tendulkar lived in Sabarmati Ashram years ago before he sought foreign lands, went to Germany, took a doctor's degree in engineering and switched on to journalism in Berlin, joining a famous paper as sub-editor.

He was arrested in June 1940 and would have been still in jail but for the active intervention of the Editors' Conference on his behalf.

Indumathi is a graduate of Karve's Indian Women's University and went to jail for a year in 1942 for leading a procession. She has been living in the Ashram for some time now.

To cap it all, today's marriage was performed in the hut in which Kasturba Gandhi used to live.

(10) Do you agree that the seven Yagnas replace the Sapthapathi?

After obtaining satisfactory answers, Gandhiji said "I am uniting you in this bond with yarn spun by my hand. Both of you preserve this garland with utmost care. And you will remember that you never break this bond. You will pray to God to give you strength in observing the pledge and in remembering rites performed here."

The first point to note in connection with today's marriage is that the priest was a Harijan, Prabhakar by name, coming from Andhra. This means a frontal attack on Bhrahminical sacredotalism and holiness and auspiciousness associated with it. When young persons so long brought up in Hindu society are married by a Harijan they are not likely to forget that the Harijan who had been kept so far away from the Hindu fold has been given a place of honour, the highest in any society.

The second point is the equality of sexes and the rights of sexes which spells emancipation of women.

Thirdly even a marriage to which Gandhiji makes himself a party, hereafter should be directed to and end in the service of Swaraj and not the creation of slaves. He wants this conception to prevail universally.

Fourthly, the medium of today's ceremony was Hindusthani and not Sanskrit.

Fifthly a breach of the pledge of service of the country involves obvious risks to the married couple.

Sixthly, old Sapthapathi goes by board with all its archaic ideology and a new one comes in with the supreme ideology of social service as the first and paramount aim of marriage, especially when winning of Swaraj and consolidating its gains is the main task before every Indian, man and woman.

The shadow of politics lay thick on today's marriage, The engagement was as old as 1940 between Tendulkar and Indumathi. However they had to wait for five years as Tendulkar was jailed under the Defence of India Rules on the suspicion of being a Pro Nazi.

Gandhiji, these days refuses to allow any marriage in Sewagram unless it is a definte departure from caste and convention but he made exception today as the engagement is of long standing. Both Tendulkar and Indumati belong to Prabhu community and come from Belgaum. Tendulkar lived in Sabarmati Ashram years ago before he sought foreign lands, went to Germany, took a doctor's degree in engineering and switched on to journalism in Berlin, joining a famous paper as sub-editor.

He was arrested in June 1940 and would have been still in jail but for the active intervention of the Editors' Conference on his behalf.

Indumathi is a graduate of Karve's Indian Women's University and went to jail for a year in 1942 for leading a procession. She has been living in the Ashram for some time now.

To cap it all, today's marriage was performed in the hut in which Kasturba Gandhi used to live.

Another cutting in the same newspaper said

NO CHILDREN TILL SWARAJ!

SEWAGRAM: Mahatma Gandhi administered a marital oath to Dr. Tendulkar, a journalist, and Miss Indumathi Gunaji who were married today in Kasturba Cottage. The ceremonial proceedings were in Hindustani specially translated from Sanskrit by Kaka Kalelkar and Acharya Vinoba Bhave.

Mahatma Gandhi blessed the couple and garlanded them with yarn garlands spun by him.

According to the special oath drawn by Mahatma Gandhi the couple pledged themselves to the service of the country with mutual aid and not to have children till Swaraj was won.

Dr. Tendulkar came out of jail last month after five years' detention while Indumathi was also recently released from jail.

NO CHILDREN TILL SWARAJ!

SEWAGRAM: Mahatma Gandhi administered a marital oath to Dr. Tendulkar, a journalist, and Miss Indumathi Gunaji who were married today in Kasturba Cottage. The ceremonial proceedings were in Hindustani specially translated from Sanskrit by Kaka Kalelkar and Acharya Vinoba Bhave.

Mahatma Gandhi blessed the couple and garlanded them with yarn garlands spun by him.

According to the special oath drawn by Mahatma Gandhi the couple pledged themselves to the service of the country with mutual aid and not to have children till Swaraj was won.

Dr. Tendulkar came out of jail last month after five years' detention while Indumathi was also recently released from jail.

It was fascinating seeing the detailed correspondence and newspaper cuttings pertaining to this very controversial wedding. The union was not merely the union of two people but represented several principles. Gandhi got them to pledge to serve the nation first and foremost. Prabhakarji, the Harijan priest, was a practising Catholic which meant that the ceremony did not only make a statement about caste, but also about respecting all faiths. My mother had once given me the prayer book from the ashram which I treasure till today and which comprises hymns and prayers from all religions, whether they be Hindu, Muslim, Buddhist, or Christian. The evening prayer sessions at Gandhiji's ashram each day would have prayers, bhajans, songs and hymns from all religions

I asked my mother about the handspun garlands that Gandhi had made for them but unfortunately they were no longer with her. My father wore Khadi till he died, my mother would wear it sometimes. Gandhiji was criticised for various aspects of the wedding ceremony, including the fact that my father had been married before. Both my parents were resolute that nothing would come between them and went through the ceremony with great respect and relief.

I remember accompanying my mother to Sevagram in 1990, she was visiting the ashram after almost 45 years. Events at the ashram had been the turning point of her life. I watched her as she knelt down near Bapu's seat that is preserved even today and saw her look of love and reverence. Later we met some of Gandhiji's followers who lived there at that time and she met someone who had been present at the wedding ceremony who said to my mother in Hindi "Indu where have you been all these years? You have forgotten us. And she turned around to me and told me 'I still remember the wedding and how we young girls passed around steel plates containing sweet jaggery with crushed peanuts to all assembled.'" She told me how simple and stark the marriage had been, and that Indumati and Tendulkar stayed in the guest hut which was decorated with flowers for that night, and the next day, Tendulkar took his bride to Bombay by train. They were to stay with Tendulkar's close friend, SK Patil. There, they would start their new life together.

The Indians Find a Sister

Although my father and my uncles spoke about Thea often, it was mostly anecdotes and incidents that they recounted to us. Up until the point my father left Berlin (in 1939) these stories were quite detailed. After that, they became a bit sketchy, so we knew little or nothing, for example, of what happened during the war: India was a British colony, and Germany and Britain were on different sides in the war, so there must, in any case, have been very little communication between the two countries during this time. Also, because my father was in prison in India – or rather in many different prisons – for nearly five years, he was cut off from the rest of the world. I always wondered how Thea had survived in Berlin after my father and Yeshwant left for India.

Fortunately, when I discovered the German web portal (htti:// thea-von-harbou.blogspot.de) which is dedicated to her life and work, I was able to fill some of the gaps in the story of Thea's life after Tendulkar's departure for India. Managed by three Germans, Dr Guenther, Dr Kleiner and Dr Kagelmann, this portal proved a rich resource. Dr Lothar Guenther has worked extensively on Subhash Chandra Bose and the Indian legions, and is the author of a book entitled *Inder, Indien und Berlin* (Indians, India and Berlin). Dr Reinhold Kleiner has written a book on Thea von Harbou and German cinema until 1933 (*Thea von Harbou und der Deutsch film bis 1933*) and Dr Andre Kagelmann's work has focused on

Thea von Harbou and the war (*Der Krieg und die Frau. Thea von Harbous Erzahlwerk zum Ersten Weltkrieg*).

When I met Dr Guenther in Berlin he told me about a wonderful woman in her eighties, called Mrs Micheala Sarma who lived in Vienna. In 2006 she was possibly one of the few people still alive who knew of Thea von Harbou's relationships with Indians. She'd been married to Bal Krishna Sarma, a supporter of Subhash Chandra Bose and they'd been in Berlin at the time.

Dr Guenther encouraged me to meet her and I travelled from Berlin to Vienna to meet this charming woman who had many stories to tell me. As we talked over tea, I learned that she had never met my father as he had left Germany by that time but everyone in Thea's household talked about him. In the two days that we spent together, she recreated for me Thea's grand personality, her generosity and her love of India. She had worked as her secretary in 1940. I quote her: "In 1940 I was living in Vienna with my fiancée Bal Krishna and then one day he got a letter from Thea von Harbou, inviting him to come and study in Berlin where he had received a scholarship at Berlin University. Someone had spoken to her about his plight of not having very much money or accommodation and she was happy to offer him support. When Bal Krishna told her that we were engaged and that I lived alone in Vienna, she invited me to Berlin and actually gave me a job as her personal secretary."

Mrs Sarma was very emphatic when she told me that Thea von Harbou did not support Nazi ideologies and that she had enrolled in the Nazi party only very reluctantly. "She joined the Nazi Party because without being a member she had no status to fight for the cause of Indians stranded in Berlin during the war." She went on to speak of how generous Thea von Harbou had been and how she had spent her personal money to look after all the Indians there. She recited small anecdotes about Thea's generosity to her, buying her dresses and other things and described Thea's lavish parties. One particular detail I enjoyed hearing was how Thea loved to eat crab and it was often served at her dinners and all the guests would be made to use their hands to eat. She also told me that my father had already left Germany when she started work with Thea. "We all knew about him, his photographs were framed in her house and people spoke about him very fondly."

Dr Guenther had also collected books written by Indians who were in Berlin at that time and were followers of Subash Chandra Bose. They got to know and love Thea because of her generosity and her support and her passion for the cause of India's freedom. One of these Indians was Captain Gurbachan Singh Mangat, who was one of the first Indian officers in the Legion, and wrote *The Tiger Strikes: An Unwritten Chapter of Netaji's Life*. Another was Dr M R Vyas who'd authored a book titled *Passage through a Turbulent India: Historical Reminiscences of the Fateful Years – 1937-1947*.

I quote from Captain Gurbachan Singh Mangat's book *The Tiger Strikes: An Unwritten Chapter of Netaji's Life*

Thea von Harbou with Indians in Berlin

Frau Thea von Harbou (TAI-JI) One evening we were invited for a dinner to Adolf Hitler Platz, Frankenallee 14. The host was a German lady in her early fifties. She was soft-spoken and hospitable. Nearly all the Indian students in Berlin were at her place that evening. We learnt later that she was at home to all the Indians in Berlin once a week, i.e. on every Friday. When the dinner was over, we wondered how she managed to get all the provisions during those days of acute scarcity of foodstuff in Germany. We also came to know that the lady used to foot the monthly bills of the Indian students who, because of the war, were cut off from their homes and were stranded in Berlin. Under the circumstances, they could not receive any pecuniary help from their parents or guardians in India. Her monthly expenditure on the Indian student community sometimes rose to well over 20,000 Reichsmarks. The only way open to the Indian students there was either to do some part-time jobs, so that they could meet their routine expenses or to accept the benevolent help of the lady. The part-time jobs available to them during the war days were not very lucrative. The lady gave them loans in the form of monthly stipends, with the understanding that they would "repay all that, and if possible, with interest." The mode of payment that she prescribed, was again something novel. She used to tell the students – 'My boys, I don't have money to throw about. I can, however, help you with this at the time of your need. I must get it back with interest, as and when you people are in a position to repay. The mode of payment will be that whenever you come across a person in the circumstances similar to yours now and you feel like helping him, please do that liberally and intimate me about the facts. You will get a receipt from me for the amount spent by you.' She is reported to have died in 1956 and I am not aware whether any Indian who availed of her generosity was in a position to repay her.

In *Turbulent India* Dr Vyas wrote a chapter titled "Indians in Berlin Find a Sister". I quote from this chapter as I feel he also offers an interesting insight on the sense of loneliness, desperation and hunger among the Indians who were students in Berlin at the start of the Second World War.

In Berlin I made no friends. I had learnt that there were a few Indians, yet I had come across only two of them: Professors Tarachand Roy who taught Hindi and Professor Bannerjee who was attached to the University's History Department as Lecturer of British History. With neither had I any opportunity for personal contact. Most of the Indians (numbering around 30) were businessmen or in other professions. Three or four studied at the Freidrich Wilhelm University. I did not know whether or how or where to contact other Indians. So I had been more or less confined to the contacts I had made at the University. They were all Germans.

Then, one day after I had been been in Berlin for about four months I ran into an Indian gentleman. He was seated in a bus when I boarded it, he came over to me and introduced himself. "I am Krishna, I live in Vienna, but I am on a visit here. How is it that I have never seen you before?" he said.

I told him I came to Berlin only four months ago.

"Then you must meet the other Indians. We all get together at the Chinese restaurant on Wednesdays at 7 pm. You must come." He got down a stop later. Kwang tung was not far from where I was staying. So I eagerly awaited the ensuing Wednesday and promptly reached there at 7 pm. Some Indians were already there in a special room. I looked for Mr Krishna. He was not there. In fact he never turned up. Some of those present there noticing me as a newcomer, a very unusual event at the time, welcomed me very warmly. They wondered how for a full four months none of them had spotted me, though quite a few lived in Charlottenburg.

While I was getting introduced to those present, a German lady accompanied by a young Indian entered. Those who were seated at the long table got up to greet her. I heard the word Tai (Marathi word meaning sister generally used as a suffix to denote respect). She replied with Namaste and took her seat at the head of the long table.

I was pleasantly surprised to see dinner being served. I asked my neighbour, an engineering student, what we would have to pay, as I had only 3 marks in my pocket. He replied "Arre bhai tamasha dekthe raho, yeh sab muftka mal hai (just watch the drama, it is all free of charge). This surprised me but it was an agreeable surprise particularly as it was a Chinese dinner. Ever since leaving London I had not eaten rice!

It was only towards the end of dinner that someone drew Tai's attention to me. She turned her eyes towards me and watched for a while. When the dinner plates were removed she announced from where she was sitting that there was a new addition to the family, welcomed me and asked me to come over to her. I went. She put a light porcelain Piggy Bank on the table and said I should break it. I did. Some coins and currency notes came out. The young Indian on her right collected them. I returned to my seat as the lady announced, "Let us see what luck our youngest brother has brought us."

As we sipped the Chinese tea someone from the top side of the table announced, "One hundred thirty seven marks." As I had not seen anyone putting anything in the Piggy Bank. I inquired from the neighbour as to who had collected the money, and from where it had come. There came the reply "Tumko khanna mila na? Ab kyon fikr karte ho? (You got your meal, why are you worried now?) but for the fact that he said it in good humour, I would have felt insulted.

The piggy bank ceremony was followed by an enquiry from 'Tai' if anyone had a problem. Then an elderly man got up, "Tai my shoes are worn out I have not been able to get a coupon for a new pair." Another one followed a little later, "I do not have a raincoat." A couple of minutes of murmur. The lady looked at me inquiringly. I did not know what was expected. Still I did not feel like asking. The lady got up, followed by the same young man who had accompanied her [and] departed with a Namaste. My curiosity about the lady was satisfied after she was left. One of the Indians present said her name was Thea von Harbou and the Indian accompanying her was Mr Shripad Samant of Goa. From 1941/42 onwards Thea von Harbou took special care of those

Indians who gathered around Subhash Chandra Bose and who worked in Radio Azad Hind or in the Indian Legion. Together with Subhash Chandra Bose she said good-bye to the eight Indian students at the Anhalter Bahnhof (railway station), who left for Frankenberg to get a military training and later on to form the core of the Indian Legion.

On the 5 June 1945, after the World War ended, the four victorious Allied Powers signed an agreement according to which Berlin was to be divided into four zones. And that this 'quadripartite' status of the city would be maintained by all of them, with each occupying and controlling its designated area. Such control also gave them administrative and legislative rights over their particular area. Along with other areas, Charolttenberg, where Thea lived, came under British control. Coincidentally the headquarters of the Indian National Army headed by Subhash Chandra Bose were also located in the same part of town and therefore fell within the British sector. It didn't take very long for the British Occupation Power to realize that Thea had supported the Indian Freedom Fighters under Subhash Chandra Bose and had been involved in the Azad Hind (Free India) broadcasts in 1941 and that she had published a novel that year in which she had portrayed the treatment of Indians by the British rulers of India in a poor light!

Within a month of taking over, the British Military Government imposed a residence ban for Berlin on Thea, on the assumption that she was a member of the Nazi party also known as the NSDAP (National-Sozialistische Deutsche Arbeiterpartei). She was then interned in a detention camp in Staumühle and her role during the Nazi regime was screened. According to Thea, it was her belief that the British had done this deliberately to punish her for her links with Indian citizens. It was only after three months that she was allowed to return to Berlin in the autumn of 1945. She was not, however, allowed to work in the field of cinema for another three years. During this time she chose, instead, to work in a construction enterprise, at the beginning as a "Trümmerfrau" or a rubble woman, and later producing roof tiles by hand. Benevolent biographers have interpreted Harbou's manual work as her desire to atone for her contribution to the NS-regime and one of them wrote: "she will amend for her believing Hitler for many years." But Thea said otherwise, for her, the reason was that she "wanted to show my will to contribute to the construction work was not only words" – this, at the age of 57.

A little over a year later, she contracted a painful tendon inflammation and had to give up this work. The owner of the construction factory, who only knew her as Thea Lang, regretted the loss of his best worker. He wrote in her certificate: "She has always carried out her work punctually and up to now never was missing a single day without excuse."

One of the things that continued to trouble me through the course of researching my parents' life and writing this book, was that I kept coming across people and books that asserted that Thea von Harbou was a Nazi sympathiser and that she had been a member of the Nazi party. I found this difficult to square with the person who both my parents, in their separate ways, loved and who loved them. Or the person who so diligently and generously helped out Indians in Berlin, often at considerable danger to herself. Whether or not claims about Thea being a Nazi sympathiser were true, to me, what became important was that she was someone my parents valued, and it is this aspect of her that I have tried to reflect in this book. Nonetheless, I do not want to pretend to be oblivious of the charge that is levelled at her, and in my own way, I tied to locate whatever information I could about her. Dr Guenther's papers also held another treasure – Thea von Harbou's 'Denazification Certificate', with notes in her handwriting along with many pages of documentary evidence that she had attached. These included details of where she had worked, the books she had written and even the royalties that she earned from all her work.

It seems that at the end of the War all Germans were required to fill out a detailed questionnaire about their lives and activities. This was called the Denazification Certificate. In her certificate, Thea speaks of being held in Staumuhle from July to October 1945 "because of my relations with Indian citizens (*"aber ich war von 10 Juli bis 10 Oktober 1945 von Brittischer Seite wegen meiner Beziehung zu indschen Staatsangehorigen in Staumuhle interniert"*). I realized that this was what my uncle Shripad had referred to in his letter to my father when he had described how he was surprised to find Thea in the same detention camp at Staumühle with other Indians after the War. Thea had indicated to him by sign language that she would be at the dentist the next morning and Shripad feigned a toothache and met her there. Thea told him clearly that she believed she had been held there not because of her work with the Nazi film industry or for disseminating nationalist socialist views, but for her support of Indians. In the questionnaire in her Denazification certificate, Thea had tried to answer all questions truthfully trying to be as 'objective' as possible. She did not use the excuse of 'gaps in memory' to avoid difficult questions as other prominent people had done.

I never thought I would have access to documents such as the Thea's Denazification questionnaire. Going through the pages written in her own hand writing confirmed to me that Thea had not supported the ideology of the Nazi regime. She had never been anti-semitic and instead had gone out of her way to help her Jewish friends and colleagues. It upset me greatly that every time I had tried to find out information about Thea von Harbou on the internet I would come across the phrase that 'Fritz Lang left Berlin for Hollywood as he was Jewish and because his wife Thea von Harbou had enrolled in the Nazi party', or 'he left due to her Nazi leanings'. I had never heard anyone in the family talk in this way about Thea. My father would say sometimes that Thea loved her Fatherland Germany and was willing to give her life for it, but that did not add up to her being Nazi, I thought. And I

THEA VON HARBOU'S DENAZIFICATION QUESTIONNAIRE

Revised 1 January, ¡

C.C.G. (B.E.) PUBLIC SAFETY (Special Bran

MILITARY GOVERNMENT OF GERMANY
Fragebogen

ACHTUNG : Der Fragebogen muss in zweifacher Ausfertigung eingereicht werden

WARNING: Read through the Fragebogen carefully before filling it in. The English text will prevail if discrepancies exist between and the German translation. Answers must be typewritten or written clearly in block letters. Every question must be answered precisely conscientiously and no space is to be left blank. If a question is to be answered by either "yes" or "no", write the word "yes" or "no" is appropriate space. If the question is inapplicable, indicate this by some appropriate word or phrase such as "none" or "not applicable." supplementary sheets if there is not enough space in the questionnaire. Persons making false or incomplete statements are liable to prosecu by Military Government.

WARNUNG! SORGFÄLTIG DURCHLESEN! In Zweifelsfällen ist die englische Fassung massgebend. Mit Schr maschine oder deutlich in Druckschrift schreiben! Jede Frage genau beantworten! Fragen mit "Ja" oder "Nein" bei worten! Falls die Frage nicht mit "Ja" oder "Nein" beantwortet werden kann, müssen eindeutige Angaben gemä werden, z. B. „keine" oder „unzutreffend". Im Falle von Platzmangel Bogen anheften! Falsche oder unvollständige . gaben sind gemäss den Verordnungen der Militärregierung strafbar.

A. PERSONAL — A. PERSÖNLICHE ANGABEN

1. Name position you hold, or for which you are being considered (including agency or firm). 2. Name (Surname) (Christian Nam 3. Other names which you have used or by which you have been known. 4. Date of birth. 5. Place of birth. 6. Height. 7. Weight. 8. Col of hair. 9. Colour of eyes. 10. Scars, marks or deformities. 11. Present address (City, street and house number). 12. Permanent resid (City, street and house number). 13. Identity card, type and number. 14. Wehrpass No. 15. Passport No. 16. Citizenship. 17. naturalized citizen, give date and place of naturalization. 18. Name any titles of nobility which have been held by you or your wife or § respective parents and grandparents. 19. Religion. 20. With what church are you affiliated? 21. Have you ever severed your connect with any church, officially or unofficially. 22. If so, give particulars and reason. 23. What religious preference did you give in the cen of 1939? 24. Name any crimes of which you have been convicted, stating dates, place and nature of the crimes.

1. Augenblickliche oder angestrebte Stellung a) Bauarbeiterin *metal + construction worker* b) Schriftstellerin *Metallarbeiterin* 2. Name von Harbou *writer* Zu(Familien)name

3. Andere von Ihnen benutzte Namen oder solche, unter welchen Sie bekannt waren oder sind. Thea Gabr Vor(Tauf)name(n)

4. Geburtsdatum 27. 12. 1888 5. Geburtsort Tauperlitz b/Hof in Bay

6. Grösse 1,69 7. Gewicht 62 kg 8. Haarfarbe blond
colour eyes
9. Farbe der Augen graublau

10. Besondere Merkmale (Narben, Schmisse, Geburtsmerkmale, Verstümmelungen, Tätowierungen) oder Entstellungen k

11. Gegenwärtige Anschrift Berlin-Charlottenburg 9, Frankenallee 14 (Stadt, Strasse und Hausnummer)

12. Ständiger Wohnsitz wie oben (Stadt, Strasse und Hausnummer)

The first page of Thea von Harbous Denazification questionnaire

found that in her certificate, Thea clearly stated that she had never been involved with any anti-semitic action but, on the contrary, had helped several Jewish actors. I quote from the questionnaire she had filled out after World War II:

> I would never have quoted these instances where I have personally helped people from the Jewish community, but I do so now to show my attitude and conviction.

1. My book *Frau Im Mond* (*Woman on the Moon*) I have dedicated to my Jewish medical doctor, Dr. Paul Fleischmann

2. I have employed my Jewish secretary, Miss Hilde Guttmann, formerly living in Berlin – Friedenau, Brunhildstrasse 3, officially even a long time after the takeover of power despite protests by the Ministry of Propaganda: later I took Erwin Biswanger former secretary of Fritz Lang, as camouflage but was only working with Miss Guttmann who accompanied me as secretary on my travels to Emil Jannings. Miss Guttmann gave up our harmonic working relations in the year 1935, if I'm not wrong, when going to London, where she got an employment with two advocates, but I do not know their names or addresses only that they were negroes. I will never forget the words Miss Guttmann said when we decided to break up our friendship and cooperation: "We will separate, my dear madam, before we will be forced to do so."

3. Through my personal intervention Alfred Abel was allowed to resume his work in film and theatre by Dr Goebbels, in spite of the fact that he was a Jew. Alfred Abel had telephoned me, in despair, and asked for my advice and help. I immediately requested for an interview with Dr Goebbels who asked me "Do you know in what strange light you are casting yourself when you speak for a Jew?" I said, "I think the racial question should not play a role when it refers to an artist and human being like Alfred Abel." Eight days later Goebbels again called me and said: "I am pleased to inform you Frau von Harbou that I have decided positively in the case of Alfred Abel. Do call him and tell him yourself."

4. Dr. Schliep my relative who lived in Annaburg, District Torgau, was suddenly taken by the Gestapo without any warning. His wife and daughter came to me for help. Since I was also under observation by the Gestapo, I called on these people who would have liked to arrest me too and fought my way through to the release of Dr Schliep. He was released and allowed to practise but later he unfortunately died of a heart stroke. I am still friends with his family until today.

I don't believe that there is anyone who can reproach me for doing any harm to them for racial reasons. I have also helped the nephew of my Jewish secretary Mrs Guttmann who now owns a hairdressing shop in Haifa, Israel. I had a long correspondence with him, though I have forgotten his name but remember that he had a young son called Wolf.

Since the 12th of January 1933 I have been closely connected by love and friendship with relatives of the Indian race, I have spoken for Indians who were staying here in Germany and for prisoners of war at the Foreign Ministry. It was only when they asked me what I could hope to achieve without being a member of the Party that I got a membership card But, as I've already said, I never attended their meetings in spite of many admonitions and just continued to do my work. However, I did work in the fields of care and help (red cross and air raid protection organsation) as I considered this to be my duty, just as I do today in reconstruction. Berlin 3rd August 1947.

In another page in the Questionnaire about her work she says:

During the years 1931 and 1945 I worked with several film companies as script writer but do not remember the exact dates. My employers were UFA, TOBIS, ROTA FILMS, NERO FILMS, CINE ALLIANCE, EUROPA FILMS, TERRA FILMS etc. I cannot remember the name of that firm where I made "Ehe in Dosen" (Boned Marriage) and "Die Frau am Scheidwege (Woman at the crossroads), the directors were named Schorcht and Pichert. The film "Die Gattin" (the spouse) I wrote for Jenny Jugo (actress).

- In the year 1941 or 1942, I wrote the novel *Aufblühender Lotos* (Blossoming Lotus) which appeared as first print in *Berliner Illustrierte Zeitung* and later as a book in the German Publishing House.
- In the year 1973 or 1938, I was working as a mediator between housewives and house staff in the Home and House department of the German Workers' Front twice a week.

- In 1942, I worked for about 6 months as a welder of anti-skid chains in the Nordland Schneeketten factory.
- In 1944, I worked at home for about three months for Siemens Precision Tools (rectifiers, microphones, spirals for deaf people).

<u>zu D.</u>

Ich habe während der Jahre 1931 bis 1945 als Filmautorin bei den verschiedensten Filmfirmen gearbeitet, ohne jetzt noch die genauen Daten zu wissen. Unter meinen Auftraggebern waren:
Universum-Film AG - (Ufa)
Tobis
Rota-Film
Nero-Film
Ciné-Alliance
Europa-Film
Terra-Film
u.a.
(Wie die Firma hieß, bei der ich Ehe in Dosen und Die Frau am Scheidewege gemacht habe, weiß ich nicht mehr, die Direktoren waren Schorcht und Pichert.)

Den Film Die Gattin schrieb ich für Jenny Jugo.

Im Jahre 1941 oder 42 schrieb ich den Roman 'Aufblühender Loto der in der Berliner Illustrierten Zeitung als Vorabdruck und s ter als Buch im Deutschen Verlag erschien.

Im Jahre 1937 oder 38 habe ich bei der Deutschen Arbeitsfront der Abteilung 'Haus und Heim' zweimal wöchentlich als Vermittl zwischen den Hausfrauen und den Hausangestellten gearbeitet.

1942 habe ich ca. 6 Monate in der Firma Nordland Schneeketten Schweißerin an Gleitschutzketten gearbeitet,
1944 etwa drei Monate als Heimarbeiterin für Siemens, Feinmec nik (Gleichrichter, Mikrophone, Spiralen für Schwerhörige),
1943-45 im Rahmen der Frauenschaft als Rote Kreuzhelferin bei Katastropheneinsätzen, (nach Bombenangriffen)
im Winter 1944-45 im Westend-Lazarett Sonntags bei den Schwer verwundeten Dienst getan,
im Herbst 1944 Heimarbeit (Füttern von Helmen) geleistet. Wie Firma hieß, weiß ich nicht mehr, es war eine Lederfirma in der Windscheidtstraße, nahe am Charlottenburger Bahnhof.

Ich war zwar ab 1941 Mitglied der NSDAP, habe aber nie irgend che Arbeit darin geleistet und, offengestanden, bis zuletzt n gewußt, zu welcher Ortsgruppe ich eigentlich gehörte. Mein Be trag wurde abgeholt und damit war die Sache für mich erledigt

- *In* 1943-45, within the framework of the Women's League, I worked as a Red Cross assistant during catastrophic events (after air raids).
- In winter 1944-45, on Sundays at Westend Military Hospital, I worked with with major casualties.
- In autumn 1944, I worked at home padding helmets. I do not remember the name of the firm, it was a leather factory in Windscheidstrasse near Charlottenberg station.
- In fact I was a member of the NSDAP since 1941 but have never done any work there and to be frank until the end I did not know which district I belonged to. My membership fee was collected and that was all.

Thea von Harbou then worked with a silversmith as a fitter until she received her Denazification certificate in April 1949. This classified her as "not charged by the NS-regime" and gave her the possibility of rehabilitation. Also, the imposed professional ban was lifted, but the stigma that she was a collaborator of the fascist government remained.

Thea was now once again able to work in the film industry and started dubbing for a few foreign films such as *Der Dritte Mann* or *The Third Man*, adapted from a Graham Greene novel. She did eventually sign contracts to write new scripts but did not maintain very good health and suffered from migraines and blood pressure. She also slowly resumed contact with my father and uncles and the many people that she had helped and loved from India.

3

After the Marriage

My parents' wedding ceremony in Sevagram created quite a stir. In particular, Gandhi's views on celibacy became the subject of considerable discussion. He had some staunch supporters in people like Jaiprakash Narayan, but there were others who strongly opposed his views on both marriage and celibacy. My parents did not accept Gandhiji's idea of celibacy but willingly conceded to his request that they would not have children till the country gained independence. I have reproduced earlier a handwritten letter that Gandhiji had sent to my mother reminding her of her vow not to procreate till the country got independence. Oddly enough, in a typically Gandhi like way, in the very next sentence he asks her: "What will you if we do not get independence?"

The controversy surrounding my parents' wedding persisted for a few months after they were married in August. Several reports appeared in the press. Gandhiji had been adamant that once he had given his word to my mother and she had produced the letter in which he had committed himself to officiating at her wedding, he would do so. Though he had announced that no press would be allowed during the ceremony, the press somehow got wind of it and several reports appeared in the newspapers. Many of these concerned what they saw as differences between my father and Gandhi on the subject of procreation. Gandhi clarified his

RIGHT TO MOTHERHOOD
V. CONTINENCE TILL
SWARAJ

A. G. Tendulkar's Letter To
Mahatma

POONA, Oct. 19. (A.P.I.): A letter
from Dr. A. G. Tendulkar to Mahatma Gandhi in connection with his
recent marriage to Miss Indumati
Gunaji at Sewagram has been released for publication by Mahatma
Gandhi.

Mahatma Gandhi in a note releasing the letter says that it speaks for
itself and needs no introduction except to remark that it virtually represents the correspondence and conversations referred to in the letter.

The letter reads: "My marriage to
Indumati on the 19th August at Sevagram at which you very kindly officiated has received considerable press
comment. A part of this comment
relates to a Press report to the effect
that we had taken a vow of continence until Swaraj is won.

"This report is incorrect and misleading. It has besides, no basis in
fact.

"Prior to our marriage, you were
kind enough to acquaint us both
with your new marriage form and
your conception of marriage ideals.
You stated that the aim and purpose
of our marriage should not be search
of pleasure or gratification but service to the country; and that you
would expect us, therefore, to make
an honest effort, according to capacity,
of not being absorbed in procreating
activity until India achieves freedom.

"We both wholeheartedly accepted
the country's service as the aim and
inspiration of our marriage.

"I said that I hold self-restraint
in great respect, but made it is perfectly clear that nothing I undertake or implied in marriage form
or ideals should impair Indumati's
right to motherhood to which she
remains entitled.

"This position was acceptable to
you, and in your talk with Indumati
on the succeeding day you assured
her that no condition of continence
was anywhere implied in your letter
to us. It was, however, your keen
desire to emphasise the ideal of self-
restraint on the occasion of our
marriage just as you had done it at
all others where you had previously
officiated.

"Many of my well-meaning and
sincere friends from different parts
of the country still continue to write
to me in regard to the report mentioned above. I feel that their
doubts and queries deserve clarification at your hands."

stand and actually sent one of the newspapers, *The Bombay Chronicle*, a copy of the letter my father had written him, mentioning the points of dispute between them. My mother kept a copy of the newspaper report which I found in her box. It's dated 19 October 1945 and here is what it says:

RIGHT TO MOTHERHOOD
V. CONTINENCE TILL
SWARAJ
A.G. TENDULKAR'S LETTER TO
MAHATMA

POONA, OCT, 19. (A.P.I.): A letter from Dr. A. G. Tendulkar to Mahatma Gandhi in connection with his recent marriage to Miss Indumati Gunaji at Sewagram has been released for publication by Mahatma Gandhi.

Mahatma Gandhi in a note releasing the letter says that it speaks for itself and needs no introduction except to remark that it virtually represents the correspondence and conversations referred to in the letter.

The letter reads: "My marriage to Indumati on the 19th August at Sevagram at which you very kindly officiated has received considerable press comment. A part of this comment relates to a

Press report to the effect that we had taken a vow of continence until Swaraj is won.

"This report is incorrect and misleading. It has besides, no basis in fact.

"Prior to our marriage, you were kind enough to acquaint us both with your new marriage form and your conception of marriage ideals. You stated that the aim and purpose of our marriage should not be search of pleasure or gratification but service to the country; and that you would expect us, therefore, to make an honest effort, according to capacity, of not being absorbed in procreating activity until India achieves freedom.

"We both wholeheartedly accepted the country's service as the aim and inspiration of our marriage.

"I said that I hold self-restraint in great respect, but made it perfectly clear that nothing I undertake or implied in marriage form or ideals should impair Indumati's right to motherhood to which she remains entitled.

This position was acceptable to you, and in your talk with Indumati on the succeeding day you assured her that no condition of continence was anywhere implied in your letter to us. It was however, your keen desire to emphasise the ideal of self-restraint on the occasion of our marriage just as you had done it at all others where you had previously officiated.

"Many of my well-meaning and sincere friends from different parts of the country still continue to write to me in regard to the report mentioned above. I feel that their doubts and queries deserve clarification at your hands."

Gradually the controversy over Gandhiji's conditions for my parents' marriage died down and they got down to a normal routine. At some point both became involved in the Goa liberation movement which sought to end the 451 years of Portuguese colonial rule in Goa. They took part in the non-violent demonstrations, while supporting the struggle and its revolutionary and diplomatic tactics.

My father loved Goa and I recall that when we were children

we would visit Goa whenever we visited Belgaum. He spoke Konkani, the local language, fluently with my uncles and cousins and had many friends. It was after he died that I learnt – from reading it in a newspaper – that he had been President of the Goa Congress Committee in 1946. The story I read was in *The Bombay Chronicle* of 29 July 1946 and it was titled "Warships and Troops won't deter Goans". The Goa National Congress was formed in 1928 by a Goan called Tristao B Cunha. At the Calcutta session of the Indian National Congress, the Goa Congress Committee received recognition and representation in the All-India Congress Committee. In 1946, Cunha helped organize an assembly in Margão, inviting the Indian National Congress speaker Ram Manohar Lohia to address the gathering. This was arguably the first and largest mass gathering in Goa which set in motion the Goa liberation movement. Along with the other organizers, Cunha was arrested by the Portuguese authorities. He was kept in a dark and damp cell at Fort Aguada prison in Goa. He was the first civilian to be tried by a Portugese military tribunal and he was court-martialled and sentenced to eight years in prison and deported to Portugal. When Tristao B Cunha was arrested in 1946, my father became the president of the Goa Congress and organized a meeting in Londa (outside Goa, On 18 May 1946,)

I also came across a small note stating that both my parents had addressed a public meeting on 3.8.46 held under the joint auspices of the Goa Congress Committee, Goan Youth League and the National Christian Party at the institute Luso Indiano Hall Girgaum, Mumbai on 3 August under the presidentship of Mr M Y Nurie, to protest against the conviction and sentence passed on Mr T B Cunha. There were several meetings of this kind though I do not have the exact details.

"WARSHIPS AND TROOPS WON'T DETER GOANS"

Dr. A.G. Tendulkar, President of the Goa Congress Committee, has issued a statement in which he says:

Portugal's reply to our struggle for Civil Liberties is already there. A Military Court Martial has sentenced our leader Tristao Braganza Cunha to a deportation of eight years and a Portuguese warship is on way to Goa to cope with the situation there.

This reply offers us no surprise. Nor is it likely to deter us from pursuing relentlessly our set objective. This objective of gaining elementary Civil Liberties has been outlined and clearly stated by Gandhiji in his statement July 24.

Signor Doctor Bossa, the Governor General of Goa, has in his letter to Gandhiji characterised our struggle as anarchical agitation. His Excellency ought to know better. Foundations for this struggle were laid down as long ago as 1928 when Mr. Tristao. Braganza Cunha founded the Goa Congress Committee and it received a concrete shape in the manifesto of March 24, 1946, which is signed by some 38 representative and distinguished leaders of public opinion in Goa, none

"Warships And Troops Won't Deter Goans"

Dr. A. G. Tendulkar, President, of the Goa Congress Committee, has issued a statement in which he says:

Portugal's reply to our struggle for Civil Liberties is already there. A Military Court Martial has sentenced our leader Tristao Braganza Cunha to a deportation of eight years and a Portuguese warship is on way to Goa to cope with the situation there.

This reply offers us no surprise. Nor is it likely to deter us from pursuing relentlessly our set objective. This objective of gaining elementary Civil Liberties has been outlined and clearly stated by Gandhiji in his statement July 24.

Signor Doctor Bossa, the Governor-General of Goa, has in his letter to Gandhiji characterised our struggle as anarchical agitation. His Excellency ought to know better. Foundations for this struggle were laid down as long ago as 1928 when Mr. Tristao Braganza Cunha founded the Goa Congress Committee and it received a concrete shape in the manifesto of March 24, 1946, which is signed by some 38 representative and distinguished leaders of public opinion in Goa, none of whom is a foreigner. Although Dr. Lohia's defiance of ban on June 18 has been unconnected with our struggle, we have welcomed it. We do not look upon Dr. Lohia as a foreigner. No Indian is a foreigner on Indian soil.

Our struggle is based strictly upon non-violent and absolutely open methods. The strength we pit against warships and Negro troops is that of voluntary and self-imposed self-suffering regardless of consequences. The main issue of our struggle and the methods by which we desire to achieve it are entirely on a moral plane and we remain assured of ultimate success as long as we do not deviate from our path. Warships and African troops will avail Goa Government as little as the mighty strength of the British Government availed them in India in Bardoli Satyagraha.

July 24 will pass in our history as the red-letter day of our struggle. Eight years deportation for having asserted a demand of Civil Liberties provides strange commentary on Doctor Bossa's lofty idealism.

of whom is a foreigner. Although Dr. Lohia's defiance of ban on June 18 has been unconnected with our struggle, we have welcomed it. We do not look upon Dr. Lohia as a foreigner. No Indian is a foreigner on Indian soil.

Our struggle is based strictly upon non-violent and absolutely open methods. The strength we pit against warships and Negro troops is that of voluntary and self-imposed self-suffering regardless of consequences. The main issue of our struggle and the methods by which we desire to achieve it are entirely on a moral plane and we remain assured of ultimate success as long as we do not deviate from our path. Warships and African troops will avail Goa Government as little as the mighty strength of the British Government availed them in India in Bardoli Satyagraha.

July 24 will pass in our history as the red-letter day of our struggle. Eight years deportation for having asserted a demand of Civil Liberties provides strange commentary on Doctor Bossa's lofty idealism.

Bombay Chronicle 29/7/1946

Some two months after he became the President of the Goa Congress Committee, my father went to visit Gandhiji in Panchgani. Following on his visit, Gandhi released a statement to the press the next day (24 July 1946) which read: "Doctor A.G. Tendulkar, President, Goa Congress Committee is the last one from Goa who has come to me with the latest news from the place. He tells me that there are several parties there, working not necessarily for its inhabitants but for power. Yet at bottom the fight is good. He has produced voluminous papers in support of the statement that confusion reigns supreme in the minds of Goans, correctly described as Gomantakas. This confusion is bad in that the inhabitants of these Portuguese possessions are novices in the art of real politics. Its separate existence, it is clear, can only depend on the goodwill of the mighty British Government and the impotence of its Indian residents. It is therefore most essential for the success of the movement that it should be conducted by the Gomantakas on the clearest possible issue, i.e., civil liberty. The larger question of swaraj should await its attainment by the whole of India unless of course the Portuguese Government wisely comes to terms with the inhabitants of the settlement through friendly negotiations. It cannot be attained by any direct action of the citizens, whether violent or non-violent. In non-violent action success is assured where every inhabitant is a hero ready to lay down his or her life. It is less to be thought of in Goa than in the more numerous and better seasoned and awakened British India. Therefore the clearest possible issue of civil liberty must be kept steadily in view.

The second condition of success is that the fight must be through non-violent and therefore also entirely open means.

Thirdly, there should be no parties struggling for power and position. Where the goal and the means are common, different parties have no meaning.

On reading the literature I find two persons called loyalists who have already made lavish declarations saying that nothing is wrong in Goa and that a false agitation is being carried on by some mischievous persons. Let not the circle of these loyalists grow larger. The best way to avoid this growth is for all parties to become one.

I was not able to find out much more about my father's involvement and activities in Goan politics although I do know that there were a series of satyagrahas in Goa Between October and November 1946. Many of the leaders of these actions were arrested, and with their arrest,. much of the momentum of the movement was lost. Subsequently, the Goa Congress began to operate from Bombay. Thereafter a number of new political parties emerged in Goa, each having a conflicting agenda and perspective in relation to the question of Goan independence and autonomy. Among the many different options that were being put forward was autonomy for Goa within Portuguese rule, independent statehood, Goa's merger with Maharashtra state, or with the southern Indian state of Karnataka.

Mahatma Gandhi sensed that an independence movement with such disparate perspectives would be ineffective and could undermine the struggle for liberation; hence Gandhi suggested that the various factions should attempt to unite under the broad rubric of civil liberties. In response to Gandhi's suggestion, the different Goan political factions met in Bombay in June1947 to formally launch a campaign demanding that the Portuguese government 'Quit India'. The Goan leadership believed that with the end of British colonial occupation, an end to Portuguese colonial occupation would logically follow. But this did not happen and Goa remained a Portugese colony till 1961

Over a period of time my father was advised by several senior politicians who wished him well that he should begin to think of moving out of politics, and follow his original dream – and one that was still dear to him – of starting up industry in India. In 1938, when he'd come back to India, my father had prepared blueprints and plans for several industrial projects. Then, he got involved in Gandhi's campaigns and had to spend several years in prison. In 1945, having spent five long years in prison, he became a free man and was eager to get back to his plans and turn his dreams into reality. And so he began to explore several options. The time seemed right: the diminishing flow of British investment in India in the lead up to the World War had encouraged Indian merchants and manufacturers and led them to believe that the moment was right to set up and develop industries in the private sector. But it was also at this time that Nehru had introduced his 'licensing policy' for industry. In awe of the Soviet model of economics, Nehru wanted to encourage state run industry but many Congress leaders, including the influential and importantVallabhai Patel, were against this and supported industries in the private sector.

My father had worked as Sardar Vallabhai Patel's secretary when he first went to Sabarmati Ashram after completing his matriculation in 1921, just before he left for Europe. On his return from Germany he re-established contact with him and they built up a good rapport and stayed in touch. Patel played an important role in India's struggle for independence and he was a well respected and loved leader. One of the tasks he was charged with was integrating over 500 princely states into the Indian Union. Despite his onerous responsibilities he remained in touch with my father and seemed to have been very fond of him and concerned about him. In one letter (see below) he shows his concern at my father's smoking and rebukes him as a father or a family member would have done. Patel was a believer in free and private enterprise and many industrialists, such as the Birlas and the Sarabhais, held him in high esteem. In the letter below he asks my father to make up his mind about what he wants to do – given that he now had the additional responsibility of looking after my mother.

Telephone : 24101

VALLABHBHAI PATEL

Telegram : POWERFARM

68 Marine Drive

BOMBAY 1

6th Aug. 46

My dear Tendulkar,

I am going to Wardha this afternoon and propose to return on or about the 14th inst. But when I return, I expect to find that you have given up smoking for good. It is a nasty habit and it is not good for a public worker or a Congressman to be addicted to such habits. You must not succumb to such petty weaknesses.

Yours sincerely,

Vallabhbhai

Dr. A.G.Tendulkar,
Congress House,
Bombay.

6th Aug. 46

My dear Tendulkar,

I am going to Wardha this afternoon and propose to return on or about the 14th inst. But when I return, I expect to find that you have given up smoking for good. It is a nasty habit and it is not good for a public worker or Congressman to be addicted to such habits. You must not succumb to such petty weaknesses.

Yours sincerely,
Vallabhai Patel

Dr. A. G. Tendulkar,
Congress House,
Bombay.

Telephone : 24101
VALLABHBHAI PATEL

Telegrams : POWERFARM
68 Marine Drive
BOMBAY 1

Camp: Birla House,
Albuquerque Road,
New Delhi. 22.8.46.

My dear Tendulkar,

I am glad to hear that you have given up smoking since receipt of my last letter. It will do you lot of good. A little firmness of mind will enable you to forget the thing altogether and after a while you will dislike it also.

I want to know what you have finally decided about your future. If you are thinking of starting business in which you consider yourself an expert and for which you have asked the Bombay Government to accept your plans and terms thereof, you must pursue it more vigorously and whole-heartedly. I hear several big companies are being floated for that purpose in Bombay and C.P. Not being experienced in the line, I am not able to judge about the future scope of business and the probable consequences of competition, both internal and external, when the aftermath of the war disappears. You can judge things better and with the help which you expect to get from Government perhaps you will be able to do better than others. If you have got full confidence you must go ahead with it without any delay.

If, however, you have any doubts in your mind or if you find any other difficulties, you must make up your mind to change

-2-

your future course of life. Business requires concentration of mind and till you
are settled firmly, you cannot afford any
divergence. At your age now, you must take
quick decisions and act upon them firmly.
Politics or public life must have no attraction for you till you have fixed your
oars firmly. You have taken additional
responsibility on your shoulders by seeking partnership with Indu and you cannot
afford to be undecided.

I wish to hear from you about the
affairs in Goa and you should keep me informed about the developments there.

Hope you are both doing well.

Yours sincerely,
Vallabhai

Dr. A.G.Tendulkar,
Tilak Mandir,
Congress House,
Bombay 4.

Camp: Birla House,
Albuquerque Road,
New Delhi, 22.8.46.

My dear Tendulkar,

I am glad to hear that you have given up smoking since receipt
of my last letter. It will do you lot of good. A little firmness of
mind will enable you to forget the thing altogether and after a
while you will dislike it also.

I want to know what you have finally decided about your
future. If you are thinking of starting business in which you
consider yourself an expert, and for which you have asked the
Bombay Government to accept your plans and terms thereof, you
must pursue it more vigorously and whole-heartedly. I hear several
big companies are being floated for that purpose in Bombay and

C.P. Not being experienced in the line, I am not able to judge about the future scope of business and the probable consequences of competition, both internal and external, when the aftermath of the war disappears. You can judge things better and with the help which you expect to get from the Government perhaps you will be able to do better than others. If you have got full confidence you must go ahead with it without any delay.

If, however, you have any doubts in your mind or if you find any other difficulties, you must make up your mind to change your future course of life. Business requires concentration of mind and till you are settled firmly, you cannot afford any divergence. At your age now, you must take quick decisions and act upon them firmly. Politics or public life must have no attraction for you till you have fixed your oars firmly. You have taken additional responsibility by seeking partnership with Indu and you cannot afford to be undecided.

I wish to hear from you about the affairs in Goa and you should keep me informed about the developments there.

Hope you are both doing well

Yours sincerely
Vallabhai Patel

Dr. A. G. Tendulkar,
Tilak Mandir,
Congress House,
Bombay 4.

My father was, however, determined to start industry. His commitment to this was immense. Nothing could stop him, not even the fact that he had no funds of his own. The first scheme that he tried to implement was for setting up a rayon factory in Dandeli in north Karnataka. It was 1946. The Congress government of Bombay appointed a committee under the late Sir Ardeshir Dalal to examine Tendulkar's scheme. They were not convinced that it was feasible and the idea then fell through. But father did not give up. The next scheme he explored was for a cement factory

Tendulkar at the construction site in Bagalkot

at Bagalkot which is situated in what is today known as North Karnataka in Bijapur District. He made a thorough investigation of limestone deposits at Bagalkot and had their suitability certified by the Geological Survey of India. He obtained estimates of capital outlay for the factory and had them scrutinised by experts from the cement industry such as the Associated Cement Companies ltd (ACC). He took up this project with great seriousness and worked hard on it. Once the preliminary work was done, a public limited company was floated. With the support of Sardar Vallabhai Patel and other stalwarts of the Congress party he was able to have a very distinguished Board of Directors from leading financiers and industrialists in Bombay such as Tulsidas Kilachand, R D Birla, R G Saraiya and Sir Vithal Chandavarkar who became directors on the Board of Bagalkot Cements pvt ltd. Tendulkar secured an underwriting of Rs 40 lakhs from the adjoining districts of Bagalkot (in Karnataka) and from the Nizam's Trust (Hyderabad) through the help of Sardar Vallabhai Patel. He also approached the public with a prospectus in 1949 and raised a subscription of Rs 75 lakhs of share capital before commencing business.

With a lot of hard work, determination and incredible tenacity he built a model cement plant which became a benchmark of efficiency and set new standards in the cement industry. The first expansion was done in 1960, doubling capacity without raising any further share capital. The cement factory had been his pet project from the start. Everyone was full of praise about his planning and implementation of a cement factory which was situated on the limestone kiln and had a rail link passing through it. He was associated with Bagalkot from its inception. Bagalkot Cement company now known as Bagalkot Udyog runs even today.

Not being satisfied with the cement plant, a few years later he decided to set up the largest aluminium smelter in India in the western ghats near Koyna in Ratnagiri. Once again after many months of searching for the correct location he identified a spot where the raw materials – bauxite and water – were abundant The largest aluminium corporation in the world, ALCOA, was to partner with him. However this dream was not to materialize due to last minute policy changes between the American giant ALCOA and the Government of Maharashtra. Tendulkar had actually believed that aluminium was one of the principal building blocks in the future for India and he spent his personal fortunes in prospecting for bauxite for the project.

Indumati Tendulkar

Time must have passed very quickly after the wedding for my parents. Tendulkar did not spare a minute till he saw his dream materialize and Indumati must have felt that her life had been seized by a whirlwind. In those early years, she was so taken by Tendulkar that she forgot everything else. After their wedding, they moved to Bombay where they stayed with Tendulkar's close friend, the politician SK Patil. In a short while they managed to get a flat in south Bombay. It was the first time that Indumati had actually lived in Bombay and she settled down very well. They also rented a house in Belgaum as Tendulkar would spend many days at a stretch in the area, working on his project.

I remember the stories my mother would tell me about how life was for her after marriage. Both my parents were Saraswat Brahmins – my father's family was from coastal Goa and it was accepted that his community, though Brahmins, were permitted to eat fish. My mother's family were strict vegetarians and she had never eaten any non-vegetarian food. Once married, she not only had to cook fish for her husband but also had to go to the market to buy the day's fresh catch. I remember once – while I was in college – being taken to dinner at the house of a friend of my mother. The lady of the house happened to be a good-hearted women who told me in her charming manner "I made friends with your mother in 1945. She was newly-married

Tendulkar and Indumati

and would come to my stall in the fish market to buy fish and would almost faint each time with the smells and with the sight of fish lying around. Everyone cheated her, they gave her bad fish or charged her too much until I took matters into my hands. I would keep the fresh fish, especially pomfret and prawns that your father liked, cleaned, cut and wrapped." Apparently our hostess owned the biggest fish stall in Crawford market and she shared recipes and gave detailed instructions to my mother on how to prepare the fish. The result was that though my parents seldom saw eye to eye in the last few years of their lives and were legally separated for many years before my father died, he would always say "Indu has magic in her fingers, she is one of the finest cooks in the world!"

Gradually, Papa sold his Mercedes and various other precious things that he had brought back with him from Germany. Both he and Indumati still wore khadi, the handspun cloth worn by the followers of Gandhi and the Congress party. Tendulkar had found a tailor who was able to style the coarse material into an elegant safari suit – a half-sleeved bush shirt and trousers which he then matched with white leather shoes. He had a fetish for white: indeed, everything he owned was white.

My mother would say that it was during this period – when he was fully preoccupied with setting up industry – that she felt that her husband was getting increasingly impatient and distant with her. He had started talking about her spending some time in an American University! "Why do you want to send me away from you, why is my education so important? You have so many degrees and qualifications – is that not enough for both of us?" she would ask him.

"Indu, please don't exasperate me any more – I want you go to America to broaden your mind. Learn how the West lives. I have lived in Europe for almost 17 years and I think you should also have some exposure."

She felt rejected and hurt by his determination to send her

away and often argued that she wanted to have children and start a family.

He reminded her: "Before independence we had promised Gandhiji that we will not have children till our country was free. We had also discussed this, and you had agreed on the possibility of going to an American University to do additional courses till India became independent. Now our country is free, but we have taken great pains to secure admission to the University and all arrangements have been made. You must take advantage of this and study for a few academic terms. When you return we can start a family! Please go Indu and make the most of this opportunity."

Indumati was not very confident about going to America. She had not been out of the country before and was more than a little apprehensive about travelling alone and staying with Americans in a University. In 1946 very few Indian girls travelled to America alone. She must have written to Bapu for his advice asking whether she should go, knowing that he would never approve – perhaps she thought that this would convince her husband not to send her off. Bapu's reply was clear and forthright, if a little unfair: "Only I know what Tendulkar brought from his stay out." Bapu's criticism was strange: he could not have been unaware that Tendulkar was working hard at setting up industry and he probably needed a little more time to prove himself. The full text of the letter is below:

Sevagram
Via Wardha CP
15.9.46

Dear Indu

I got your letter I am glad to hear that you are feeling better. How can you ask for my blessings to go to America? I didn't know you were that kind of a person. I understand that Tendulkar also feels that you will gain something. If both of you feel that way than who am I to say anything? Since you both ask me I have only one thing to say – first do something here then go. Only

I know what Tendulkar brought from his stay out. He brought nothing, but this is my personal opinion. Others may not agree with me

Bapu's blessings to you both
My blessings to you both

I also came another note on the subject of her going to America written by Gandhiji to my mother in Gandhiji's *Collected Works* (Volume 91). There is no date on the letter but I presume that it was written roughly at the same time, It may have been a hand written note as Gandhiji mentions that he was glad that Tendulkar visited him, and it could be that he handed it over to my father to pass on to my mother.

Letter to Indumati G Tendulkar

CHI. INDU,

Why do you want to go to America? For a person like you, the field of service [here] is vast. Spending a year or more in America would be a waste of time for you. You haven't yet moved through the length and breadth of India. I shall understand it if you go abroad after settling down in a particular job. Then you can go to Afghanistan or Central Asia to gain experience. Asia is always there. I am positive that America or Europe is not for you. You will learn about these countries from Tendulkar.

I had absolutely no idea where you were, nor where Tendulkar was. I was therefore glad when he visited me today. I hope you are well.

Blessings from
BAPU

(From a copy of the Hindi: Pyarelal Papers. Courtesy: Pyarelal)

Notwithstanding Gandhi's advice, my mother did go to America. Perhaps she did not have it in her to stand up against my father's determination. As the arrangements were being made for her departure, she heard the news that Jawaharlal Nehru would declare independence for India from the British on 15th August 1947. When Indu heard this, the first thing that came to her mind was that now she would be free to have children. Tendulkar and she had kept to the promise they had given to Gandhi not to have children till independence.

Both Tendulkar and Indumati were in Mumbai when Jawaharlal Nehru addressed the nation on the 15th of August at midnight with the famous words "Long years ago we made a tryst with destiny, and now the time comes when we shall redeem our pledge, not wholly or in full measure, but very substantially. At the stroke of midnight hour, when the world sleeps, India will awake to life and freedom."

They were sad that Gandhiji was not in Delhi whilst power

was being transferred from the British Raj to India. Gandhi, who had played such a sterling role in the movement, was in Kolkata. Saddened by the Partition of the country, he had spent the day fasting and in prayer. This was something that the whole country had worked towards. But the moment of euphoria was also marred by the terrible violence that accompanied it as the country was divided into two, India and Pakistan, a decision that resulted in huge loss of life and property, violence on a scale never seen before in India and untold grief and suffering.

My mother was already 35 years old and wanted to start a family, she had pleaded with my father that she stay back in India. But he was adamant. All arrangements for her journey to America had been made, her college fees had been paid in advance, her boarding arrangements were in place. My father refused to change his plans. He was working very hard on the cement plant and genuinely felt that an exposure to a good American university would help Indumati.

My mother's journal has a detailed piece about her voyage to America in which she describes her shock and sorrow at learning about Gandhi's death.

30th of January 1948; a day I will never forget. After days of listening to the eerie silence of the sea, the loud cries of seagulls, the noises of the Shanghai port and the hustle and bustle of loading and unloading luggage came some welcome relief. I had embarked on the P & O ocean liner from Mumbai, my destination was San Francisco and we had stopped in Shanghai for a few days. The sea voyage hadn't been very comfortable and I had spent hours simply lying on my bed in my cabin. This was my first trip out of my country! I was waiting patiently in the queue at Shanghai harbour for my turn to have my passport stamped at the immigration counter. The cold air bit through my overcoat. I tried to cover my head with the loose end of my sari.

The broadcast from the overhead speaker announced ship arrivals and departures. Suddenly I heard a different announcement.

"We regret to announce that Mahatma Gandhi, the Father of the Indian nation, is no more. He was assassinated today in Delhi on his way to a prayer meeting." A sudden deep throbbing filled my head. It felt as though all my blood was being drained and everything seemed to spin around me. "Just an old man in a loincloth in distant India. Yet when he died, humanity wept," were the last words I heard as I dropped to the floor unconscious.

A few minutes later, I was revived by the paramedics in the immigration office at the harbour. I was asked a few questions but my replies were inaudible to the people around me. The health officer, though, could see that I was in shock after hearing the traumatic news. "Yes, I knew Gandhi personally," I replied to his inquiry. "He was like a father to me. He officiated at my wedding in his ashram in Sevagram and before I left for America he had told me not to go. He wanted me to dedicate my life for the service of our country – India. He spent his life fighting for the independence of the country and yet when we got our freedom it was divided into two countries – a Muslim-dominated Pakistan and a Hindu-based India. He was devastated with the violence that ensued that he didn't participate in the celebration of India's independence…" I babbled incoherently, clearly in shock, as though my words would drown the sorrow of losing someone so loved and revered by thousands of Indians.

I was inconsolable for the remaining journey to San Fransisco. I looked back at my life and realized how pivotal Gandhiji had been for me. He was like a father to me and I remembered all my visits to Sevagram and how he had performed our nuptial ceremony in spite of opposition from the senior members of his ashram. During the wait in the immigration lounge in San Fransisco I saw clips of Gandhi's funeral procession relayed on television. Thousands of people had followed the procession. Gandhi's body had been placed on a truck and was accompanied by members of his family and politicians as it moved towards the cremation ground in Rajghat which lay on the outskirts of Delhi. I saw the flames of the funeral pyre and the police trying desperately to control the crowds. The Indian Prime Minister,

Jawaharlal Nehru made a speech. "The light has gone out of our lives, and there is darkness everywhere, and I do not quite know what to tell you or how to say."

I was glued to the news and listened with a mix of fascination, awe and horrible unbelief as all world leaders made public pronouncements of their grief over Gandhi's death. Members of governments as well as dignitaries flew in from all over the world to pay homage to this "little brown man in the loincloth who led his country to freedom". Pope Pius, the Archbishop of Canterbury, President Truman, Chiang Kai-shek, the Foreign Minister of Russia and the President of France were among the millions worldwide who lamented Gandhi's passing. In the words of General George C. Marshall, the American Secretary of State, "Mahatma Gandhi had become the spokesman for the conscience of mankind, a man who made humility and simple truth more powerful than empires." Albert Einstein added "Generations to come will scarce believe that such a one as this ever in flesh and blood walked upon this earth."

I tried to explain to my fellow passengers as we boarded

Indumati at University in Ann Arbor, Michigan, USA

the ship from Shanghai what Gandhi's death meant for India. I narrated to them the struggle for Independence, and the small role that I had played in the freedom movement. I regretted not having had a last glimpse of my beloved Bapu before he was cremated. He was one person who had supported me all my life. I couldn't deal with the fact that he was no more. I remembered the last letter that he had written to me in which he had said that he didn't understand how travelling to the USA would help me in any way. And I regretted not having taken his advice. His advice rang in my ears. He had told me that if I ever found myself in a dilemma I should "remember the face of the poorest man in India. If your decision helps him, then you are on the right track!"

My husband had spent a lot of money on me for this trip to the US. He had sold the newspaper he had started in Belgaum and had kept aside money for this purpose. It was my first time abroad and I took a long time to adjust to the culture shock. I found the curriculum very different from my University days in Pune. Initially, I was a little self conscious and shy, but soon warmed up to my American room mates who found me a bit of a novelty as

Indumati and her friend in the USA

they had never met an Indian before but gradually grew fond of me. They mischievously decided to make me shed my sari and my Indian ways. They convinced me that my husband had sent me to America to learn how to 'become' a western lady as he had lived in Europe for so many years! Part of this 'westernisation' was to even encourage me to smoke cigarettes with them. I gagged on my first puff, but in a very perverse way, it made me feel closer to my chain smoking husband! Perhaps, I thought, on my return he would approve of my new-found habit and we could smoke together. My friends made me laugh, they helped me to buy a new wardrobe which included slacks, skirts and dresses.

The weeks passed sooner than expected and it was now time for me to return to India. However, a few days before I was scheduled to leave, my friends had organised a surprise party in my honour. They assembled in a restaurant and waited while I was accompanied there. I had no idea that I would have a chance to say goodbye to all my friends and professors that evening. It was a grand party and I was touched by their affection. My course had ended on the 19th of August 1949, the day was significant as it coincided with the date of my wedding anniversary, I had been married in Sewagram exactly four years ago. India had been independent from the British for two years and now I was returning to India – it all seemed like another life

Indumati returned home to India by ship. She was glad to be back and began soon to settle down to her old routine. But Tendulkar continued to be busy setting up industry and she hardly saw him as he travelled between Bombay, Belgaum and Bagalkot all the time – this latter was the site of the proposed cement plant that he was setting up. She was disturbed at his behaviour towards her – he was preoccupied all the time and she began to feel that they were steadily growing apart. But a few months later, she found herself pregnant.

My aunt, Anuradha Kittur described to me the conversation she had with her about this. One day, shortly after her return from America, she met my mother and found her relaxed and happy. Asked why she was smiling so much, Indumati replied, "I am finally expecting a baby Anuradha."

"Oh Indu, I'm so happy for you. You have been married for almost four and a half years and I know how much you wanted a baby. Look at me, I already have four children! Have you told Tendulkar?"

"I will when he comes home this evening. But don't worry Annu, I'll catch up with you in the number of children you have soon enough," she replied. My aunt was worried for her as she was already almost 38 years old and this would be her first baby. "Take care and call me when you are due, I will come and look after you," Anuradha told her.

Tendulkar was overjoyed when he heard the news. "The child will be a boy, my son," he announced proudly. "He will be called Gautam, after the Buddha." Indumati was excited at how happy her husband was. He was in his mid-forties and would finally be a father. "Everything will work out wonderfully, Indu," he said. "I would love to give this news to Thea!" he added. I know that my mother requested him to wait a little while and to break the news only after the baby was born.

A few months later in September 1950 Indumati was returning to Bombay from Belgaum by plane. The flight was bumpy because of the overcast sky. After a particularly strong air pocket she suddenly felt a strong sensation in her stomach. By the time she had reached home, contractions had begun and she had to be rushed to the hospital. She gave birth to a son in her seventh month of pregnancy. The baby was premature and the chances of him surviving were slim. The following is from my mother's account of my brother Gautam's birth

> I remember seeing my little baby son in the incubator, and I had resolved that he would live. I eventually brought him home and spent most of my day nurturing my little premature baby. Only after five weeks, when I was certain that my baby was out of danger did I entrust him into a nurse's hands. He was born on

Gokulashtami, the day that is celebrated as the birthday of Shri Krishna and I felt that it was an auspicious day for his birth.

Tendulkar arrived the next evening and was relieved that his son was doing well and looked better. He gave me a quick embrace and was glad that I was more relaxed. "You must take care of yourself," he told me that night. I was happy to be by his side although of late I had been so preoccupied with the health of our son that I hardly noticed Tendulkar's absence from Bombay. His total preoccupation had been on the setting up of his new cement plant in Karnataka. He was in a hurry to set it up as quickly as possible. He had taken to working day and night to raise funds for this plant from the governments of Karnataka and Maharashtra.

"Indu I wanted to tell you that I have been in touch with Thea von Harbou. She is well but her health has not been too good. I asked her to contact various machinery manufacturers for the cement plant. She says that after the war Germany is in a bad state and the large firms that once were the pride of industrial Germany are looking for business."

"Have you told her that we have a son?" Indumati asked.

"Yes she was very happy and sends you her best greetings. She has asked me to tell you to take lots of rest." I smiled, I had forgotten about Thea. Tendulkar had always said that she had been the strongest influence in his life, but I had never imagined that she would resurface in our current life! I had grown a little more secure in my relationship with Tendulkar after the birth of Gautam.

"I will have to go Germany soon to visit various cement factory manufacturers. I will also meet Thea again. But this should not upset you Indu, you know that my relationship with her is over. It was over from the time I met you in Belgaum in my newspaper office. You are my wife."

I turned on my side. Somehow the words seemed strange, I had taken it for granted that one day he would meet her again, why was it necessary to pacify me at this stage and that too in the middle of the night? I said nothing, and waited for him to fall asleep, I then went quietly to my baby's room and picked up my little son who was the joy in my life and that was all that mattered now. He snuggled in my arms and reached out to be fed.

Another event that occurred in 1950 that also had tremendous impact on the life of my parents was the passing away of Sardar Vallabhai Patel. Sometime in the middle of that year Sardar Patel became very ill. Both my parents were very disturbed to hear about this. He had stood beside them and been a real support from the time my father had met him as a young man in Gandhijis ashram in 1922. Now the circle had completed itself and it was with the support of Sardar Patel that my father had received a head start in his industrial ventures. He had been a mentor and a guide to my father and had introduced him to various industrialists who had either subscribed to shares in my father's company or had joined as Directors on the Board. My mother too narrates that she even went to visit Vallabhai Patel when he was ill and took her infant son with her to take the great man's blessings. Sardar Patel breathed his last in December 1950 in Bombay and they both were saddened, having lost a father figure and friend. I remember my father recounting how he had gone for Sardar Patel's cremation in Bombay where a crowd of about a million people had gathered in the presence of Prime Minister Nehru, and President Rajendra Prasad.

Return to Germany

Papa travelled to Frankfurt in 1952. He was visiting Germany after almost 14 years. He had often talked about his earlier time in Germany and it was only when I was older that I came to understand what it must have meant to him. I wonder what thoughts went through his mind when he thought of all that had happened since he'd left – the Second World War, the rise and fall of the Third Reich, the occupation of Germany by allied forces, and at the other end of the world, his marriage with my mother, India's Independence, the Partition of the country and then, Gandhi's assassination. The one thing he never spoke about was the time he spent in various prisons in India as a political prisoner, waiting for the war to get over so he could get started on setting up his industrial ventures.

The business part of his 1952 trip involved travelling to Rheinhausen in northern Germany to order machinery from a Krupp subsidary for his cement plan. He had recently procured all the necessary permits and licenses from the Indian government which allowed him to go ahead with the project.

The British may have left India by then but they left behind their bureaucratic system of governance which involved elaborate paperwork and red tape which often led to huge delays in the execution of business plans. Tendulkar had been able to get a clearance 'in principle' from the state of Karnataka and the Trust of the Nizam of Hyderabad to invest in the plant he was setting up. With the uncertain situation in India, perhaps a less determined man would have been easily disheartened. Tendulkar had grown impatient, but now that everything was slowly falling into place, he was convinced he could fulfil the promise he had made Thea, of using his learning and his skills to build industry in India. Tendulkar was also looking forward to meeting Thea – they'd started communicating again once the war had ended and things had opened up between Germany and India.

After Independence, Tendulkar had travelled extensively across India for almost four years, exploring the various potential sites for the projects he had in mind until he finally narrowed his focus to the cement plant which he planned to build in a yet undeveloped part of India. He was certain that thousands of poor villagers would benefit from his venture.

I can just imagine Thea calmly waiting in the arrival enclosure at Berlin airport for Tendulkar. I sometimes try to imagine her from descriptions my father and mother gave me: I see her in a woollen overcoat, with a hat and gloves, a bunch of flowers in her hand. She has brilliant blue eyes, somewhat faded by the travails of time and the difficulties she had lived through, and an air of reserve that makes her look older than her sixty five years.

She must have been surprised to see Papa, almost 50, severely tanned by the Indian sun, his salt-and-pepper hair, and his receding hairline. I have heard many people say that her love for Papa was unconditional. The years of separation had tempered her emotions but her devotion to Tendulkar remained intact.

I wonder what they must have spoken about. Perhaps they talked about themselves, the growing Tendulkar family, common acquaintances who had stayed behind in Berlin. She must have taken him around the Berlin they had known, visiting the old places they were familiar with. My father, in his usual intense and distinguished style, must have painted for Thea a picture of India emerging from the old idea of a British colony to one that would soon be alive and buzzing with industry, marching ahead on the path to development. Thea must have been eager to hear all about the latest developments in India and about how Tendulkar's cement project was progressing. She would have wanted to know every detail of the wedding ceremony, and about their relationship with Gandhi.

Tendulkar must have seemed so much more mature than before. Intense and passionate, but he would have seemed calmer and wiser, like a man who had seen life in all its nakedness and who had suffered. Both of them must have been apprehensive about how this 'first' meeting would be. Thea had waited impatiently to meet Tendulkar again, and perhaps she was overcome with emotion, but struggled to control herself, fearing that an emotional outburst could upset Tendulkar.

From what I could gather from family lore, Tendulkar's eloquence had not diminished with the years, and once again, this time, he managed to mesmerise Thea with his stories about the freedom struggle, the simplicity of his wedding, and how the young nation was stabilizing under the regime of Prime Minister Jawaharlal Nehru.

For his part, Papa found that Thea had become slower and more deliberate in her actions. The harshness of the war had taken a toll on her health. Though they both still felt a strong affection for each other, neither of them tried to rekindle their earlier romantic relationship. Thea looked at Tendulkar with a sense of pride. She felt that he was her protégé. Tendulkar, too, had always had great respect for Thea. He was aware of the turmoil she had been through over the last few years and wished there was something he could do to make her feel better. In fact, he wanted Thea to light the cement kiln at his recently completed factory to launch his new venture. This, he felt, would be appropriate and would also acknowledge her important contribution to the project.

My mother had once told me that Thea had promised to visit India and light the kiln on condition that my father send her (Indumati) and her baby son to visit Thea in Berlin first. The request had been made spontaneously. Thea didn't think for a second that Indumati might possibly resent visiting her husband's former wife.

My father had agreed to this request but I am sure he wondered how Indumati would react to it. Perhaps it dawned on him that this would probably be the best option to allow him to really focus on his work without feeling guilty about not paying enough attention to his wife and son. He must have thought that Thea and Indumati would get on well with each other. Both women were extraordinary in their own way. Both had made tremendous sacrifices for him and had unconditionally accepted everything about him. What they shared in common was their love for him, and for India.

But of late, Tendulkar found himself in a situation where he couldn't give Indu and his son the attention they deserved. He had waited so long to set up his cement plant that it had soon become an overriding obsession. He could only think and dream about cement. Until very recently, Indumati had been busy with their son, but now that she had a nurse, she was getting increasingly resentful of Tendulkar's constant preoccupation with work.

Tendulkar promised to send Indumati and their son to Berlin to spend some time with Thea. He described what a delight his son was and Thea, who had already seen pictures of him, was as excited at the prospect.

In the years that had passed since they parted, Thea too had been through an interesting time. In her own way, she had waged a battle against British rule in India. In July 1945, after the Second World War had ended, the British Military Government interned Thea in the camp at Staumühle and subjected her to sustained interrogation on her role in the Third Reich. She was questioned not only for working for the film industry in Berlin but also because she had supported Indian students during the war. Thea told my father that after hours of cross-examination she was able to establish the fact that she was innocent of any accusations that may have been made about any association with the Nazi administration. She had never done anything anti-Semitic in her life and it was on record in several places that she had often risked her life to plead for the release of Jewish friends under detention. The interrogators had been a little surprised by her preoccupation with the Indians, especially the dark-skinned non-Aryans. Her support to Indian students and to Subhash Chandra Bose was well known. The British had kept her in the detention camp because she had published a novel titled *The Blooming Lotus* which was based in India and showed the British in a poor light. In the autumn of 1945 she was released and permitted to return to Berlin, but restricted from working in cinema.

Thea volunteered to work as a 'Trümmerfrau', this was a German word for women who, in the aftermath of World War II, helped clear and reconstruct bombed buildings in Berlin by picking up and separating bricks from rubbish. She described to him how by volunteering to be a Trummerfrau she had contributed her mite towards the reconstruction of her beloved city, Berlin. She told him how "Gandhi's words – that no work was too small for him" – rang in her ears. She also told him how a lot of her critics made fun of her, especially people who knew the kind of life she had lived before. They would talk about her and say that 'Thea von Harbou is now reduced to doing back breaking work like collecting and sorting out the bricks from Berlin's rubble.'"

All too soon it was time for Tendulkar – who'd been busy meeting people from the Krupp subsidary at Rheinhausen, ordering machinery for his factory at Bagalkot and setting up various things – to leave for India. Thea and my father must have met often during this time, they were hungry for each other's company, and at each meeting Thea reminded Tendulkar that she was keen to meet Indumati and their son. I have often wondered how she must have felt when my father left – they'd met again after so long and she probably knew that it was unlikely they would meet again.

Two Women

My father managed to persuade my mother to visit Thea in Berlin. My mother wrote in detail about her stay in Berlin with Thea von Harbou.

Two weeks later Tendulkar returned to India. Back home, he told me details of his trip, especially his meeting with Thea. I was initially perplexed by Thea's strange invitation, she wanted me and my son to go and stay with her for a few weeks!

"Why don't I go with you on your next trip, and then I can meet Thea. Is it necessary that I visit her without you?" I asked my husband, totally confused. "After all, I have never met her. I don't how to interact with her – she may resent the fact that I am your wife and the mother of your son."

He was irritated by my lukewarm response to what he had thought was a grand idea. He did not understand my hesitation, nor my concern about Thea being a stranger.

"All these years you've heard stories about her," he said, agitated. "And you empathized with her! Suddenly she has become a stranger to you?" I said nothing.

The topic of my visit to Germany was not under constant discussion, but it hung over all our interactions and conversations. Tendulkar started to lose his temper very easily with me and the atmosphere at home became somewhat strained. Finally, in a desperate bid to find understanding for my side of the issue, I confided in my sister. At first when she heard about my strange predicament, Annu burst into laughter. The whole idea seemed too ludicrous to be taken seriously. As she grew to understand the implications of the situation I was in, she became more sober and concerned.

"Indu, whatever the situation may be today, you must remember that your husband was once married to this Frau Harbou and that for several years, they lived together as man and wife. How is she going to receive you?"

I had hoped my sister would be able to shed light on the issue so that Tendulkar's position would seem more reasonable, and frankly I was startled to hear my sister voice my own fears. I was even more convinced now, that it was a poor idea for me and my baby to travel to a distant country and put ourselves at the mercy of a woman I did not know. But when I brought up the subject with Tendulkar again, later that week, he managed to convince me that Thea had gotten over that aspect of their relationship. All she wanted was to feel like a part of the family.

"Thea really wants to meet both of you. She will grow to love you and treat you like her younger sister. I know Thea, she is a warm woman with a large, generous heart," Tendulkar reassured me.

I believed Tendulkar was right that Thea had got over their marriage. As far as my sister's warning was concerned, I accepted the idea that Thea would indeed receive us with warmth. Still, I did not quite understand why I should be going there in the first place. But Tendulkar was so intent on seeing the proposal through that a few weeks later, I reluctantly found myself boarding a flight to Frankfurt, with my two-year old son in tow.

I looked out of the window as the airplane took off, wondering how I had managed to allow myself to be bullied into this. My little son lay fast asleep on my lap, oblivious to the significance of the journey we were both making.

"You will be so much bigger next time you see India, my baby," I cooed to him. The plan was that we would spend three months as [Thea's] guests in Berlin. As the plane lifted into the clouds and I settled into my seat, tuned into the soft rhythmic breathing of my sleeping son, I began to open up to the idea of the trip. I had seen America, why not Europe? This was a golden opportunity. I had often pictured Berlin as Tendulkar had talked about it, and now I would have a chance to see it with my own eyes. The more I thought about it, the more convinced I became that Thea would indeed be a wonderful hostess. She would be more than happy to see us and we would receive a warm reception from her as from an old family member. It was ridiculous to fear Thea as a rival, she was at least 24 years older than me. A whole generation lay between us.

Finally, the plane landed at Frankfurt signalling the end of the long journey. As the doors of the aircraft opened, I was met with a burst of cold air that penetrated every single pore of my body. I was not accustomed to the cold European winters. Even Michigan had not felt this icy.

As I entered the arrival hall at the airport I saw Thea von Harbou waiting for me. She stood with a board that had my name on it, but I would have recognized her anyway. She was just as I imagined her – distinguished and aloof – and as I went up to her, she smiled and embraced me warmly.

"Welcome to Germany, Indumati."

"Thank you, Tai," I replied, meeting the elder woman's eyes briefly, before lifting the baby up for her to look at.

"Ah, I see his father in him," Thea remarked. I was touched by Thea's warmth. Although we both belonged to completely different backgrounds, we seemed to have struck an instant bond with each other. Surprisingly, what could have been a potential conflict of interest between us – the fact that we loved the same man – became the thread that bound us together.

Our conversation on the way home was somewhat hesitant. Thea's English was rusty, as she was a little out of practice

"Indumati, tell me more about Shripad and Elizabeth and my little nephew Klaus. I believe Klaus has a little sister too, I remember now Shripad had written to me and he'd said her name was Shanta. Where do they live? And where is Shripad working now?"

I filled Thea in on the details. Shripad and Elizabeth had stood by Thea through thick and thin. Thea wanted to know about the youngest Tendulkar brother, Yeshwant who she had treated like a son while he was in Germany.

I told her that Yeshwant worked in an engineering company and was married to a lovely Indian woman from the same community as the Tendulkars. She was nice and friendly and they made an interesting couple, he so tall and thin and she so short and petite. Thea was pleased to have news of them and smilingly said about Yeshwant, "yes, that's right, he was always very thin."

Thea had a maid to cook and clean the house and hired a nanny to look after my baby. Within a few days we had slipped into a routine and both felt very much at home. I had been looking forward to trying out Western clothes again. Thea had a few fancy blouses and coats tailored for me, but wanted to see me in saris. She was fascinated by the manner in which the sari was draped. She would often make me wear my sari in front of her just so she could watch in fascination.

Thea had a huge collection of artefacts, especially from Asian countries, and loved the crafts of the Orient. I felt so much empathy for this wonderful German woman who had helped so many people and came to admire her more every day. I was happy to be with her for the time being, knowing I would be home after a while.

Thea's bedroom had a big photograph of Tendulkar on the wall across from the bed. Each time she would walk by the photograph, she would stroke the surface with her fingers and say, "Mein Leibling." Initially I thought that Thea was trying to provoke me but then I began to notice how her face would light up when she said this. I realized that what Thea was doing was almost performing a small ritual of stroking the photograph of the man she loved. It didn't make a difference to her that someone was watching her and that that someone was me, the wife of the man whose picture graced her wall.

Thea continued to take up job assignments in films like dubbing voice-overs from English to German. She was often

Thea von Harbou and Indumati

Indumati, the German nurse and infant Gautam

invited for meetings and to speak at film appreciation workshops. I accompanied her a few times and would sit quietly and listen attentively. I was amazed by the body of work that Thea had amassed throughout her life. It seemed to me that she must have published at least a hundred novels and written scripts for at least 30 films but Thea rarely spoke about this.

One day, while still with her, I felt violently ill. I vomited several times and had an acute pain in my abdomen. "Indu, I think you are pregnant,"Thea teased me. "This time you will have a daughter.You have to promise me that if you have a daughter you will name her after me."

Feebly, I promised I would. I was, however, in too much pain to think clearly.As the hours passed I felt worse and worse. Finally, Thea realized that my condition was not to be taken lightly. She rushed me to the hospital where it was determined that instead of being pregnant as Thea had hoped, I was suffering from acute appendicitis and had to have immediate surgery.

Whenever I received a letter from my husband I would give it to Thea and ask her to open it first. I had really started seeing Thea as an older sister and I wanted to include her in everything. Thea read my letters with much excitement.We would get into animated discussions on India andTendulkar which would carry on late into the night. Thea wanted to hear about Gandhi and his campaigns and how he had led the struggle for freedom, she wanted to know about Tendulkar's life in prison.

I was not the only one who told stories. Thea shared with me anecdotes about the 'Tendulkar boys'. She told me the story of *Aufblühender Lotos*, the novel she had written in 1942 during which time she had had a grip on contemporary India.Through her close interactions with the three Tendulkar brothers and with the other students, she was able to understand the various issues that affected India. She had begun to understand some of the complexities of the caste system, child marriage, the dowry system, the plight of widows and particularly the plight of child widows and this was what inspired her to write the book.

The two of us were from totally different backgrounds, and

Thea von Harbou and Indumati

yet we had grown to appreciate and respect each other. Whatever apprehensions we had both had about meeting each other had vanished. Tendulkar formed the crux of our bond. Yet, after spending so much time talking to each other and sharing our experiences, we both realised that Tendulkar himself was like an enigma. We knew him so well, yet neither she nor I fully understood him. Once I remember distinctly I saw her lost in thought and said to her, "Thea, why don't you go to India and visit Ayi? I will stay back in your house in Berlin and look after your pets Schonheit and Pumpernickel."

"No my dear, you don't know what you are saying. It is your duty to stay at the side of your husband, work with him and nurture his dreams. The dreams are more important than anything else. I too have a dream of Tendulkar building industries in India and leading the country to prosperity. He has a great vision and the tenacity to achieve what he wants to, Indu. Don't worry if the going is tough, remember he has lived for many years in the West. I was with him when he was much younger and I have seen how women throw themselves at him. My dear, life will not be easy, I understand that you are noble and generous and have suffered with him, and I know he will never let you down. Don't worry, stay by him shoulder to shoulder. I am old now, this December I will celebrate my 65th birthday. I have had a good life, I have been successful and have met many wonderful people, don't worry about me, my dear."

She was smiling as she said this. She had come so close to the Indian people and had realized their suffering and their courage. She did not want her fantasy of India to be destroyed. I understood that she would never leave Germany. She knew that for her, India would always remain a dream.

Indumati and her son returned to India in due course. Tendulkar was happy to have his family back. He was busy setting up the cement factory in Bagalkot which was reaching completion. It was almost a year later in July 1954 that Tendulkar received a telegram from his friend Conrad Molo that told him the sad news that Thea had passed away. Both he and Indumati were devastated, they had lost a real friend.

Thea died on the occasion of the Fourth Berlin Film Festival in 1954. Her film "Der müde Tod" (The silent death) had been screened as part of a retrospective at the Delphi Palace. Thea von Harbou enthralled a packed audience of cinema lovers and admirers as she spoke about the production techniques of the film which had brought her and Fritz Lang international fame in the early twenties. She was excited, the audience had greeted her with thundering applause, the now 66-year-old film maker and writer must have felt honoured and validated, she spoke of her memories and her her long association with the German cinema industry. She had been at the receiving end of much criticism for her involvement with the State in pre-war Germany, and this tribute to her talent must have felt like it was long overdue. Unfortunately, as she left the packed auditorium she tripped and fell on the staircase and was admitted to hospital as she had suffered a fracture of her hip and had other internal injuries. A few days later Thea von Harbou died in the hospital from cerebral apoplexy. The headlines in the Berlin newspapers referred to her masterpiece "Der müde Tod" and wrote that "the never tired death" had finally caught up with her.

Tendulkar and Indumati could not make it to Berlin in time for the funeral. A few months later, in May 1955, I was born to my parents. My father was successful in completing his project, the Bagalkot Cement Company, but Thea was not there to fulfil her long cherished dream of lighting the cement kiln. Instead, my parents did the next best thing and dedicated the firing of the kiln to her memory. My mother tells me that my father asked her to climb the stairs of the kiln with me, a one-month-old baby and that it was I who 'lit' the flame in the cement kiln in Thea's name.

Postscript

This is where my story ends, and in a way, this is where it also begins. Life is not like fiction, it does not have neat endings and all the threads never unravel in the hands of the writer. I have tried to tell the story here of two, actually three, unique people from different backgrounds, brought together by history and circumstance. Thea von Harbou's fascination for India and her love of my father, and Indumati and Tendulkar's love of India and their fierce desire and passion to see their country free, as well as their deep love of and friendship with Thea bound these three characters together. The Second World War catalysed my father's return to India and brought him to Belgaum where he met my mother. It was the same war that drew the attention of Thea, one of Germany's most celebrated authors and script writers, towards Indians trapped in Berlin, and to writing a novel based on the British Raj in India.

My mother believed in her husband's brilliance and was convinced that he would achieve their common dream of seeing an India that had industry and jobs for its poor and education for its children. She was willing to wait and fulfil Gandhi's conditions of not having children till independence as they were equally desirous of creating their own lives, of building a home, of nurturing a family.

My father in his mid-forties, finally had a home and children in

Indumati and Tendulkar

the country of his birth. His impatience and frustration during his long confinement as a political detenue must have been immense. But both my parents stuck to their commitment to Gandhiji and the Gandhian principles of self rule and ahimsa. Both felt equally committed to building India after the exit of the British and both were devastated to see the violence of partition.

It was time to build a new nation. They both believed in the new self reliant, free and prosperous India. Both of them were passionate about what they did. My father had a mesmerising personality and was articulate and convincing. He was a linguist who spoke several Indian and European languages fluently. I feel he was one of the unsung champions of post-independence India who contributed his energy and skills towards building industry in the country. At heart he was an entrepreneur, always ready to accept the challenge of setting up new projects.

His association with the Bagalkot Cement Company lasted for over 17 years. The first five years in setting it up and the remaining ones in successfully running it. This in itself was a great achievement considering that when he came out of prison in 1945 all he had was his determination and will to succeed. The Bagalkot factory from its inception was run by a 'Managing Agency' which was called Tendulkar Industries pvt ltd and had been instituted by my father. 'Managing Agencies' were a popular practice established by the British before independence. As an example, several British concerns were appointed as Managing Agents to run tea estates and other concerns without actually owning them. However by the mid-sixties Indira Gandhi who was then the Prime Minister abolished all Managing Agencies and gradually my father's managing agency, Tendulkar Industries pvt ltd, no longer handled the day-to-day running of the plant. The timing of this move also coincided with the change of heart on the part of his American collaborators, ALCOA, for the aluminium project in western India. His visionary outlook with regard to the importance of aluminium even as far back as then and his efforts and investments in surveying, and analysing the suitability of the project came to a grinding halt with last-minute policy changes on the part of the Indian government and its decision to not allow foreign collaborators to have more than 49 per cent investment in any company in India.

Both these unfortunate events happened when my father was nearing 70 and he was also suffering from a heart ailment. It was then that he decided to spend more time developing his 300 acre mango farm in Belgundi village where he had been born. However his undying enterprising spirit did not diminish despite disappointments and he remained active till the end. In 1970 he once again made plans and gained a license and permission to set up a new cement factory after prospecting for limestone in the forest of Aurad in Chandrapur, in the state of Maharashtra. This was not to happen at his hands though the project did eventually go through and other industrialists were able to profit from it.

My mother was busy bringing up her children – my brother and I. We spent a few years in London as my father was keen that my brother and I get a British education. Indumati realized that she had a talent for painting and spent many hours developing her talent. Once my brother was admitted to Westminster school in London, she brought me back to India with her – I was just 9 years old. As a child I witnessed the turbulent marriage of my parents. The differences in their personalities and the differences in their backgrounds soon surfaced. My mother, being the more traditional one, spent many hours in her prayers and rituals. My father was more western in outlook and they very rarely saw eye to eye in anything. Eventually they were legally separated. However towards the end of my father's life they maintained a cordial relationship and had tremendous respect and regard for each other.

I remember when I was in boarding school in Kodaikanal in the late 1960s my mother reconnected with her associates from the Gandhian movement. After the demise of Gandhiji some of his followers continued working to promote the kind of society that he envisioned, and their efforts came to be known as the Sarvodaya Movement. Acharya Vinoba Bhave known for his non-violent activism led the Sarvodaya movement which was considered the social movement in post-independence India which strove to ensure that self-determination and equality reached all strata of India society.

Some of the Sarvodaya workers associated with Vinoba Bhave, were J P Narayan, Dada Dharmadhikari, Dhirendra Mazumdaar, Shankarrao Deo, K G Mashruwala. In the 1950s and 1960s they had undertaken various movements such as the 'Bhoodan' movement. The mission of the Bhoodan movement was to persuade wealthy landowners to voluntarily give a percentage of their land to lower castes. Vinoba Bhave walked across the whole country on foot, to persuade landowners to give up a piece of their land. Crowds followed him nearly everywhere he went.

In the early 1970s my mother joined Shankar Rao Deo, a staunch follower of Vinobha Bhave, and other Sarvodaya leaders in their travels to various parts of India to spread the message of Sarvodaya. I remember that she went all over the country and I think once again felt the pulse of the country as she had done when she was a young woman attending various meetings. She must have yearned to recreate the feelings that she had experienced during the independence struggle, though India as an independent country had changed drastically and she too had changed and was now the wife of an industrialist.

I met Shankar Rao Deo as a young teenager and remember my mother telling me that he was a staunch follower of the philosopher J Krishnamurthy. She had mentioned to me that J Krishnamurthy had miraculously healed him and had got him out of a deep depression during which he had not spoken for several months. When I was in St Xavier's college J Krishnamurthy would often come to Bombay and give public talks. I remember attending several of them and each time being impressed by his distinguished and elegant persona and his brilliant mind. It was many years later that I read his biography written By Pupul Jayakar where she mentions Shankar Rao Deo's close connection with J Krishnamurthy. I remembered my mother recounting her travels vividly.

I reproduce an excerpt from Jayakar's book, *J Krishnamurthy a Biography*

> In 1962 in the midst of the Chinese conflict and the traumatic confrontation between Kennedy and Khrushchev, Shankar Rao Dev decided to lead a peace march to China. His friends tried to dissuade him, but he was adamant. So a small band started walking the dusty overland trail. No one was clear what route they were to take; frontiers were forgotten, but the spirit had decided and so they marched. Poet Allen Ginsberg and his friend Peter Orlovsky founders of the 'Beat movement' with its revolt against the establishment and its questioning of all material values, were in India at that time, also marched. They were stopped at frontiers of Burma had to turn back.

I remember my mother telling me that it had been such a shock to him when Shankar Rao Deo had been stopped at the border of Burma that he fell into a long silence and a very disturbed state of mind, He was in a deep depression and refused to utter a single word to anyone for several months. J Krishnamurthy eventually met him a year later in 1963 and was able to get him out of his depression.

I was happy when my mother finally came home from her travels, she had gone up and down the country for almost a year with the Sarvodaya leaders. As a child I was scared I would lose her to the movement but now I understand why she had gone with them – to recreate the excitement of the freedom struggle for which she had spent many years.

My father passed away peacefully in his sleep in June 1975 at the age of 72 in Belgundi village. Hundreds of people from the nearby villages and all the workers of Bagalkot Cement company came to pay homage to a man who had given them a livelihood and had instilled in them a spirit to carry on his work of developing industry in the hinterlands of India. His life had come full circle and he died in the house on the top of the hill that he had dreamed that he would build as a young boy, in the village where he had been born.

Till the end he maintained that one of the strongest influences in his life had been Thea von Harbou. He always spoke about her as being a very generous and big hearted woman. He was able to fulfil his promise to her that he would set up industry in India. Thea was a much loved name in our family and it was something of a shock growing up to read that she was considered a Nazi sympathizer. Writing this book and meeting Dr Lothar Gunther and his associates gave me access to her Denazification certificate and statements and I learned so much more about her multi-faceted personality. I have not written about her illustrious career as a writer and film maker as this book is about her relationship individually with both my parents and the other Indians that she came across.

My mother moved to Belgundi after my father's demise and lived there for almost 30 years before she passed away in 2006. She died at the handsome age of 96, an elegant and energetic woman active and restless till the very end. She loved Belgundi village and was closely involved with the villagers. She re-established ties with two women from the village, Kamla and Godavari. They had been her favourite 'students' when my mother worked in the village during my father's incarceration. She supported a crèche for small infants that Godavari had started. Women would leave their small infants in the crèche before going to work in the fields, She started a school called Tendulkar High School in the village and dedicated to the memory of my father. Today it has over a thousand students and has classes till matriculation. She helped educate young students who lacked funds and paid for the weddings of those who had no parental support. She even went to the extent of calling the police when women were mistreated either by their in-laws or husbands. She gave talks in schools and donated to various charities. She was constantly writing poems, and articles and notes. Towards the end of her life she handed her notes, letters and most important her memories to me with the wish that I put it all down in a book. This is that book.

Appendix
How I Came across Thea von Harbou and Laxmi Dhaul

Lothar Günther

Mr Gunther was employed in the International Friendship League of the former German Democratic Republic where he dealt with Asian countries – China, the Peoples Republic of Korea, later with South- and South-East-Asian countries including India and Indonesia. In 1969 he accepted an offer of the Foreign Ministry of GDR and got an assignment in New Delhi with the then Consulate General of the GDR in India, which from October 1972 became the Embassy of GDR. He was responsible for cultural and social affairs until 1973 and again from 1979 to 1980.

India was not my subject whilst I was in University, my focus was China. However my love for India developed many years later when I worked in India and lived there for several years. It took me a few years to understand the diversity of culture of India. It was with the help of many Indian friends that I was able to appreciate the people, their philosophy and last not least, their history. Back in Germany, I could not forget the friendship and support of all these Indian friends and I started with some research on modern Indian history, in particular the history of Indian-German relations during the past century. Although, I had read and learned about Germans in India, I could not find much information about Indians in Germany and therefore, concentrated on this topic. One result of this research was a book *Inder, Indien und Berlin* (Indians, India and Berlin) which I wrote together with a friend of mine. Berlin was also the home and centre for Indian Freedom Fighters during the two World Wars and also several young Indians chose Germany, especially Berlin for technical education over other European countries.

During my studies of the history of Indian students in Berlin and Germany I came across the names of Thea von Harbou and Ayi Ganpat Tendulkar. Thea von Harbou was known to me because of her novel *The Indian Tomb* which was later made into a black and white silent film with the same name in 1921.

I later learned more about this famous lady, also how she became fascinated by the handsome and brilliant Indian student and journalist AG Tendulkar who she met in the early '30s. I also came across several instances when she helped many Indian students who were stranded in Berlin during the Second World War. They were not able to avail of financial support from their families. These incidents are hardly known in Germany or in India and there was no awareness on what Thea von Harbou did for the many Indians in Germany during the war to help them survive in this difficult situation.

I also read Thea von Harbou's novel *Blossoming Lotus*, which was published in 1941 and which was a story based on the Indian Freedom Movement. I came across other books written by former officers of the Indian Legion about their time in Germany with Subhas Chandra Bose who had set up base in Berlin for a short time. In Germany I was lucky to also come across two persons who were doing research on the life of Thea von Harbou and we jointly started a web blog dedicated to her (http://thea-von-harbou.blogspot.com). I joined them in their endeavours and was given the responsibility for dealing with that part of her life that related to India and Indians.

A few years ago I was very excited when Mrs Laxmi Tendulkar Dhaul, daughter of Dr A G Tendulkar saw the web blog and sent us an email. She was happy to find a person in Berlin doing research on Thea von Harbou and her father during the time he was in Germany. We exchanged emails till we met personally here in Berlin. In the beginning, Laxmi Dhaul was only keen to know more about Thea von Harbou and her father in the years 1932 to 1938, what her father did here in Berlin, how and when both of them met and how and where they lived. Together we went to pay our respects to the grave of Thea von Harbou. It is situated where other celebrities are buried and is designated as an 'honour grave' by the city of Berlin. We also visited the building where Thea von Harbou lived till her death. We exchanged ideas for a possible book before we concluded our first meeting.

Although Mrs Dhaul had already written some books on Sufi shrines in India, this project was totally different because it was . historic in nature and was about her family, a personal matter. There were many aspects to be considered in such a book. For instance it should describe the life of her father who was a wanderer between worlds and women and who finally returned to his Indian roots and also to an Indian wife.

Laxmi Dhaul wanted to honour not only her parents, Ayi Ganpat and Indumati, but also Thea von Harbou, who had become part of the Tendulkar family because of her relations with AG Tendulkar and her love of India. So this book has evolved into two main parts. The first a 'West-East' love story in Germany before and during the fascist time and World War II, and the second a story based in India which was controlled by the British Raj at the time, and an emerging freedom movement headed by Mahatma Gandhi. Finally Laxmi concludes her book with Thea von Harbou and Indumati meeting and exchanging their experiences with each other.

She has used incidents in a historic setting based on the personal experience of her family and reflecting the political, cultural and social situation of that time. The aim of this endeavour has been to inform readers in India and possibly in Germany and elsewhere about life and love in both countries, thus giving an example of Indian–German relations and history in difficult times.

Laxmi Dhaul did not spare any effort to search for relevant sources and material in India and in Germany, to research in archives and in literature, and I know she has written several drafts of this book. She was able to collect substantial information about Tendulkar and Thea von Harbou. Fortunately her mother Indumati shared many incidents in her life which Laxmi has narrated as well.

So we learn that Dr. Tendulkar was not only a brilliant journalist and an excellent student but also very gifted in the fields of science and technology. Thea von Harbou was a prominent figure in the field of art and literature in Germany and a person who wrote film history in her country. One can say that Thea von Harbou and Ayi Ganpat Tendulkar were real ambassadors of their countries and peoples concerned. A better witness and chronicler of that than Laxmi Dhaul is difficult to find. What I personally could contribute to her book I did with pleasure, and it was an honour for me.